The Echo from Dealey Plaza

The Echo from Dealey Plaza

The True Story of the First
African American on the White
House Secret Service Detail and
His Quest for Justice After the
Assassination of JFK

Abraham Bolden

 HARMONY BOOKS • NEW YORK

Published in the United States by Harmony Books, an imprint of the
Crown Publishing Group, a division of Random House, Inc., New York.

www.crownpublishing.com

Harmony Books is a registered trademark and the Harmony Books
colophon is a trademark of Random House, Inc.

Library of Congress Cataloging-in-Publication Data

Bolden, Abraham.
  The echo from Dealey Plaza : the true story of the first African American on the
White House secret service detail and his quest for justice after the assassination of
JFK /Abraham Bolden.—1st ed.
    p. cm.
  1. Kennedy, John F. (John Fitzgerald), 1917–1963—Assassination.
  2. Kennedy, John F. (John Fitzgerald), 1917–1963—Friends and associates.
  3. Bolden, Abraham. 4. African American police—Biography. 5. United States.
Secret Service—Officials and employees—Biography. 6. Psychotherapy patients—
United States—Biography. 7. Whistle blowing—United States—Case studies.
  8. United States. Secret Service—History—20th century. 9. Racism—United States—
History—20th century. 10. Conspiracies—United States—History—20th century.
  I. Title.
  E842.9.B59 2008
  363.2092—dc22
  [B]   2007040887

ISBN 978-0-307-38201-6

Printed in the United States of America

Design by Leonard Henderson

10 9 8 7 6 5 4 3 2 1

First Edition

This book is dedicated to:

My beloved wife, Barbara, who through forty-nine years of our marriage has been a source of strength and help to me as I struggled to overcome the many obstacles of this life;

My father, Daniel, and mother, Ophelia, who will always be remembered by me for their tireless labor, sacrifice, and parental diligence;

My three children: Ahvia Reynolds, Abraham Bolden Jr., and Daaim Shabazz, who brought me so much joy and happiness as children and great pride in their accomplishments as adults;

My two grandchildren, Ismail Tariq Bolden and Cydni Rhea Bolden, who must now carry on the works that were begun by our forefathers;

Brother Elijah Phillips Israel, who walked with me through the valley of the shadow of death and comforted me in my time of great trepidation;

And finally to William R. Wagnet and the many friends and acquaintances who had faith in my innocence and my ability to overcome the challenges placed before me.

Author's Note

All events and testimony occurring in the trial section of this book are footnoted and authenticated by transcripts and documents from each separate trial. In order to avoid some repetition and redundancy of citations pertaining to the same witnesses, all testimony and comments by the witnesses and trial judge are recorded from the transcripts of the second trial except in cases where the second trial included allegations that the first trial violated my constitutional rights and guarantees or where there were conflicts in the testimony of a witness between the two trials, in which case relevant testimony from the transcripts of the first trial are also referenced.

—AB

The Echo from Dealey Plaza

Introduction

THE IMPACT OF John F. Kennedy's assassination radiated out in all directions, like the ripples from a stone dropped into water. The event had such force that we still feel it today, nearly forty-five years later. The echo from Dealey Plaza reverberated around the world and altered the course of American life. It also affected countless individual lives, one of them mine.

I knew John Kennedy. I shook his hand and looked into his eyes, and I served, for a brief but critical time, at his side. I sensed in my heart, as many people did, that he understood the troubles of the common man and shared the pain of all downtrodden and oppressed people. He labored to make the promises of a better country a reality for all Americans. Born into great wealth and privilege, he did this not for any personal gain but simply because he knew it was the right thing to do. He wanted to do his best to foster equality of opportunity for all the citizens under his charge, and even those beyond our borders. John F. Kennedy entrusted me with his life, making me the first African American to serve on the Secret Service White House detail. No one can ever take that honor away from me.

I can't say for certain who fired the fatal shots on that day, November 22, 1963. The government rendered its official opinion, and legions of authors and researchers have offered theirs, but we are likely to debate the whys and wherefores of this event for a long time to come. What I do know is that the president died because of a failure of the security around him, a situation that some of us saw

1

coming. I wasn't there that day, but I saw what went on among the agents who were pledged to protect him to the very best of their ability. I was one of those agents. This is my story, the story of my journey from a small town in southern Illinois to the door of the Oval Office, and then to the depths of personal crisis in the aftermath of that service. Although I have changed some names to protect the identity of certain people, the story is true, and speaks to us today about the state of the society that we asked John Kennedy to lead, and the kind of country he left behind.

Chapter 1

I ENTERED THE Secret Service in 1960, after a number of years in law enforcement, first for the Pinkerton Detective Agency and then as an officer in the Illinois state police. It was as a state trooper that I first encountered the special agent in charge of the Springfield, Illinois, office, Fred Backstrom of the United States Secret Service. Massachusetts senator John Kennedy was on his way to Peoria for a presidential campaign stop, and I had been assigned to escort SAIC Backstrom around the city for security preparations.

As we rode along one of the intended motorcade routes, I turned to Agent Backstrom. "Are there any Negroes in the Secret Service now?" I asked.

Backstrom and I had worked together before and were on friendly terms. "I don't think so, Abraham, but I'm not sure. I heard that there may be one in New York or New Jersey, but I've never met him," he replied. "I can tell you this: we are looking for new agents, and if you're interested, I don't see any reason why you shouldn't apply. I can send you an application in the mail, and the Civil Service Administration will guide you along the way."

We went back to our duties, but a few weeks later I received the application, just as Agent Backstrom had promised. In the early fall of 1960, I drove down to Springfield, where I was escorted from Secret Service headquarters to take the civil service test. I learned several weeks later that I had just missed passing the test, but the next time SAIC Backstrom came through Peoria, about a month before

Kennedy was to visit, he stopped by my house. Backstrom suggested that I could enter the Secret Service under a Schedule A appointment, meaning that my previous experience would qualify me to become a probationary agent. The probation period would end after completion of two years of satisfactory service. Agent Backstrom was very encouraging, as was my wife, Barbara, and so I left the Illinois state police and joined the Unites States Secret Service.

I first saw John Kennedy when he came through Peoria on a campaign swing in October 1960. I was assigned to traffic control and caught a glimpse of the young senator sitting perched atop the backseat of a big white Lincoln convertible as his motorcade came in from the airport. I watched Kennedy hop down from the car about fifty feet away from me to shake hands with locals crowded along the side of the road. Agents from the convertible directly behind fanned out to protect him as he waded into the excited crowd.

By the following spring, I myself had been through training at the Department of the Treasury, under which the Secret Service resides. President Kennedy was now scheduled to visit Chicago on April 28 for a thank-you dinner with Mayor Richard Daley at McCormick Place. Daley's political machine had helped deliver a victory to Kennedy, through means not everyone considered legitimate. An advance detail of Secret Service agents worked with the local office to plan security, and assigned the Chicago field agents to various protective duties and positions. While some agents got the coveted spots inside the McCormick Place banquet room near the president, my assignment was to guard a basement rest room that had been set aside for Kennedy's exclusive use while he was there. I searched the bathroom and the surrounding area, and when I was satisfied that it was secure, I quietly took up my post.

At about 8:30 P.M., a half hour after the event was scheduled to begin, I heard a sudden commotion at the top of the stairs near the rest room. It seemed a group of people was heading downstairs, trailed by the sounds of a cheering crowd and the flashing of cameras. Before I knew it, John F. Kennedy was striding toward the rest room, surrounded by an impressive entourage, including Mayor Daley, Governor Otto Kerner, Senator Paul Douglas, Congressman William Dawson, and a handful of prominent local politicians. As he got to the door, the president surprised me by stopping directly in front of me and looking me in the eye with a slight smile creasing his lips.

"Are you a Secret Service agent or one of Mayor Daley's finest?" he asked, causing the mayor to chuckle lightly.

Collecting myself, I replied, "I'm a Secret Service agent, Mr. President."

"He's assigned to the Chicago office," a more senior agent offered. "His name is Abraham Bolden."

Kennedy nodded slightly in acknowledgment and continued on in his crisp Boston accent. "Has there ever been a Negro agent on the Secret Service White House detail, Mr. Bolden?"

"Not to my knowledge, Mr. President."

"Would you like to be the first?" Kennedy asked, his eyes twinkling under the bright hotel lights.

I didn't try to hide my enthusiasm. Smiling broadly and nodding, I answered, "Yes, sir, Mr. President."

After a short while, my attention was diverted back to the entrance of the rest room as President Kennedy walked out of the washroom in a hurried pace. Led by two Secret Service agents, President Kennedy and the other members of the group climbed the steps leading up to the main floor amid the blinding flashes of light from the photographer's cameras, turned left in the direction of the banquet room, and disappeared from my view. The band played the presidential fanfare. I heard the thunderous applause that filled the corridors of McCormick Place as President Kennedy entered the banquet hall.

* * *

SIX YEARS LATER, I stood desperate with fear in the dimly lit corridor of a prison psychiatric ward. Kennedy was dead, felled by an assassin's bullet, and the glory of that electric moment in Chicago barely survived in my memory. I waited for the guard to walk me to one of the barren cells, and listened to the soft moans, unintelligible babble, senseless ravings, and occasional harrowing screams of the unfortunate souls consigned to that terrible place. I was about to become one of them.

Chapter 2

WHEN I LOOK back at my childhood, I am able to make eerie connections to the troubles of my adult life, shadows that hinted at the darkness that was to come. I am also lucky enough to be able to see the foundations of my character being put into place, and I am filled with pride and gratitude toward my parents for the ways in which they prepared me.

A record snowfall fell on East St. Louis, Illinois, on January 19, 1935, preventing my mother from going to the hospital when she went into labor. When I came into the world late that night, it was through the ministrations of the neighborhood midwife, who lived down the street. The blanket of white snow would have added an unreal air of cleanliness and tranquility to the rows of wood-framed shanties along the unpaved streets and the cornfields lying just beyond. When the snow melted, the mud in the streets would suck the shoes right off your feet. Making it to the outhouse was an ordeal in such weather in the years before my dad dug the trenches and laid the dull maroon clay pipe that brought us indoor plumbing.

While the circumstances of my birth might seem extraordinary from the vantage point of the twenty-first century, they weren't particularly so for my mother, a stout, resourceful woman with light brown skin. She kept house for my father and their six children, including me, sewing our clothes and quilts and linens on an old Singer pedal sewing machine, and putting up canned fruit and preserves to sustain us. My mother ran a tight ship, maintaining a strict schedule of household chores for all the children and generally making sure that her brood stuck to the straight and narrow.

I can't imagine a woman more ideally suited to go through life with my father, a strong, stern man of quiet intelligence who seemed unable to ever stop working. When I was a boy, my father would ride a bicycle between two full-time jobs, at the B&O Railroad during the day and the Swift Packing Company at night. Even in those precious hours at home, Dad was always building or improving something. We became used to the sound of hammering and sawing and to the sight of Dad digging up the ground to lay pipe, pulling wire, or mixing cement. I think my father found something therapeutic and soothing about the hard physical labor, and he saw to it that each of his children learned something about these manual trades, not only for the focus and discipline they required but also so that we would have those skills someday if times got hard.

My parents were quite a team. We children grew up knowing that our father wouldn't tolerate any of us straying even slightly from his strict code of proper behavior. There was to be no disobedience, lying, fighting, cursing, gambling, smoking, drinking, or hanging out with unsavory characters. We also knew that he wouldn't hesitate to enforce his code with a few strokes of his belt. Most of the time, just the thought of being punished by Dad was enough to keep us in line, and he was able to leave the day-to-day management of the family to my mother. In contrast to her no-nonsense, laconic husband, my mother's jocular, fun-loving personality kept the home in high spirits. We kids knew that if we were in trouble, we could go to Mom to help smooth the way with Dad if necessary.

My father used to say, "Your family comes first," and he lived by that principle every day of his life. When there wasn't quite enough food to go around, he'd sit quietly by himself in the living room while the children ate. He wore his only suit, gray and threadbare, for years and years, all the while making sure that no expense was spared on books for school, educational outings such as our annual trip across the Mississippi River to the Forest Park Zoo in St. Louis, or on the finest musical instruments, which he insisted that all of us learn. I myself had chosen the trumpet, and though our cupboard was skimpy, my father found a way to bring home the best trumpet he could get his hands on. I got to be pretty good, eventually earning the nickname "Little Satch" for my fondness for Dixieland jazz, and winning music scholarships to Milliken and Lincoln Universities. As a teenager, I played with a touring group and occasionally on the radio.

As it happens, music was the spark for another brush with greatness. Before I was old enough for the high school band, I used to sneak into their practices to watch my older brother and listen to the music. Whenever Mr. Elwood C. Buchanan, the band director, would stop the music to talk something over, there would always be the lingering sound of a lone trumpeter in the back of the room, playing jazzy riffs on the march they'd been rehearsing. It was coming from a skinny, very dark-skinned boy who always looked as if he were transported to another world when he played. I asked my brother who he was.

"Oh, that's Miles Davis," he said. "Dr. Davis' son. He has a brother in the band who plays sax."

It was important to show equal respect to any adults we might encounter, not only our parents, as I learned the hard way one evening. I was fourteen, a boy, but starting to think of myself as a young man. Adding to my pride that day was a new pair of hobnailed boots on my feet, which in those days was like sporting a pair of the latest Nike basketball shoes. A bunch of my friends, including Floyd, Moses, Spook Eye, and Aaron, and I were playing ball out in the street in front of Brother Albert's candy store. I let one get by me, and the ball bounced onto the porch, striking one of the wooden window frames just below the glass.

Brother Albert came limping out of his store and snapped at me, "Little Bolden, move on down the street from in front of my store before you break one of the windows."

He don't own this street, I thought, *and I'm not moving anywhere.*

Of course, it wasn't long before another throw sailed over my head and hit one of the windows with a loud bang. Brother Albert shot out of the store as fast as his lame legs allowed.

"I told you boys to move on down the street a little bit! All of you know better than to play hardball in front of my store." He shook a finger at me. "Now move on like I said."

I turned to Brother Albert and sneered, "You kiss my ass."

Brother Albert stood seething for a moment but didn't say anything. A minute later, he closed up his store and marched down the street in the direction of my house. At this point, I was determined to stand my ground, even as Spook Eye and Moses urged me to move down the street. Even after Brother Albert returned to his store, followed by my sister Cecelia telling me that "Daddy wants to see you," I stayed where I was, tossing my ball in the air and catching it in my glove. When Cecelia came back a second time, I slowly made my way home, dragging the toes of my boots across the street.

As soon as I walked in the door, my dad's big black hand took me by the strap of my bib overalls and yanked me right out of my boots. In a flash, he was laying his belt hard against my backside. He kept at it even after my mother cried out, "Don't kill the boy, Daniel!"

"I'm not going to kill him, Ophelia." Dad spoke calmly even though he was breathing hard and sweating with the effort of the whipping. "I just wanted to kiss his ass for Brother Albert." It was the last time I played ball in front of Brother Albert's store. And I've never spoken that way to anyone since.

*   *   *

THERE WAS NOTHING fanatical about my parents' faith, but church was an important part of our lives, and years later, I would rely on my faith to carry me through moments of despair. Mom took the lead in our religious education, shepherding us to the raucous and emotional services every Sunday at St. Paul Baptist Church, teaching us to read the Bible, and holding spontaneous Bible sessions around the house. She helped me deal with my own youthful doubts about God.

I recall confronting her one day. "Mom," I said sorrowfully, "I hear the preaching and the singing and the people shouting and crying around the church, but nothing is coming of it. Things are not getting any better for our people. If God loves everybody, why is there so much misery and unhappiness all around us? It's as if God doesn't care about us."

Mom believed that the people in church were all doing their best to do the Lord's work and be good Christians, and she told me so. She comforted me with something I must have heard her say a thousand times: "God will make a way somehow."

But I suppose my mother's answer never fully satisfied me, and I began to search the Scriptures myself. I needed somehow to reconcile the obvious deprivation that permeated our little world with the great and beneficent God I heard about from my parents and preachers. I had found a beaten-up paperback copy of the New Testament in a trash pile near the vacant lot where my friends and I played ball, and began to study it methodically. Every morning before school, I'd get up early and read several chapters in my mother's favorite rocking chair behind our black potbellied stove. I'd pick out one verse to memorize, and all day during school I would repeat it to myself until it became a part of me. My parents dictated the presence of religion in our lives, but I didn't see it as onerous. I took to it naturally, willingly, and later even contemplated attending the seminary.

Perhaps I was predisposed to a more spiritual perspective on life.

Even as a child, I accepted the notion that there was more to the world than what I could see or hold in my hand. I sensed other, unseen spheres of parallel existence, shadowy entities that I felt present in times of illness or danger. I didn't fully understand these specters, and feared them, even as they amused and sometimes comforted me.

I knew these presences, though undefined, were to be taken seriously. Throughout my life, I have been visited by dreams and have experienced what some people would call visions, which have figured prominently in my consciousness. One dream from my youth, perhaps when I was about thirteen, has haunted my life. I was imprisoned, lying faceup in a rectangular steel enclosure with a glass window at eye level. The enclosure was resting in the center of a large bare room with no doors. Outside the window, I could barely make out four figures that seemed to be a woman and three small children. I tried to call out to them, but they did not answer. I woke up sweating and terrified, alone in the darkness.

The next morning I told my mother about the dream. When she asked what I thought it had meant, I told her, "I'll be dead before I'm thirty."

"Don't say that, son," Mom responded calmly. "No one knows when that time will come but the Lord." And yet I was never able to shake that dream, even when I told my wife about it many years later. In 1962, when our third child was born, the sense that the time was drawing near was with me all the time. I was twenty-nine.

Not long after, I had my first experience with an unexplainable phenomenon. I was playing ball in the sandlot about four blocks from my house, as I often did, when suddenly I heard a voice calling my name. I looked around but saw no one. When I heard the voice again, it was clearly my mother's voice, calling for me. I bolted for home, stopping long enough to explain where I was going.

"Aw, come on, man," my friends said. "You can't hear your mother from here." And yet I kept on going, as fast as I could. When

I got to the house, I found my mother sitting in an armchair on the back porch, sobbing softly. In one hand she held my dad's old pliers. Her other hand was dripping blood onto a pile of old newspapers. I came closer and saw a fat sliver of porcelain wedged underneath one of her fingernails. I took the pliers and yanked the shard out before she could even protest, and was rewarded with a chorus of "Thank you, Jesus!" I don't know how it was that my mother was able to make her need known to me, but I do know how good it felt to have been there for her.

As I grew into manhood, my life didn't take me too far from home. I attended Lincoln University in Jefferson City, Missouri, graduating near the top of my class, and married a local girl. While on semester break in my hometown after driving my mother to church one Sunday, my eye was drawn to a beautiful young woman walking down the street with her mother. I recognized her as someone I knew, but couldn't imagine that this lovely young lady was Barbara, the little girl with skinny legs I remembered skipping rope in front of the local movie theater. I was smitten, and wasted little time courting her. We married very soon thereafter, and set about starting our family. Not a day has gone by when I haven't felt grateful for the good fortune that put Barbara in my life.

At first, I capitalized on my musical ability to find work, teaching lessons part time at a local accordion school. I even had the chance at a full-time job as a high school music teacher, but I'd already begun to feel that this was not my calling. My introduction to law enforcement was through a classified ad that Barbara spotted in the *St. Louis Post-Dispatch*. The Pinkerton National Detective Agency was looking for investigators. I decided to apply, which led to an experience that was to presage many later episodes in my professional career.

I went to the St. Louis office of the Pinkerton Agency on a cold Monday in January 1957. One of the two women at the front desk asked how she could help me. I told her I had come about the ad for investigators in the newspaper. Barbara had wisely counseled me to take the ad with me, in case there was some confusion, and I held it out to the receptionist. She turned to her colleague and said, "He's looking for a job application."

The other woman, a small blonde who had been pecking away at her typewriter, looked at the ad, then looked at me, then shook her head. "I don't think they're hiring."

I protested, holding the newspaper ad from just the day before. "The ad says that Pinkerton is looking for detective investigators, and it gives this address at the bottom of the ad."

"Well, as far as I know, they're not hiring people like you."

I didn't feel like letting that slide. "But the ad doesn't specify a white investigator or a Negro investigator," I said coldly. I turned on my heel and had one hand on the exit door when I heard a man's voice.

"What seems to be the problem out here?" A tall, well-dressed, middle-aged man had come out from the main office and was taking in the scene. The woman explained how I had come in looking for a job and how she was handling the situation, but he stopped her short.

"Give him an application, and when he finishes filling it out, show him into my office." I was interviewed on the spot and learned that while the Pinkerton Agency employed some black uniformed guards, none was working as a detective. They seemed to be impressed by my college record and by my pledge to work hard so that they would never regret the decision to hire me. A week or so later, I was hired as a Pinkerton detective, the beginning of my life in police work.

A year later, I joined the Illinois State Highway Police, stationed in Peoria, and eventually moved out of traffic control, becoming one of the first members of the Illinois Criminal Investigation Division when it was formed. There, my knowledge of police work deepened. Many of the investigations in which I participated had to do with gambling and helped prepare me for my work later with the Secret Service.

By the time I made it into the Secret Service, at the end of October 1960, I not only had a fair amount of law-enforcement experience under my belt but also had learned a thing or two about breaking down color barriers. It seemed that each job brought with it the opportunity to become a racial pioneer. At Pinkerton, I had been the first black detective, and as a state police officer, I'd had the prestige of becoming the first black patrolman assigned to work District 8 in Peoria. There wasn't much I hadn't seen or heard. I knew what to expect from the other agents, and I had an idea of what they'd expect of me.

The Secret Service at that time was a relatively small organization, with about three hundred agents, a third of whom were assigned to Washington, D.C., either as part of the White House detail or to other protective research positions. The rest of us were field agents, scattered to various offices around the country and in a handful of foreign countries. We were required to provide protection for the president and vice president if they were in our area, but our primary day-to-day responsibility was to investigate counterfeiting, the transfer of American and foreign currency and other negotiable documents, and the forging of checks and instruments issued by the U.S. Treasury Department.

I served primarily in the Chicago field office, although from time to time I went to other cities on undercover assignments to investigate counterfeiters. These were dangerous operations that required an agent to assume a false identity and act his part with great skill, lest he be unmasked and threatened. I enjoyed the work immensely, even though it took me away from my family, and found I had a talent for it, posting a 100 percent rate of success in these cases.

Of course, the Chicago office was not free of racial issues. At first, I was assigned to work with three postal inspector aides in an effort to clean up a large backlog of check forgery cases in the city's densely populated black ghettoes. I didn't encounter any serious problems, but within the office itself, I began to get hints of the kind of racism that seemed fairly standard in those days, especially after the agent in charge departed and was replaced by Harry Geighlein. Geighlein held weekly staff meetings and liked to keep things light, usually opening with some banter and jokes, some which had clear racial overtones. He would casually refer to black males as "colored boys." Eventually I complained, only to be told that I needed to relax, to develop a thicker skin. My superiors seemed to feel that their making such jokes actually reflected how completely I had been accepted in the "club," but I wasn't buying it, and extracted a promise that such behavior would cease immediately.

That didn't stop everyone in the office from indulging in the usual antics. One agent, named J. Lloyd Stocks, had a habit of making "colored boy" jokes when he knew I could hear him. He liked to horse around, pantomiming the shuffling gait and slow drawl that formed the caricature of an uneducated southern Negro. Again, I made my resentment known, and although no official action was taken, Agent Stocks did stop his clowning. Over time, he and I developed what I thought was an amicable relationship.

Chapter 3

THE SECRET SERVICE made little mention of my status as the first black agent on the presidential detail, either within the Service itself or to the general public. I had received my orders to come to Washington shortly after my conversation with President Kennedy in that Chicago basement. The assignment was for an initial thirty-day probationary period, after which I would have the option of remaining as a permanent member of the detail or returning to my position as a field agent in the Chicago office.

In fact, another agent in the Secret Service had been touted as the first "Negro" in the agency. That agent, however, viewed his Negro heritage with disdain, pointing out that he was a fluent Spanish-speaker who was the offspring of a Hispanic mother and a "mixed Negro" father. I worked with him in 1963, and he wasted no time in making his feelings clear. While we were on an undercover assignment in Cleveland, Ohio, this agent punched a handcuffed black prisoner in the face. I took immediate exception to the unnecessary brutality and reminded him that the prisoner was a "black brother" and shouldn't be receiving that kind of treatment from his own Negro kindred.

"Don't call me a Negro. I'm no Negro. I'm Puerto Rican, so don't ever call me a Negro again! Look at my hair and the color of my skin. Do I look black to you?" He added a few uncomplimentary remarks about blacks in general, comments that stuck with me a long time and tainted my association with him for the rest of my tenure with the Secret Service.

In April 1961, just days before I met him, President Kennedy issued the following order:

Memorandum for the Heads of All Executive Departments and Agencies

Executive Order Number 10925, promulgated March 6, 1961, reaffirms that "discrimination because of race, creed, color or national origin is contrary to the Constitutional principles and policies of the United States" and that "it is the policy of the Executive Branch of the Government to encourage by positive measures equal opportunity for all qualified persons within the Government." I want immediate and specific action taken to assure that no use is made of the name, sponsorship, facilities, or activity of any Executive Department or Agency by or for any employee recreational organization practicing discrimination based on race, creed, color, or national origin. Current practices in each Department are to be brought into immediate compliance with this policy, and a report by the head of each Executive Agency filed to that effect before May 1, 1961.

I believed that Kennedy's commitment to racial equality was deeply felt and sincere. Suffering is a great equalizer, and I had seen something in Kennedy's eyes that made me understand that he had known suffering of his own and could empathize with people of vastly different experience. It would have been easy to see the appointment of a black agent to his personal detail as a political attention grabber, but in truth, he didn't need a stunt like that to win over African American voters. They loved him already.

If anything, the president's efforts in the area of civil rights hurt him politically more than they helped him. He alienated Southerners and conservatives around the country, most of whom were already suspicious of him. In this, the Secret Service reflected the more backward elements of America. Many of the agents with whom I worked were products of the South. Time and again I overheard them making chilling racist remarks, referring to Kennedy as "that nigger-lover," whose efforts to force integration in the South and enforce other civil rights initiatives were "screwing up the country." I heard some members of the White House detail say that if shots were fired at the president, they'd take no action to protect him. A few agents vowed that they would quit the Secret Service rather than give up their lives for Kennedy.

These were, of course, volatile times for race relations in America. A month before I was to report to Washington, violence erupted in several southern cities. In May 1961, the Congress of Racial Equality (CORE) staged a series of "Freedom Rides" in Alabama in an effort to integrate buses and bus terminals. One bus was burned by a mob in Anniston, Alabama. An angry segregationist crowd attacked a group of civil rights demonstrators in Montgomery, injuring several people. Several hundred U.S. marshals, sent in by Attorney General Robert Kennedy, arrived to protect the demonstrators. National Guardsmen, with fixed bayonets, scattered a mob that had challenged them outside a black church where Martin Luther King Jr. was speaking.

Elsewhere, the Student Non-Violent Coordinating Committee (SNCC) would face opposition from more radical black nationalist and black power organizations. The Nation of Islam, led by the Honorable Elijah Muhammad, would rise in prominence, bringing in many new recruits for a new "Black Nation of Islam," as more and more flourishing Muslim businesses challenged the status quo of white dominance in America. Images of violence and upheaval sparked by simmering racial tension were electrifying the airwaves and print media across the country and around the world.

Such was the climate when I arrived in Washington on the night of June 5, 1961. I only had a couple of hours until I was to report for duty at the White House at midnight. The guard at the gate checked my credentials with great care, and I felt his eyes on my back as I entered the building. Turning to look at him, I saw in his face the understanding that my arrival there was historic.

Inside the White House, I was greeted by Stu Stout, a broad-shouldered, middle-aged agent neatly dressed in a dark suit. As Agent Stout led me through the building, past the portraits of Abraham Lincoln and George Washington and the presidential seal etched into the floor, I marveled at the elegant furnishings, the marble and polished mahogany, the sheer grandeur of the place. He sat me down in the small Secret Service office and gave me some initial instructions.

"The president is going to Palm Beach Thursday. We don't know exactly when, but we should be leaving before noon. When I show you around in a few minutes, you will notice that some agents are carrying small tote bags with them. They have a few extra changes of clothing in them because on this job you never know when the president might decide to leave the White House for a while. I would advise you to get a tote bag if you don't already have one. Put a change of shorts, a shirt or two, and a few toilet items inside."

I told him that I knew where I could get one right after my shift ended, and he quickly told me that I wouldn't need it that soon. I wouldn't be going to Palm Beach, but would be assigned to the president's Glen Ora Farm compound in Middleburg, Virginia, where the First Lady would be staying while the president was in Florida.

Stu showed me around. We walked past the office of press secretary Pierre Salinger and his assistant, Andrew Hatcher, the first black man to hold the post. Passing other Secret Service agents, we came to a highly polished dark wooden door bearing the seal of the president of the United States. Stu opened the door just wide enough for me to glimpse the president's large desk and the rocking chair that had received so much attention. Immediately past the Oval Office was the Cabinet Room, dominated by a great long mahogany table, where, Stu said, "decisions are made that affect the whole world." I saw immaculate meeting rooms, salons used for entertaining, the spotless kitchen, and the elevator that led to the First Family's living quarters. We descended below ground level and walked along long, brightly lit corridors, where uniformed personnel moved around purposefully or sat in front of computer consoles and television monitors. Brightly colored maps and displays lined the walls. It seemed otherworldly.

Stu paused in front of a set of heavy gray steel doors and told me that what I was about to see was one of many things I would learn about that were never to be discussed outside the Service. He opened the door and showed me "the president's office in case of extreme emergency," a room furnished nearly identically to the president's office upstairs, but with computer-animated maps on the walls and a communications office.

I spent the rest of that first night in the Secret Service office within the White House, studying the appropriate sections on protection in the agency manual and getting to know the other agents, who would stop by and introduce themselves. One agent in particular, however, seemed to be keeping his distance. He never introduced himself or even acknowledged me. I said something to him as he walked by my desk for the second or third time, but he didn't respond. I hated to be guilty of the same kind of stereotyping that had been directed at me so often, but this agent just had the look of trouble about him. He was large and paunchy, with his stomach hanging over his belt. But he held himself with the bearing of a military man and the confident movements of a former athlete. When he spoke, I heard the unmistakable accent of the Deep South. I wondered if perhaps I had inadvertently sat at his desk, and moved to another desk in the office, but he showed no reaction.

Later, after he had left, I asked another of the agents about him. "That's Harvey Henderson," Agent Edward Tucker told me. "He takes over when Stu is off. He's been around a long time on the detail. He has a quick temper and has a problem with some people. If he gives you any trouble, just let me know."

In the morning, on the way to my apartment after my first White House shift, I bought that tote bag Stu had mentioned, and a pair of sunglasses. I phoned Barbara to share the excitement of my new assignment and to tell her about all that I had seen. Over the next couple of days I familiarized myself with my duties. One of my tasks, like all the White House agents, was to stand post at various locations in and around the building. I had studied the manual carefully on this point and knew the regulations. An agent was required to be inside (if the post was one of the small enclosed guard stations) or in very close proximity to his post at all times until relieved by another agent. According to the manual, failing to secure a post of duty, leaving without permission, or drinking on a post of duty were all grounds for immediate dismissal from the Secret Service.

John Kennedy had already left for Palm Beach when I arrived for work on June 9, which I thought must have accounted for the fact that no agents were manning the two security posts in the White House lobby. I went straight to the Secret Service office to resume studying the manual, as I had been instructed. I found my copy, with the strip of paper I had stuck between the pages to mark my place.

Inside the book, right next to my bookmark, was a surprise. It was a copy of an office memo, folded in half, with a crude caricature

penciled on the back. The drawing showed a man with obviously exaggerated Negroid features—a large, flat nose, wide lips stretching
from ear to ear, and tight beads of hair. The face had been colored in,
black except for the big white eyes and oversized lips. And the
tears . . . the man in the picture was crying.

It wasn't the overt racism that surprised me, but rather the fact
that something like this had happened so soon, after only a few
days on the detail, and in the White House of John Kennedy, the
man who never missed a chance to demand publicly and forcefully
that racism and bigotry be eliminated throughout America. This
was a president who was prepared to send troops into the South to
ensure justice for black people and who had seen to it that I was
brought into his personal protection detail. I had sworn an oath. I
had left my wife and family halfway across the country to be in this
dangerous place, prepared to sacrifice my own life for the president's, and there I sat in the stillness of the office, listening to the
pounding of my heart, staring at a cartoon of a crying, buffoonish
black man. The memo on the other side of the picture compounded
my anger.

```
OFFICE MEMORANDUM       UNITED STATES GOVERNMENT
TO: SAIC—WH DETAIL     (AIR MAIL) DATE: JUNE 6, 1961
FROM: SAIC MARSHAL—MIAMI              3-11-602-111
SUBJECT: VISIT OF THE PRESIDENT TO PALM BEACH, FLORIDA


    This will confirm my long distance telephone
conversation today with ASAIC Behn relative to
securing reservations at Woody's South Wind Motel,
West Palm Beach, Fla.
    I advised that I had conferred with Mr. R.
McCarthy of the above named motel and he advised
that he would not accept a colored agent at this
```

motel but that he could find housing at a first
class colored motel at Riviera Beach, Fla.

ASAIC Behn was further advised that the
exclusive Palm Beach Towers accommodates
Assistant Press Secretary Hatcher and that
possibly the colored agent could share a room with
Mr. Hatcher.

As an alternative, two shifts could be
accommodated at Woody's Motel and, if integration
is an issue here, reservations for the entire
working shift employing this Negro agent could be
housed together at the Negro Motel.

This is a very explosive situation which may
bring unfavorable publicity to the President and
this service if not handled carefully.

                                         John A. Marshal

Chief 2cc   SAIC Miami

Reading the memo left me totally deflated. It was all too clear to me that the racism that Kennedy wanted so much to stamp out in the country was alive and well in his own government, in this very service. Here was an opportunity to put Kennedy's words into action, but it was clearly not a priority of the old guard at the Secret Service, whose attitude was no better than that of the hotel manager in Palm Beach, not to mention the duly elected governors who were actively resisting integration in places such as Mississippi, Alabama, and Arkansas.

I hand-copied the text of the memorandum, folded the memo, and placed it back in the book. I was going to keep cool, say nothing, and see if my lack of response might lure the prankster out into the open. Maybe he would give himself away with some more overt and direct racist comment or action.

Chapter 4

A WEEK AND a half later, having moved off the midnight shift to more reasonable hours, I was standing post directly outside the president's office, where a meeting was going on. The door opened, and Senators Hubert Humphrey and Barry Goldwater walked out of the Oval Office. I reached in to close the door behind them, and the president, who was talking with his brother Robert, looked up and noticed me.

"Mr. Bolden, I see you made it here. How do you like Washington?" He extended his right hand to me.

Stunned that the president remembered our conversation, no less my name, I stammered, "F-fine, Mr. President."

Kennedy smiled broadly. "How's Mayor Daley?"

"Fine, Mr. President."

He motioned to Senators Goldwater and Humphrey, who were still standing outside the office, and we walked out toward them.

"This is Mr. Bolden." He raised his hand in a gesture of formal introduction. "He's the first Negro to be assigned to the Secret Service White House staff."

Humphrey greeted me with warmth and enthusiasm, pumping my hand and asking how I was finding Washington. Goldwater, on the other hand, made no audible greeting, nor did he try to shake my hand. I got the sense that he thought meeting me wasn't nearly as important as the conversation with Humphrey that the president had interrupted.

"Have you met my brother Bobby?" the president asked, leading me back into the Oval Office, but the attorney general appeared to have left. Still smiling, apparently enjoying my presence there, Kennedy introduced me to his secretary, Evelyn Lincoln, and to his press secretary, Pierre Salinger, to whom he described me as "the Jackie Robinson of the Secret Service." When Kennedy and Salinger began to get back to business, I returned to my post. I was relieved by another agent about five minutes later.

I returned to the Secret Service office, where Agent Henderson, in charge of the shift that day, was reading a newspaper.

"We sent your relief," Henderson drawled. "You weren't on your post. You're not supposed to leave your post for any reason." He barely looked up from his paper.

"President Kennedy took me into his office," I said.

My explanation seemed to further inflame Henderson. "You're not supposed to leave your post until you are relieved," he continued, his voice rising in anger. He now folded the paper and laid it on top of the desk.

"President Kennedy called me into the office and I was with him for a while," I said again, my own agitation now showing. "What am I supposed to do when President Kennedy gives me an order or asks me to do something? I can't tell the president what to do."

"If something happens in your area and you're not on your post, your ass is going to be in the wringer," he warned, waving his finger at me as I walked out of the office. I stopped and turned, and Henderson and I stood for a moment staring unblinkingly at each other. I felt with sudden certainty that he had been the one who had left the cartoon and the memo in my manual. I had the fleeting thought to rush him, to have it out right then and there. Henderson tugged at the top of his pants but made no move to sit back down or advance toward me.

I knew I couldn't challenge him. It would have been a disgrace and an embarrassment to the president. More important, it would have played right into the hands of men such as Henderson, helping them make their case that blacks were unfit for such a position. Besides, Agent Henderson was the shift supervisor that day, and so he was legitimately in a position to comment on how I did my job. With the tension still simmering, I walked away.

Not all the agents on the White House detail were like Henderson, for which I was thankful. Stu Stout, for example, the agent who greeted me when I first got there, represented the other side of the coin. He and I were among the agents who accompanied the president a few days later on a cruise on the Potomac aboard his yacht, the *Sequoia*. As the boat motored along the river, trailed by a Coast Guard patrol boat, Agent Stout and I sat together in some leather fishing chairs on deck.

Stout was a veteran agent. He had served on the presidential detail under both Truman and Eisenhower. He had traveled around the world and had met more prominent leaders and dignitaries than I had even seen on television or in the newspapers. Still, he never boasted about his career, but talked to me about it in a thoughtful and friendly way. Stout described the attempted assassination of Harry Truman at Blair House in Washington, when he had been on duty. Truman had been living there while the White House was under renovation. On November 1, 1950, two members of the Puerto Rican Nationalist Party, Oscar Collazo and Griselio Torresola, stormed the hotel. Several uniformed White House police officers were wounded in the ensuing confrontation, and one of them, Private Leslie Coffelt, died from his wounds. Agent Stout had been one of the Secret Service agents who had sealed off access to the president's quarters, where Truman was taking a nap.

I had read about the quick and courageous actions of the agents at Blair House. In fact, the account of that incident helped fuel my interest in becoming a Secret Service agent, back when I was a state police officer in Peoria. To hear this man describe it with such matter-of-fact calm made me again feel proud that I had been able to join the Service. He represented the quiet courage and simple decency that I had always imagined would define the men in this job. I watched Agent Stout as he told me the story, and noticed that even while we chatted, he was relaxed but always alert, never forgetting his duty.

When he finished the story, Stout took off his tie pin and held it out to me. "Did you ever get one of these?"

I examined the tie pin. It was shaped like a PT boat making its way through water, and on it was etched "Kennedy, 60."

"That was Kennedy's campaign pin," Stout said softly. "He gave that to me personally, and now I'm giving it to you."

"No, Mr. Stout," I protested, trying to hand the pin back to him. "If I take this, then you won't have one, and it's from the president."

"That's okay, Abe. I have plenty of souvenirs from Kennedy and other presidents. This is your first one. Take it. I can get another one. And stop calling me 'Mr. Stout,'" he added with a smile. "Call me Stu. Everyone else does."

"Thanks, Mr.—uh—I mean, Stu," I laughed. "Thanks a lot."

We could see the sun setting as the boat began its return to the dock. Stu Stout laughed, too, for the first time during the trip.

Chapter 5

W HEN THE PRESIDENT returned from Palm Beach, he went to join his wife and family at Glen Ora Farm in Virginia. Kennedy needed to rest his back for a few days, having aggravated a lingering problem. Dr. Janet Travell, the president's personal physician, attended him there, which, along with the crutches he occasionally used, sparked a great deal of speculation in the press regarding his condition, although the press generally refrained from using photos of him on crutches. Dr. Travell's presence was significant for other reasons, at least to me. She represented another gesture on Kennedy's part to create opportunities for all Americans. By placing women and members of minorities in high-profile positions, he was leading by example.

It seemed that the president was always on the move. After returning from Virginia, he intended to spend the Fourth of July holiday at the Kennedy family compound at Hyannis Port, on Cape Cod in Massachusetts. I would be traveling there with the Secret Service detail.

Standard procedure on such a trip was as follows: The Secret Service detail that had direct responsibility for the president would fly ahead on a chartered plane, so that they could be on the ground and ready to assume their protective duties as soon as the president walked off his plane, Air Force One. A few senior agents would fly with the president, and another detachment of agents would remain at the airport of departure in case some emergency required Air Force One to turn around and come back.

Customarily, the advance flight also carried a sizeable contingent of the White House press corps, who also wanted to be waiting on the ground when the President landed, especially the photographers. The press corps and the Secret Service agents had been through this routine often enough and all seemed to know one another. The revelry began as soon as the plane was in the air, with lots of noisy joking and chatter. Pretty soon, a stewardess came walking down the aisle, passing out liquor in those little airplane bottles free of charge to anyone who wanted it. Soft drinks were also available. I asked for soda. The rules forbidding agents from drinking on duty were as clear as they could be.

As I've said, the Secret Service isn't a very large organization, and like everyplace else, people talk. Within the Service, the drinking and carousing on the part of the White House detail was nearly legendary. I had heard plenty of stories about the agents assigned to the White House detail, and decided this was my chance to see if there was any truth to the stories. In the course of the short flight, I managed to stroll the length of the cabin. Several agents had what appeared to be mixed drinks in their hands. Two empty liquor bottles were sitting on the tray table in front of Agent Harvey Henderson, who happened to be acting as the shift supervisor that day.

As soon as we landed at Otis Air Force Base, agents took up positions by a roped-off area of the runway where a substantial crowd had gathered to greet the president. Massachusetts state police officers provided additional security. When Air Force One arrived, Kennedy stepped off the plane and walked straight toward the crowd, reaching over the barricade to shake hands with the many well-wishers, while the state troopers, with arms outstretched, held them back. The mood was light and friendly. Kennedy was clearly happy to be back in Massachusetts on this hot summer day.

Suddenly, I felt a tug on my coat sleeve. I turned quickly to discover that my arm was in the grasp of one of the uniformed state troopers.

"Let me see some ID," he demanded.

I simply pointed at the Secret Service identification pin on my lapel and tried to keep moving, to maintain my position in the line of protection as the president moved along in front of the crowd. The trooper, however, didn't let go. I forcefully jerked my arm free and strode off toward the president, but out of the corner of my eye, I could see the trooper taking a step to follow me.

"Leave him alone!" another agent shouted, trotting over. "He's with Kennedy." That agent stayed at my side until Kennedy climbed into the helicopter that was waiting to ferry him to his compound.

My shift of agents piled into a big station wagon to head toward Hyannis Port. The smell of alcohol filled the car, and it seemed to me that several of the agents were slurring their speech and showing other effects of their in-flight drinking. At least three of them were clearly in no condition to respond properly to any emergency that might develop.

We drove past an administrative building on the base and could see Air Force men and women strolling in their neatly pressed uniforms, prompting comments about the good-looking Women's Air Corps members. Suddenly, one of the agents in the car, Bob Foster, pointed out the window and shouted in his thick southern accent, "Thar goes a nigger!" Foster quickly reached up and cupped his hand in front of his mouth as if trying to catch the words he had just spoken. "Oops!" He was pointing at a young African American woman walking through the base, seemingly proud and happy in her Women's Air Corps uniform, unaware of the slurs aimed at her by this representative of the U.S. government.

I said nothing, nor did anyone else in the car, although one agent flinched noticeably at the comment. Others were clearly startled and turned to stare at Foster. Foster gave me a sidelong glance. My blood was boiling, and once again I had to resist the temptation to reach over and punch one of my colleagues.

At the compound, Agent Henderson took over the wheel of the station wagon from the driver who had picked us up, and drove the agents on our shift to a large white cottage in town, about five minutes away. After the memo I had read back at the White House, I had been apprehensive about the living arrangements, but there was nothing unusual here. Secret Service agents used this cottage whenever the president was in Hyannis Port. It had a large wooden porch across the front, a sitting area with a number of bedrooms off it, and a well-equipped kitchen. The large backyard had a patio and a brick barbecue pit, and led into thick woods. The cottage was relatively secluded, about fifty yards from the nearest house. As we hadn't eaten since we left Washington, everybody chipped in some money, and Henderson and Foster drove off to buy food and drinks. They came back in about an hour with the groceries, along with a healthy supply of beer and bourbon.

We spent the afternoon and evening eating, drinking, chatting, and watching television. About 8:00 P.M., I overheard Henderson asking agents—not including me—if they wanted to go into town. He drove off with a couple of other men. In addition to the drinking, the White House detail also had a reputation for womanizing. Stories circulated throughout the service about arrogant agents in Washington who fancied themselves playboys, and sure enough, I was awakened at about 2:00 A.M. by the sounds of women's voices. I got up, used the bathroom, and wandered to the windows overlooking the front of the cottage. I heard the laughter of a woman and some men coming from one of the bedrooms, and a little later on saw two agents drive away with a couple of women in the station wagon.

THE SCENE AT the Kennedy compound the next day seemed straight out of a *Life* magazine photo spread. Large, stately homes were spaced out along a lawn that sloped down into a sandy beach. Children were playing everywhere. The president's father, Joseph Kennedy, sat on a porch overlooking the ocean, his legs wrapped in a blanket, with his wife, Rose, at his side. On the water, a small sailboat with a group of boisterous passengers tacked back and forth, expertly piloted by Ted Kennedy. Later in the afternoon, adults and children joined in a happy game of touch football. Fittingly enough for the president of the United States, John Kennedy quarterbacked his team, despite the evident pain in his back.

One morning, I was seated at a post of duty near the compound's beach when Jacqueline Kennedy and her little daughter, Caroline, came strolling hand in hand down the path from the house. Mrs. Kennedy offered a cheerful "Good morning," which I acknowledged a little nervously.

"Will you please watch Caroline for me while I take a swim?" she asked with a smile as she guided the girl to a chair next to me.

"I'd be happy to."

"I won't be gone long," Mrs. Kennedy said. She spread out her blanket, adjusted her bathing cap, and slid gracefully into the water.

Caroline sat quietly for a few minutes, looking at me from across the table, then got up and went to play in the sand. Finally, her curiosity got the better of her, and she walked back to me.

"What's your name?"

"My name is Abraham," I told her in the playful voice I used with my own small children.

"Abraham?" she repeated.

"Yes. Like Abraham Lincoln."

She regarded me for a moment, pondering her next question. "Do you have a little girl?"

I told Caroline that I had a little girl about the same age as she was. "Her name is Ahvia."

"Can she come and play with me?"

"She's far away in Chicago," I answered, gesturing up over the ocean toward the sky.

"I can go to Chicago," Caroline offered.

"Okay," I said. "When you come to Chicago, the two of you can play together."

Caroline went back to playing in the sand, but later, after her mother had finished swimming and the two of them were walking back up toward the house, I heard Caroline ask, "Mommy, can we go to Chicago?" I never heard Mrs. Kennedy's answer.

Later that afternoon, the president took a cruise around Nantucket Sound on his fifty-two-foot yacht, the *Marlin*. It was one of many boating excursions he and his family took during this holiday visit. I wasn't assigned to the yacht or to the follow-up Coast Guard boat, but remained behind, patrolling part of the beach. When the yacht returned, the president was met on the dock by his brother Robert. As the two men approached me, I turned my back to them in order to secure the perimeter, as was my duty. To my surprise, the president stopped behind me and called out, "Mr. Bolden."

I turned and walked toward them.

"Have you met my brother Bobby?" he asked, just as he had back in the Oval Office. "Bobby, this is Mr. Bolden. I'm sure he knows who you are, since both of you are in the same business," he joked. "Mr. Bolden is the first Negro on the White House detail."

"Glad to meet you, Mr. Bolden." Bobby Kennedy held out his hand to mine. "I'm glad to see the Secret Service making progress in this area. It's long overdue. Where's your home office?"

"Chicago, sir."

"Oh, that's Mayor Daley's territory."

"Yeah," laughed President Kennedy. "He's one of Mayor Daley's enforcers."

Bobby Kennedy asked me why I hadn't come into the FBI.

"We're always looking for good people. We have several Negro agents and they've been with us for many years."

When I answered that I had indeed thought about the FBI but felt I couldn't qualify without a law or accounting degree, he said, "Things like that can always be waived. If you are still interested, you should make out an application in the Chicago office. We're looking to hire more Negro agents very soon."

The president kept the conversation going. "Do you intend to make a career in police work, Mr. Bolden?"

"No, Mr. President. Someday, I would like to be a diplomat to one of the African nations."

"Do you speak any of the African languages?"

"No, sir."

"Well," the president said, "I'll be around for seven or eight more years. You should enroll in a school of languages. I think Berlitz has a school of languages right in Chicago." His brother mentioned that they sent some agents there for training.

"Look into it when you get back to Chicago," the president continued. "Let me know when you have completed one of the courses. If you qualify, I may be able to help you achieve your goal."

As I thanked the president, I was taken by the contrast between the two brothers. While John Kennedy's eyes were soft and welcoming, Robert's were hard and piercing. Robert had a reputation for ruthlessness in those days, and now that I was in his presence, I could understand why. He gave the impression that he could and would do whatever needed to be done, regardless of the consequences or of the pain his decisions might cause. I sensed that the president's first considerations would always involve mercy or compromise, whereas Bobby's instincts were to achieve total victory. If one was a natural diplomat, the other was a warrior. They complemented each other perfectly, and it seemed that the president had chosen the ideal attorney general for those turbulent times.

The president turned and began walking toward the house but stopped abruptly and clutched at his right hip and lower back as a grimace crossed his face. His brother offered to get a golf cart for him, but Kennedy looked back over his shoulder at the little flotilla of boats offshore, full of press photographers with high-powered cameras. Determined to show the nation a strong, able leader at all times, he pushed back his shoulders and stood nearly perfectly straight.

"I'll walk."

As the two men strode away, I looked up and saw Harvey Henderson standing some distance off, his arms folded across his chest and his gaze fixed on me. My shift was just about over, and as we drove back to the cottage together a short while later, Henderson was unusually quiet. Clearly, there was something on his mind.

I was on duty the next time Kennedy took his yacht out for a cruise. I was about to climb down into the follow-up boat when I noticed Agent Henderson on the yacht, in conversation with the president. When they finished, the president disappeared into the cabin, and Henderson motioned for me to leave the follow-up boat.

"There's been a change in your assignment today," he said. "You're on the yacht."

I sat down in one of the leather deck chairs as the yacht made its way out into Nantucket Sound. Not too long into the journey, the galley door swung open. A crisply dressed U.S. Navy sailor stepped out carrying a silver tray laid out with a silver bowl, some crackers, and a glass of juice. He marched straight over to me and set the tray on my lap.

"Sir, the president would like you to have some lunch." The sailor did an about-face and was gone before I could answer. My astonishment didn't stop me from making short work of the bowl of delicious clam chowder.

The sail was uneventful, highlighted by a short stop to allow

Mrs. Kennedy to swim. Afterward, Agent Henderson again said next to nothing on the drive back to the cottage, but once we arrived and settled in to relax for the evening, I could sense his restlessness, which seemed to border on agitation. Agents were breaking out the drinks. Henderson sat on the living room couch, opened a beer, and leveled a cold, hard stare at me, which I did my best to ignore. He kept it up through two or three quick beers, until he suddenly spoke.

"Bolden."

"Yeah, Harvey?"

"I'm going to tell you something, and I don't want you ever to forget it." The sound of the South was heavy in his voice. "You're a nigger. You were born a nigger, and when you die, you'll still be a nigger. You will always be nothing but a nigger. So act like one!" Henderson spaced the words out slowly for emphasis, but his voice was rising.

The words hung in the room as every agent stared silently at Harvey Henderson. He had moved his body to the edge of the couch. His feet were flat on the floor and he was clutching his beer bottle. You could hear him breathing hard through his nostrils. He was like an animal, poised to spring forward if I made any move toward him.

If I had ever doubted that Henderson had planted that memo and cartoon back in the White House, I knew it for certain now, as surely as I knew that he was baiting me, trying to lure me into a fight. Thoughts of Jackie Robinson raced through my mind. I do not mean to equate myself with a hero of Robinson's stature, but in that moment, I thought about the years of locker room taunts that he had endured, and the many times his white teammates had tried to pick fights with him, just so that they could humiliate him. I'd dealt with racism my entire professional life, once even having to pull my gun on a motorist who refused to be ticketed by a "nigger." But here I was faced with a representative of my own nation's government, the acting head of our president's personal guard . . . my supervisor. I'm sure he wanted nothing more than to beat me bloody, but he also wanted me to disgrace myself by losing control. I eyed Harvey Henderson—a big, powerful man, drunk and full of hatred—and knew that if we were to go at it, there could be no mercy. I would have to send him to his God before he sent me to mine.

I looked him squarely in the eyes. "I love you, too, Harvey," I said, and walked out to the porch.

"You shouldn't have said that, Harvey," said Agent Tucker, who then followed me outside.

"Don't pay any attention to him, Abe," Tucker told me. "He gets like that when he's drinking." Tucker went back into the cottage. I kept on walking for a long time. When I got back to the cottage, I sat awhile longer on the porch steps, weary in body and soul, and realized that I was ready to go back to Chicago. My mother had taught me not to remain where I was clearly not wanted.

THE FOURTH OF July was a big event at the Kennedy compound, with a picnic that seemed to last most of the day. The rich and famous were arriving, including Sargent Shriver and Peter Lawford, but none of them held any appeal for me. I had met John F. Kennedy, and that was all I needed. My shift was over, and while most of the off-duty agents returned to the compound that night for food and drinks and fireworks, I stayed behind at the cottage and ate some sandwiches in solitude. I couldn't wait for morning to come, and with it my chance to return home.

At the compound the next day, I was told to report to the helicopter pad in front of the mansion. I would be returning with the president. The helicopter ride was a first for me and all but took my breath away. Air Force One made an even bigger impression, with its multitude of suites and rooms, all elegantly appointed, and the banks of elaborate communications equipment staffed by uniformed personnel. Usually, the Secret Service agents who flew with the president on Air Force One were the most senior personnel, veterans of long standing on the White House detail, but someone had assigned me there that day, and I had a notion of who was behind it.

As he walked through the main cabin where the agents were seated, John Kennedy acknowledged me with a nod and a smile. My intuition told me that he wanted me to remain in Washington, to become a permanent member of the White House detail, and my presence on the plane was a gesture toward that end. As gratified as I was by this idea, I couldn't shake my deep sadness over recent events. It seemed to me that I had no choice but to cast off any thoughts of staying on.

Chapter 6

I N M I D - J U L Y , T H E chief of the White House detail, James Rowley, asked me to report to the Treasury Building for an exit interview with U. E. Baughman, chief of the United States Secret Service. Chief Baughman, a veteran of more than thirty years in the Service, was a tall, distinguished-looking man. Upon entering, I noticed that his office appeared to be in disarray. Documents were scattered all over his desk and stacked on every surface, including the tops of the file cabinets. Without looking up from the papers in front of him, he asked me what I thought of my assignment on the White House detail.

"Meeting the president and being around the White House were okay," I answered, "but I think that I prefer to work out in the field on counterfeiting and check cases. I like the investigative side of the job more than the protective."

"You were only here for the thirty-day period. Sometimes all of the travel is hard, especially on one's family," Baughman said. "Do you have any particular observations that you would like to make?" Even as he asked the question, the chief was reaching into a drawer for a fresh stack of papers, and kept himself busy thumbing through them. I didn't know it at the time, but the chief had resigned from the Service, effective within the next thirty days. I was probably watching him page through the residue of his career.

I explained to Chief Baughman that I had expected to encounter some form of racism when I came to Washington, but was nonetheless surprised by what I found. "My biggest disappointment was that the only racists I ran into were members within the Secret Service. There were a couple of incidents where the word *nigger* was used in my presence," I said. Without hesitation, I identified the agents involved and described the times and places of those instances.

"I think you took the right course of action," Baughman said. "You can bet that I will look into the matter and discuss it with Chief Rowley over there when I see him." He looked up from his papers, his attention now focused on me.

I went on to tell him that I thought the training I had received during the thirty-day stay was inadequate. "Every time I asked an agent what to do in case of this or that situation, the response was always, 'Play it by ear.' " I described how at one point, when the president went to the State Department auditorium for a news conference, another agent handed me an AR-15 automatic weapon. When I told him that I didn't know to operate the weapon, the agent had just smiled and said, "Fake it."

The chief was leaning back and looking at me, apparently disturbed by what he was hearing.

"Something like that should never happen. You should not have been given the gun unless you were qualified to use it."

Finally, I said that there was too much drinking of alcohol by the agents guarding the president, and that I had witnessed agents drinking liquor on the press plane going to Hyannis Port. "Two of the agents were high, in my opinion."

The chief took a small notebook out of his desk drawer. "And who were those agents?"

He wrote down the names as I spoke them. The drinking and partying by the agents on the presidential protection detail were common knowledge throughout our agency. It wasn't my intention to get any particular agents in trouble, and I told the chief so. I got the sense that he wasn't in a forgiving mood any longer when he said somewhat icily that while there was no prohibition against agents relaxing when not on duty, the shift supervisors were responsible for seeing that everyone on duty was able to perform their duties to the fullest, especially around the president.

I shook hands with Chief Baughman, signaling the end of my tenure on the White House detail, and at 9:00 P.M. that night, I boarded a plane for Chicago.

The very next morning, I was back at my desk in the Chicago office. I had barely begun sifting through a month's worth of mail and new case assignments when my superiors summoned me to find out about my stint in Washington. I sat down with SAIC Harry Geighlein and James Burke, his second in command. In contrast to his unkempt appearance and sloppy manners, Burke had a reputation as an absolute stickler who knew the Secret Service manual backward and forward and let it guide his every action and decision on the job. He was single-minded and detail-oriented, notorious around the office for making agents redo entire reports because of a single misspelled word or misplaced comma. And God help the poor soul who ever dared to question Burke's methods or his unwavering certainty.

I gave Geighlein and Burke a thorough account, speaking favorably of my meetings with the president and most of the other agents. I spoke about the trips to Glen Ora and Hyannis Port, eventually getting around to the drinking I'd witnessed on the detail, on the press plane, and in Hyannis.

Agent Burke pounced on this information. "They shouldn't be drinking during duty hours under any circumstances. The manual clearly forbids that. Did you report that to Rowley?" he asked, referring to the chief of the White House detail.

"No, I didn't say anything to him, but before I left Washington, I discussed it with Chief Baughman," I answered.

"You should have spoken directly to Rowley about the drinking. That's serious, and if what you say is true, someone should be fired."

Then I told them about the incident at the cottage, when Agent Henderson had thrown the word *nigger* in my face.

"What a big jerk," Geighlein commented.

Burke nodded in agreement but said only, "You can't be too thin-skinned." I suppose the Secret Service manual didn't cover this kind of thing. "Now, you take our other Negro agent in New York. He's not offended by those kinds of words. As a matter of fact, I have heard him use the word *nigger* myself."

"Yeah, Abe," Geighlein chimed in. "You're going to run into all kinds of people on this job, and you just have to let it roll off your back."

"But I'm me, not another agent, and I think that for a supervisor to tell an agent something like that—"

Burke interrupted. "I personally think you're being too sensitive about this whole issue. Things like that are going to happen, and you're going to have to learn not to let it bother you."

"I wonder what your attitude would be if I had called Harvey a white, honky, fat pig," I shot back angrily.

"All we're saying is that you can't be too thin-skinned over these racial issues." For Burke, there was nothing left to discuss.

I SOON SETTLED back into my old routine, handling a substantial caseload for the Chicago field office of the Secret Service. Over the next few years, I uncovered more counterfeiting plants and made more arrests involving the forgery of government checks, than any other agent anywhere in the country, according to Agent John Hanly, who had become the special agent in charge of our office. Hanly, a physically imposing former admiral in the U.S. Navy who still retained his military bearing and attitude, liked and respected me, which unfortunately didn't always work to my advantage. During the period of his stewardship, he appeared on television concerning several of the big cases that I solved in the Chicago area. At meetings he would openly refer to me as his "top agent" and tell other agents either to ask for my input on their cases or to try to learn from my example. I grew uncomfortable, sensing the resentment of the other agents. Before long, it was clear that few of the agents in our office were eager to cooperate with me.

The arrival of Agent Maurice Martineau complicated office dynamics even more. Martineau transferred to the Chicago office in early 1963 as assistant SAIC to Agent Hanly, and eventually he took over its leadership. Animosity between Hanly and Martineau simmered from the start of their tenure together, reportedly connected to some association earlier in their careers. Hanly made no effort to hide his contempt for Martineau, and the friction between them would occasionally escalate into heated arguments that we all witnessed.

I suffered personally from the tension between the two men, getting caught in the cross fire, so to speak. At one point, while I was investigating a counterfeiting case involving suspects named Frank Jones and Lee Braughton, Hanly called me into his office and instructed me not to turn in my reports to Martineau anymore. The manual was clear on this point; normal procedure required agents to hand over reports to the assistant agent in charge for review, and I had always done so.

I protested mildly, citing the manual, and Hanly replied, "I'll take care of Marty. I'm the agent in charge. If I tell you to give your reports directly to me, that is what I want you to do." He continued in his authoritative tone, "You're doing a hell of a job here, and I have put you in for a raise. I'll discuss everything with Marty."

Sure enough, Martineau called me into his office after one of our weekly meetings not long thereafter, and warned me that I was not following procedures as set forth in the manual.

"Mr. Hanly told me to bring my reports directly to him," I said in my defense.

Martineau pounded his fist on the desk and shouted, "Mr. Hanly is not the manual! Read this!" He shoved an open copy of the book at me, open to the appropriate page.

I jumped up from my chair and rushed to the door of Agent Hanly's office, which was actually connected to Martineau's. I was sure he had overheard the exchange between Martineau and me. Barely able to contain my own anger, I started to speak, but Hanly interrupted.

"Marty, let's talk."

Martineau and Hanly went at it behind the closed door of Hanly's office. One of the stenographers came over to ask me why the two men were screaming at each other, and when I explained what I knew, she said with genuine sympathy, "Ah, Abe, they're putting you in the middle."

After the argument was over, Mr. Hanly sat at his desk, red-faced and sweating, obviously still fuming from his argument with Martineau.

"Don't give Marty a damn thing," he thundered. "If he wants to know something about the investigations you are doing, let him come to me. You understand that?" He stood up to his full height. Knowing that Martineau could hear everything he said through the open office door, he added, "I'm the agent in charge, and as long as I am agent in charge, I'm running this goddamn office as I see fit."

"Yes, sir." I spoke in a soft, placating voice.

"Okay. Go back to work and bust some more asses." Hanly waved me out of the room, and as I walked out, past Martineau's desk, the assistant special agent in charge shot me a terrifying look. *If looks could kill,* I thought at that instant, *I'd be one dead black man.*

I was always on the wrong side of Maurice Martineau. Rather than praise me for clearing so many cases, as Hanly did, Martineau would call me into his office and complain that I was "hogging" cases. He suggested that if I had some cases that were winding up, getting close to a successful conclusion, I could turn them over to agents in the office who weren't having the same kind of "luck." When I flatly refused, he accused me of being too ambitious and uncompromising.

One episode in particular cemented the bad blood between us. On November 17, 1963, I flew to Washington at the request of the Intelligence Division of the Internal Revenue Service. Joseph Harmon was the chief of the division at the time. Having been instructed that this mission was top secret, I checked into the local YMCA under an assumed name and reported to my contact agent at the Treasury Building the next morning.

The agent, a tanned, middle-aged gentleman with a southern accent, politely ushered me into his office and offered me a seat. "The reason that we sent for you is that we are in the process of putting together an undercover agents program within the Intelligence Division of the IRS. We asked several of the other agencies in the government to recommend one or two of their best undercover agents for the program. These agents will be on loan to the IRS for extensive undercover operations in Washington, D.C., and in other parts of the country. The Secret Service recommended you to become part of the program."

"When will the program start?" I asked, surprised.

"It's already in progress. We have an assignment for you right now, here in Washington."

The prospect of transferring from Chicago to Washington began to interest me. "What kind of assignment, and where is it?" I asked.

"The initial assignment will be inside the Capitol Building. There are very influential and well-connected employees in the Capitol Building that are running skin games and loan sharking on other employees. We need a man inside to infiltrate the group and get information as to who is behind the operation and how much money is

being raked in. These people aren't paying any taxes and are draining the lower workers of their paychecks. These are, as I said, well-
connected people, and some of them work directly for senators and
congressmen on Capitol Hill."

"And when will I have to start?"

"You can't start until we have everything set up for you to go in.
There has to be a lot of preparation made for you to infiltrate this
group of people. They are smart and know how to get things done in
Washington, and there's a lot of money involved here."

I couldn't help being intrigued. "So what kind of preparations
are we talking about?"

The agent explained that the first step would be a complete
change of identity for me. I would be given another name, and all official references to Abraham Bolden—birth and marriage certificates,
employment records, everything—would be erased. "There would,
in fact, be no more records of an Abraham Bolden that could be
traceable to you," he explained, "or to anyone that has been associated with you in the past."

My eagerness quickly turned to uneasiness. *If they can actually
do that,* I thought, *I'll never even be able to prove that I am who I really am.* Something felt vaguely wrong about the whole proposition.

"I'll have to think this over," I said.

"Okay, think it over and let us know your decision as soon as
possible. We'll be looking to hear from you through your proper
channels."

I left the Treasury Building and began walking back to the
YMCA. My route on this sunny and mild November day took me
down Pennsylvania Avenue, past the White House. My mind filled
with thoughts of Kennedy, who was in Florida at the time. Throughout the Service, rumors were flying about threats on the president's
life. Reports had circulated in the agency about Cuban dissidents
and right-wing southerners who were stalking him and plotting his

assassination. Each weekly meeting brought information about some new organized group with a plot of its own. Suspects had actually been detained in Chicago and in Palm Beach. At the beginning of the month, in fact, a high-powered rifle had been confiscated from a suspected assassin in Chicago. Concerns for Kennedy's safety in our city were so high that Kennedy was forced to cancel a trip during the first week of November.

As I turned my gaze to the White House, I saw something that stopped me cold. The front gate and the first floor of the building were in sharp and vivid focus on this bright, clear autumn day. But the upper floors were strangely indistinct, obscured by a thick white mass, as if a single cloud hovered over the president's window on this cloudless day. I looked away quickly and saw nothing like that cloudy obstruction near any of the other buildings nearby, but when I turned back to the White House, there it still sat. I closed each eye in turn, again checking my vision, but the cloud remained, covering only the upper floors of the White House.

I can't say why, exactly, but I was immediately overwhelmed by the conviction that what I had just seen was a vision, and that this vision had meaning. Knowing that the Secret Service and other agencies were at that very moment investigating grave conspiracies against the president that were highly organized, I felt certain that Kennedy's life was in mortal danger.

I flew home the following day and told Barbara about my vision as soon as I arrived. She reacted somewhat cautiously, either because she was suspicious of the very idea of such a phenomenon or because she believed in the reality of the vision but didn't trust my interpretation of it. The next morning at the office, Charlotte, a secretary to whom I often confided such things, was even more skeptical.

Later, Agent Martineau, who had been appointed acting special agent in charge after Hanly was transferred to the Paris, France, office, summoned me to his office and listened intently as I recounted my meeting with the IRS and explained their proposed assignment.

"Well, what are you going to do?" Martineau asked.

"I'm going to turn the assignment down," I answered quickly. "I'm not accepting any assignment that will change my identity and involve moving to Washington, D.C. I joined the Secret Service. I'm not interested in being an IRS undercover investigator."

Martineau exploded, almost as if he had been expecting something like this. "Damn, Abe! Where do you come off choosing what you're going to do around here? What are you, some prima donna or something?" His anger seemed to erupt from nowhere. "You don't decide what you're going to do around here. That bullshit might have been okay when Hanly was here, but it's going to stop now," he said angrily.

"I'm not accepting the investigation," I repeated firmly as I stormed out of his office.

I shared the story of my vision with some others, including another black agent in the Chicago office, Conrad Cross. Cross took it no more seriously than he had my previous observations about the inept protection provided by the White House detail. He had the same kind of cavalier attitude as the Washington agents, contributing to my growing certainty that Kennedy's days were numbered.

And then it happened. On the afternoon of November 22, 1963, I was in a bar on Thirty-eighth and Indiana in Chicago, interviewing the owner in the course of an investigation. The drone of the small black-and-white television behind the bar was interrupted by words that most of us will never forget: "President Kennedy has been shot."

In the silence that followed, every person in the room turned toward the screen.

"The president has been shot," the announcer repeated. "We will now join Walter Cronkite in New York. . . ." I didn't wait to hear Cronkite, but rushed out to my car and sped back to the Secret Service office.

"They shot the president!" Margie called out to me as I got off the elevator. Inside the office, Agent Joe Noonan was pacing back and forth in a barely controlled rage. He had served three years on the White House detail and shared my view of the conduct and over-confidence of the agents on that detail.

"I knew it would happen," he shouted, waving his arms. "I told those playboys that someone was going to get the president killed if they kept acting like they did. Now it's happened." Noonan's pacing grew more rapid as he resumed his rant. "I'd like to see the faces of all those guys on the detail now, who told me that nobody wants to kill President Kennedy," he sneered.

Martineau, for his part, instructed the secretary not to admit anyone into the Secret Service offices, and then shut himself in his own office, muttering, "This could mean the end of the Secret Service."

June Marie Terpinas, one of the agency's pool stenographers, came up to me with tears in her eyes, and told me that when she heard that President Kennedy had been shot, she rushed into Martineau's office and gave him the news. According to June, Martineau's response had been a cold "So what else is new?" Sobbing, June said that Martineau "acted like he didn't care one way or the other."

At a meeting of all the Chicago agents during the week of Kennedy's state funeral, we received orders from the chief's office in Washington. We were not to discuss Kennedy's protection, regardless of who asked us. We were told to channel all inquiries concerning the protection of President Kennedy through the chief's office. I remember thinking, *Protection? What protection?* The message from Washington made it clear that anyone who violated the directive would be dealt with severely.

The assassination of John F. Kennedy on November 22, 1963, represented a turning point in my own career in the Secret Service.

Before Dallas, I had voiced my opinion of the president's protection detail to colleagues and superiors in the Chicago office. I told anyone who would listen that I didn't believe the agents on the White House detail would act swiftly or appropriately to stop an attempt on the president's life. A long line of superiors, from Harry Geighlein and James Burke to Maurice Martineau, tried to tell me that I was over-reacting, that things appeared lax to me only because I was new to the detail. The senior agents struck me as arrogant and overconfident, and saw to it that nobody acknowledged the apprehension of any less experienced agents regarding the president's safety. I even told my story to a Secret Service inspector, Thomas J. Kelley, who visited the Chicago office just after I returned from the White House detail. I told Kelley everything I had seen and everything that had happened to me in Washington, and although he promised me that he'd look into it all, I heard nothing from him or from Chief Rowley prior to the assassination. The senior agents' cocksure attitudes governed right up to the moment of Kennedy's death. One of the younger agents riding on the car behind the presidential limousine heard what sounded to him like a rifle shot. He started to jump from the running board to assist the president, just as Agent Clint Hill had run to protect the First Lady. But the young agent was called back to the follow-up car by a more senior agent, just as the third and fatal shot tore into the back of the president's skull. The same inspector, Kelley, to whom I had previously complained about the laxity of the Secret Service agents surrounding the president, oversaw the Dallas investigation of Kennedy's assassination.

After the assassination, I saw one suspicious action after another on the part of Secret Service personnel, all of which left me convinced that the Service wanted to present its own carefully orchestrated version of its performance to the Warren Commission and other official bodies that were investigating the assassination. By this time, my own disenchantment with the Service was no secret. Beginning in January 1964, just after the assassination, orders started coming down from my supervisors that hinted at an effort to withhold, or at least to color, the truth.

The first involved a suspect in the actual assassination. I was the night duty agent that week in November, which meant that all calls that came in to our office after working hours were routed to my home phone. Two nights after the events in Dallas, I received a call from SAIC Forrest Sorrels of the Dallas office at about 10:00 P.M., looking for Agent Martineau. Sorrels said he was in the Dallas police station and that he and Inspector Kelley had interviewed Lee Harvey Oswald, who had mentioned the name John Hurd.

"I don't know if it's spelled H-e-a-r-d, H-u-r-d, H-e-r-d, or H-u-r-t. I'm giving you the phonetic sound," he explained. "I want you to tell Martineau to drop everything he's doing out there and put every agent possible on tracking down anyone who has the name John Hurd. This is top priority and we need to get this done as soon as possible." He went on to ask about the outcome of the investigation of a Chicago gun shop called Klein's, as if he assumed that any agent in our office would have been aware of it. I couldn't tell him a thing, because I had never heard of the case.

"Well," Sorrels concluded with some urgency, "tell Martineau to get on this right away. Every agent should be assigned to identifying this man."

I couldn't reach Martineau until around midnight, and when I did, he was none too pleased.

"What the hell does he want us to do, run out in our pajamas? We'll take care of it tomorrow morning." In fact, Martineau did mobilize every agent and secretary in the Chicago office first thing the next morning. We pored over every file and register in our office, compiling a list of people named John Hurd, Heard, Herd, Hurt, or similar. ASAIC Martineau instructed us to track down every person who fit the profile and to notify him when we had located each one.

He also made it clear that we were not to interview any of these suspects unless we cleared it with him.

The search turned up several likely candidates, and we turned over the information to Agent Martineau. Yet not only were no arrests ever made connected to this investigation, but we never heard another word about it from Martineau—no follow-up, not even any feedback—even though he had demanded we turn over every scrap of paper, every note and scribble, generated by our search. I couldn't help wondering how we could have gotten an urgent nighttime call instructing us to drop everything and chase down this John Hurd, as other Secret Services offices around the country presumably did as well, and yet that name never came up in any official report or investigation nor in any press account of the assassination.

The second episode troubled me even more. Immediately after the assassination, several newspapers reported the presence of an unidentified man in the area now known as the "grassy knoll" in Dealey Plaza. According to some of the accounts, a Dallas police officer had run to the grassy knoll just after the president was shot, and encountered a neatly dressed man there. When questioned, the man reportedly presented a leather-bound commission book identifying him as an agent of the U.S. Secret Service. At the same time, rumors of the possibility of a lost commission book were circulating within the Service. The story that we heard from some agents in Washington featured several of the agents who were traveling with the president going to a strip club on November 21 and staying until the early morning hours of November 22. At least one of them was reported to have become quite inebriated and could have either lost his Secret Service identification or had it lifted off him that night.

In January 1964, ASAIC Martineau announced that the Secret Service intended to update identification books throughout the agency, and that all agents needed to turn in their current identification books right away. We received newly engraved identification books about thirty days after the old ones were sent back to Washington. To the naked eye, the new books were virtually identical to the old ones except for a new photograph and the addition of a single word, *the,* to the front cover. Now, instead of "Treasury Department," the front cover bore the words "The Treasury Department." To anyone who wasn't a member of the Secret Service, the old books would have been just as credible as the new ones. It seemed fairly obvious to me that the Service was looking to sweep under the rug the fact that some agent had lost his identification, and the best way to do so was to issue new ID to all personnel. The Service was circling its wagons at a time when many members of Congress felt the FBI should take over the protection of the president. A lost commission book could have been the last straw: how could the Secret Service protect the life of the president when it couldn't even protect its own identification books?

The third instance related to a Secret Service investigation that we had begun just before Kennedy's assassination. Toward the end of October 1963, while preparations were being made for the president to visit Chicago to attend the annual Army-Navy game at Soldier Field, a phone call came into our office for ASAIC Martineau. He took the call during one of our regular meetings, so the agents present heard his side of the conversation. He said that he didn't have enough personnel to look into whatever matter had been discussed.

"All of our agents are tied up at the moment, and we don't have anyone to send over there," he said firmly to whoever was on the other end of the line. When he hung up, Martineau explained that the call had been from the Chicago office of the FBI, which had information possibly concerning the president's upcoming trip. A woman who owned a rooming house on the city's North Side had gone into one of the rooms to do some housekeeping and had discovered two rifles equipped with telescopic sights. She had rented the room to two men she believed to be Hispanic, and had also seen two white men going in and out of the room. Knowing that the president was due to visit Chicago, she grew concerned and called the authorities.

Martineau professed to believe that this was not yet a Secret Service matter, in that there had been no direct threat to the president in connection with these rifles. He felt strongly that this problem fell under FBI jurisdiction, especially since the Service didn't have the resources to investigate every individual who had a rifle and disliked John Kennedy. As we all sat there listening, Martineau called the office of James Rowley, who had become chief of the Secret Service. When he got off the phone, he told us that we were, in fact, going to investigate the case.

Three agents were dispatched to interview the woman at the rooming house. I was not involved, since they anticipated tailing the suspects in a predominantly white part of Chicago, but at one point, I was able to listen in on the car radio for several hours while our agents followed the suspected assassins. Amazingly, they botched the surveillance and lost the suspects. One of the agents had neglected to turn off his two-way radio, which went off with a loud squawk—a transmission from Martineau back at the office—as the agents drove past the suspects in an alleyway behind the rooming house. The suspects bolted, and our guys promptly lost them in traffic. The investigation was abruptly terminated, and the chief was notified.

Just a few days before the shooting in Dallas, the Secret Service received even more threatening information, this time about a group of anti-Castro Cuban activists allegedly plotting to assassinate the president. Homer S. Echevarria had been overheard to make a statement to the effect that Kennedy was about to be taken care of. Instead of immediately contacting the White House detail, which was with the president in Fort Worth, Texas, ASAIC Martineau assigned several of his agents in Chicago to look into the matter. None of our agents was able to get next to Echevarria, and the investigation fell apart.

Later, when the Warren Commission convened to investigate the assassination, the chief of the Secret Service feared that agents who were on duty in Dallas that day might be held accountable in some way. With the president dead and his alleged killer, Lee Harvey Oswald, known to have had Cuban connections, the investigation of Echevarria took on new urgency, and some of the Chicago agents tried to revive the case, but to no avail. I sat in the cubicle next to one of the agents who had been involved with both threats in the Chicago area, so I could overhear his conversations. I listened to him dictating his reports and complaining about the progress of the investigation. It seemed that this agent thought Echevarria was a gunrunner for the CIA and that a contact agent from the CIA had called Martineau to inquire about the Echevarria case. The agent was "unhappy," concerned that whatever the connection was between Echevarria and the FBI or CIA, one or both of those agencies might have been interfering with his investigation.

In early December, Agent Martineau called us together to tell us that the FBI was taking over the Echevarria case and that our investigation was to terminate immediately. He told us to turn all documents, reports, notebooks, scribblings, and support files in to him, and he would in turn forward them to the chief's office by special courier. He warned us not to discuss the case with anyone, anywhere. In fact, he said, we should forget that the Echevarria case had ever existed. Reports in this case had been dictated by agents in Martineau's office and typed by a particular secretary. When they were delivered, with all the other relevant paperwork, by special air courier to Washington, D.C., they were delivered into the hands of Paul J. Paterni, deputy chief of the United States Secret Service.

One week later, the chief's office in Washington sent an order that all copies of reports relating to the advance security arrangements for President Kennedy in Chicago be removed from the files and delivered to Washington. My understanding, from conversations that I heard between the office secretaries, was that the chief's office communicated this same order verbally to field offices across the country. The field reports referred to by this order were the reports that Secret Service advance teams prepared prior to any presidential visit to any location. The reports covered all necessary precautions in that location, determined who would be responsible for those precautions, and specified transportation plans and routes to and from each location, each stop within that location, and other security details. A copy of such a report would be filed with the field office with authority over a location, and other copies would be distributed to the upper echelons of the Service. If all copies of all such reports were removed from all offices except that of the chief, he would be the only one in a position to provide investigators, such as the Warren Commission, with information regarding the security around the president at any given time or any given location. And there would be no way to verify or refute that information.

MY RELATIONSHIP WITH Maurice Martineau continued to decline. It was like our own private Cold War that occasionally erupted into open confrontation. He never made any effort to hide his contempt for me, and I can't say I did a lot better. One morning, I was sitting at my desk when the phone rang. I picked it up and leaned back in my chair to have a conversation. Looking up I saw, tied to the ceiling light above me, a rope . . . a hangman's noose. The moment Martineau came to work, I walked him into my office and showed him the noose.

"Aw, someone's just joking around," Martineau said, rather lightly. "I'll call maintenance and have it removed."

The fact that he didn't seem to be taking it seriously outraged me. "I think we should call a meeting and find out who tied this rope over my desk."

"Don't be so thin-skinned," Martineau answered, as if I had never heard that before. "They're just having fun with you. Don't make a mountain out of a molehill. You'll get the whole Service in trouble over a joke like this." As he stalked out of the office, he added, "I'll call maintenance and get them up here."

I asked each of the agents assigned to the office about the noose hanging from my ceiling, but of course nobody knew the slightest thing about it. To be sure, Maurice Martineau, assistant special agent in charge, made no further move to get to the bottom of things. The rift between us widened by the day.

Overt gestures of racism such as this were rare, but the normal course of work offered Martineau plenty of opportunities to let me know where I stood with him. By way of example, there was a case in February 1964 in which I was investigating an alleged counterfeiting operation in the basement of a church. The pastor of the church identified the young man to whom he had entrusted two small presses and other printing equipment for the printing of flyers and programs for the congregation. I picked up the suspect, who promptly confessed to using the equipment to make counterfeit money. He went with me to the church, unlocked the basement, and showed me the array of printing and photographic plates he used in his operation, not to mention some of the actual counterfeit bills. It would all have to be seized as evidence.

I radioed the office from the car, got Agent Martineau on the other end, and asked him to send some agents to the church to help me collect, catalog, and transport all the seized materials and equipment.

"We don't have anybody to help you, Abe." With a slightly nasty chuckle, he added, "When did you start needing help, anyway?" It was the middle of the afternoon, the time of day when agents usually returned to the office to prepare their daily reports.

I slammed the radio down and drove back with the suspect actually holding some of the confiscated machinery in his lap. Later, he helped me unload the instruments of his own undoing into the back room of the Secret Service office. In the main office, we found Martineau sitting around making casual chitchat with no less than four other agents, half of them lounging with their feet propped up on their desks.

Chapter 7

My real troubles began in 1964. In May of that year, I flew to Washington for a long-overdue stint at the Secret Service training school. Previous attempts to attend had been cancelled because of case assignments or court appearances, and since my bosses had generally rated me as an outstanding agent, nobody ever pressured me about it. But the time had come.

Shortly after lunch on my first day of training school, the personnel director of the Secret Service, Howard Anderson, poked his head into the classroom and motioned to me and Gary McLeod, another Chicago agent, to come speak with him.

"Bolden," Anderson said urgently, "I just got a call from Mr. Martineau in Chicago, and he wants you and McLeod to return to Chicago immediately."

"What's it all about?" Gary asked.

"I don't know all of the details yet. It has something to do with an investigation of a counterfeiting operation in Villa Park, Illinois. Mr. Martineau has sent for Agent Jordan out of Milwaukee, and he's trying to call in all the agents that he can," Anderson explained somewhat breathlessly. He went on to tell us that we needed to pack our stuff up from the classroom and head directly to the airport, where we were already booked on a flight back to Chicago that was leaving in an hour's time. Since there'd be no time to return to our hotel, other agents were on their way to collect our bags and belongings and would meet us at the airport.

We had heard about Agent Anderson. Rumors around the Service were that at one time he had been the agent in charge of the New York office, and that whether it was the pressure of that post or for some other reason, he had suffered a nervous breakdown. Watching him twitch and perspire, his speech and movements nearly frantic as we drove to the airport, I found that easy to believe. It never occurred to me to wonder whether something else was agitating him, to ask myself if perhaps he knew more than he was saying. He said nothing else about the reason for our return to Chicago except that he expected the investigation to be over quickly and that he looked forward to our coming back and completing the training in Washington.

At the airport, Inspector Gerard McCann greeted us, carrying the bags he had retrieved from our hotel. Seeing how hastily he had jammed everything in, I took my bag and began to open it to straighten it out. McCann took the bag right out of my hand and said, "The plane is waiting for us on the runway." He also told us that he had paid our hotel bill, for which I reimbursed him on the spot.

On board the jet, McCann led the way to our row of three seats. He sat at the window, and Agent McLeod stepped aside so I could sit in the middle. McLeod took the aisle seat. When Inspector McCann saw me hesitate for a second, he offered me his window seat. It suddenly dawned on me that these two men were not my traveling companions but an escort. Some sort of deception was at work, and I sensed danger. I thought about my boyhood dream, and about being dead by the age of thirty. I was twenty-nine.

McCann and McLeod said virtually nothing and sat eerily still as we flew to Chicago, while I tried to put the pieces together. I couldn't imagine any reason they might need a black agent to help in an investigation in all-white Villa Park. I couldn't even think of any ongoing investigations in that community, much less one that would need me.

Chicago was sweltering with temperatures in the high nineties when our plane hit the tarmac. Agent Richard A. Jordan, a well-respected but excitable young man whom I had known in Chicago before he became the special agent in charge of the Milwaukee office, was waiting for us as we disembarked.

McLeod walked straight up to Jordan and demanded, "What the hell is going on?"

Jordan seemed nervous. "We got this counterfeit plant located out in Villa Park. We need all the help we can get, so we had to call you guys out of school."

"Are there any Negroes involved in that counterfeit operation in Villa Park?" I asked.

"Yeah, Abe," said Jordan as he hurried us to a Secret Service car.

"That doesn't make sense to me. I didn't know Negroes lived in Villa Park. I can't see a Negro going to Villa Park to pass counterfeit money, because he would be too obvious." I didn't ask the other question on my mind: why would Inspector McCann become involved with a Chicago counterfeiting case, anyway?

Inside the car, the heat had us all sweating freely. On the way into town, Agent Jordan stopped at a gas station to fill up the tank, and I took the opportunity to call my wife from a pay phone. I hadn't even dialed half the number when Jordan hurried up from behind, his anxiety plain to see.

"Who are you calling, Abe?" he shouted.

"I'm calling my wife to let her know that I'm in town."

"We don't have time for that. We have to get back to Chicago now. You can call her from there. Everybody else is all loaded up and ready to go, and you are holding us up."

This just didn't sound like any counterfeiting investigation I had ever seen. Inside the car I could hear Maurice Martineau's unmistakable voice coming over the two-way radio. "Have them wait in the U.S. attorney's office," he was saying.

The U.S. attorney's office was on the same floor of the same building as the Chicago office of the Secret Service. Inspector McCann led me to the grand jury room and asked me to wait there. I had given testimony countless times in this room, but everything about that moment felt unfamiliar—the stillness of the empty chairs around the long mahogany table, the sweat-soaked shirt clinging to my skin, the gnawing in my stomach. I was overcome with weariness.

"All I want to do is call my wife," I said to McCann, "and get something to eat. I haven't eaten since about five this morning, and that was only a cup of coffee and two donuts." It was now late in the afternoon. While McCann opened one of the windows in the stuffy room, I told him I was getting a drink of water.

"You can wait a few minutes, can't you, Abe?"

"I guess so," I replied, "but I can't see what's wrong with going to get a drink of water."

"Well, we'll only be here a few minutes, and besides, if you leave the room, the informant might see you in the hallway," McCann said, referring to the alleged Villa Park investigation. As a general rule, an undercover agent would not be introduced or identified to the informant as an agent until the informant had been thoroughly debriefed and registered by the Secret Service. I asked if it would be all right to use the phone in the main office of the U.S. attorney to call my wife.

"No, Abe. Mr. Martineau will be here in a few minutes, and when he comes in, I don't want him to have to wait around for you."

Something was very, very wrong. No undercover operation I'd been on, whether as a Pinkerton detective, a state police officer, or a Secret Service agent, needed this level of precaution. They weren't letting me eat. They weren't letting me drink. I couldn't even make a phone call. I understood that I was being held in that room against my will, and I couldn't contain myself any longer.

"What's this Villa Park case all about?" I demanded.

McCann walked over the window and stood silhouetted against the light, a tidy government man in a neat gray suit. "I don't know what this is all about, Abe. I was told to come to Chicago just like you were. All I know is that Marty wanted me to stay here with you. That's all I can tell you at this time."

"Well, hell!" I fumed. "We've been here for over an hour now. It looks like Martineau isn't coming. Could you go get him? I'm tired and hungry and would like to call my wife."

Of course, there was no Villa Park investigation. That was obvious to me now. I waited another hour in that stifling room, with no food or water and no chance to use a phone. Martineau didn't arrive until after 6:00 P.M., and when he did, he was not alone. Accompanying him were Inspector Michael Torina and Edward Hanrahan, the United States attorney for the Northern District of Illinois. The three men sat across the table from me. Martineau, looking ruffled as if he had a long, hectic day, wore a slight smile on his face. He wasted no time on pleasantries, but just pointed a finger in my face and started shouting.

"You've been trying to sell the file of the Spagnoli bond case."

I hadn't known what to expect, but I certainly hadn't expected anything like this. "You can't be serious," I said. "That's ridiculous."

"We have a signed statement from Frank Jones naming you as the agent who he received a portion of the Spagnoli file from. Jones said that you sent him to Spagnoli's house and told him to try to get fifty thousand dollars for the whole file."

"You can't be serious," I repeated. "Are you talking about the same Frank Jones I arrested twice in the past year for passing and making counterfeit money?" We had been dealing with Jones for some time, always plagued and frustrated by his constantly changing stories and excuses. His case had caused some friction in the office, especially between Martineau and me, but then again, there was always friction between the two of us. The Jones case was a ragtag operation so far as the quality of the counterfeit notes was concerned, but it was important in that it involved a close network of people who passed the counterfeit notes made by Jones working primarily on the South Side of Chicago.

I remembered Jones very well. In early 1962, Chicago police detectives had caught a member of his gang passing counterfeit five-dollar bills and arrested him. I was assigned the case and after interviewing the passer convinced him to cooperate with the Secret Service. Hiram McCann became an informant for the Secret Service and gave information on other members of the counterfeiting ring. Jones' name came up as one of the main cogs in the scheme. Another person in the gang, a man called Slim, was thought to be a Negro pimp whose real name was Horace Foster. My information was that Foster worked with a very nice-looking lesbian called Princess when passing the counterfeit notes. After Jones' arrest and during his conversation with me on May 11, 1964, Jones also claimed to have known a "dago" counterfeit plate maker also called Slim. I didn't believe Jones and didn't trust his information. Another counterfeiter named Arthur Rachael did use an alias of "Slim," but I seriously doubted that was the same man.

Based upon Hiram's information, I arrested several members of the counterfeiting ring while continuing to keep Jones under periodic surveillance.

Finally, in the summer of 1962, I got a call from a tavern owner on the South Side of Chicago who had been hit with two counterfeit five-dollar bills the night before. Immediately suspicious, the owner waited until the passer left, then went outside and copied down the license number of the car in which he drove away. I interviewed the tavern owner and checked out the license number. The car was traced to Frank William Jones. I arrested Jones and brought him into the office for an interview.

Jones vehemently denied that he had intentionally passed counterfeit notes, claiming that his wife had cashed a check and probably received the bills from a currency exchange where she did
business. I didn't believe Jones, and presented the case to the United
States attorney's office for prosecution. Prosecution of Jones was
denied, however, on the basis that there was not enough evidence to
sustain a successful prosecution for knowingly passing counterfeit
documents.

I was convinced that Jones was the leader of the counterfeiting
ring, and when in early 1963 Jones was identified as the passer of another counterfeit five-dollar bill, the Secret Service raided Jones'
home, working with SAIC John Hanly. We hit pay dirt. In the basement of Jones' home, we found the counterfeiting press, paper, and
inks. There were fragments of counterfeit five-dollar bills jammed in
the roller of the press.

Knowing that conviction for a third felony could mean a life sentence without parole, Jones agreed to cooperate with the Secret Service in identifying other members of his gang who were passing the
counterfeit notes. Over the next several months, Jones called me at
the office and at my home offering information, but when I found
that much of the information could not be verified, I suspected that
Jones was taking me for a ride. I thought he might still be holding
batches of counterfeit notes that he needed to unload.

In order to test Jones, I sent a longtime informant with the Secret
Service, Richard Walters, to Jones' home to attempt to buy any of
the five-dollar bills that Jones might have hidden away. Knowing
what I was dealing with, I filed meticulous reports of my encounters
with Jones and discussed every move that I made with Hanly, the
special agent in charge.

When Jones called my home on the night of May 10, 1964, I refused to meet with him, explaining that I was going away to Secret
Service school and would not have time to follow up on any new

information that he might have. Jones was disappointed, and on the morning of May 11 he called the Secret Service office and complained to Agent J. Lloyd Stocks that he had valuable information and that I had refused to meet with him.

After being dressed down by ASAIC Martineau and threatened with termination if I did not meet with Jones as ordered, I met Jones in front of his home around noon. When Jones complained that some of his neighbors might see him seated in a "detective car," I drove to Marquette Park, where Jones complained that I was going to send him to prison for the rest of his life. We had just arrested Joseph Spagnoli, Arthur Rachael, and several other members of a well-organized counterfeiting bond gang. During the conversation, Jones contended that he knew one of the people arrested by the name of "Slim." During our conversation, Jones was leafing through a Phillips 66 Fishing Guide. On Saturday, May 9, I had used the guide to note down, on the back cover, the addresses of both Joseph Spagnoli and Arthur Rachael. My assignment was to participate in the arrest of either Spagnoli or Rachael. I placed the fishing guide next to me on the front seat for quick reference in case I had to go from one address to the other.

When I saw Jones thumbing through the guide and making reference to Spagnoli, I took the guide from him, tore off the back cover, shredded the cover, and threw the pieces in a trash can in the park. I instructed Jones to do nothing about Slim or anyone else until I could discuss the matter with my superiors.

Later that night, May 11, Jones phoned me at my home and spoke vaguely about talking to someone about some "suits." Jones asked me to meet him the next day and he would explain everything.

I met Jones at a McDonald's restaurant on the afternoon of May 12. Agent Conrad Cross was seated in the Secret Service car, as we had been working together during the morning. I stood outside the restaurant talking with Jones, who again said that he was in contact with Slim and was on to something that would help the Secret Service a whole lot. Jones was deliberately vague about the information, saying that he would give me more information only if I could promise that he wouldn't go to jail for the rest of his life. I told Jones that I would bring his cooperation to the attention of the prosecuting attorney but could make no promises beyond that.

I returned to the Secret Service office and dictated a report covering my contact with Jones over the past few days. Afterward, I went straight into Martineau's office. I explained in detail what had transpired between Jones and me, and the information that Jones professed to have in hand.

"Close down the investigation and stay away from Jones," Martineau said, almost shouting. "He's just trying to get out from under his own case."

The next morning, I went to work and telephoned Jones.

I told him the investigation was over. Jones made no reply, and suddenly the dial tone hummed.

Now, there in the grand jury room of the U.S. attorney's office, Martineau confirmed that this was the man and the case in question. "When is the last time you saw Jones?"

"You know that I saw Jones almost a week ago." I was feeling defensive and angry. "You know damn well that when I came to work on Monday morning, May 11, Stocks called me into the office and told me that early that morning Jones had called the Secret Service office and told him that he wanted to talk to me but that I had refused to meet with him. I told Stocks then and there that I didn't have the time to fool with Jones and that I had two cases pending against him. You know all about it because when Stocks jumped up and went into your office and told you that I had refused to talk to Jones, you sent for me and chewed my ass out. You accused me of trying to 'run the show' and pick and choose what I wanted to do. Now you're sitting here asking me when the last time I saw Jones was."

It was all I could do to keep a lid on my rage. "You and Stocks demanded that I see Jones, and you know it. I went to see Jones because you ordered me to go. When I got to Jones' house, he told me that he wanted to help us catch other counterfeiters and the 'dago' that helped him make the plates for his operation. The next day, I came into the office and discussed the whole interview that I had with Jones with you, and you told me not to see Jones again. I haven't seen him since you told me not to. And now you're sitting here in front of these inspectors and the U.S. attorney asking me when I saw Jones like you had no knowledge of what I was doing."

I was too angry to be afraid at this point, or even to realize that there was any reason to be afraid. Martineau just sat there looking at me with that peculiar smirk on his face. None of the others spoke, nor met my eye.

"Well, that's not what Jones said," Martineau responded. "Jones tells a different story altogether."

"I don't give a damn about different stories Jones told!" I shouted. "Jones told a different story when I arrested him for passing counterfeit five-dollar bills at the Tiger Lounge. Jones told a different story when Mr. Hanly and I went into his house and found the counterfeiting plant in the basement. Jones told a different story when he went around collecting money from people on the South Side of Chicago, claiming to be working for Alderman Charles Chew. Jones was pocketing all of that money, and when Chew found out, he had him arrested. Jones has a case in state court right now for soliciting money under false pretenses. So don't tell me about any different story that Jones might be telling." I was almost winded from my diatribe.

Nobody said a word. Some of them scribbled. Inspector McCann got up and paced. Martineau shuffled papers.

"Wait just a minute." Something occurred to me. "Am I under arrest? If I am under arrest, I request that I be granted the right to call my attorney right now."

Hanrahan, the U.S. attorney, visibly flinched but said nothing.

"We do have a warrant that was issued at 2:00 P.M. today by Judge Campbell," Martineau said. "When we told him what we had, he got out of his sickbed and came to court and issued this warrant."

"I don't give a damn about that! If I'm under arrest, I want to be represented by an attorney, and that's that!"

Night was falling. The heat and the exhaustion were catching up to me, making it harder and harder for me to keep my composure, but the seriousness of the situation was coming into focus.

"You know that I'm not guilty of the charges you're making," I said, as calmly as I could. "I've been set up."

The half-smile on Martineau's face convinced me that this was the moment he had been waiting for. His answer was a challenge. "Prove it."

Martineau and his gang left me alone with Inspector McCann for a while. I managed to get a glass of water out of him, but not much else. When Martineau returned, he asked for permission to search my house. As calmly as I could, I told him that if I could call my lawyer, I'd let them search the house. I even offered to help, if that would help clear the matter up faster. Neither Martineau nor Hanrahan responded, and they abruptly left the room.

A little while later, Agent Jordan returned and Inspector McCann walked me back to the Secret Service office. Jordan sat me down and began to grill me.

"Who did you call when you were in Washington last night?"

"I called my wife."

"You called the White House, didn't you, Abe? We have the records and we know that you tried to call someone there. Who were you trying to contact?"

"I don't think that's any of your business," I said curtly.

When I'd arrived in Washington, D.C., on May 17, Agent McLeod and I had walked to a small coffee shop and had sandwiches. On the way back to the Willard Hotel, where we were staying, I decided to call the White House switchboard. I needed to contact J. Lee Rankin, counsel for the Warren Commission, but I didn't know how. I needed to let some member of the commission know that I was interested in giving testimony as to my observations and complaints about past Secret Service agent conduct.

EVERY AGENT IN the Chicago office knew my feelings about the White House detail and that I believed its "protection" of President Kennedy was a complete sham. The detail was an unhealthy conglomeration of cocky senior agents, few of whom showed much respect for Kennedy, and inexperienced probationary agents and trainees who may or may not have fully understood the gravity of their assignment. Just as important, it was impossible to believe that anybody in the Secret Service could say with a straight face that nobody was out to get the president. We had seen far too much evidence to the contrary.

The way I saw it, there were at least three factions in America actively trying to get at Kennedy. First, the organized Cuban émigré population based in Miami resented him for his ineffectiveness with Castro, and specifically for the complete fiasco at the Bay of Pigs. Second, Mafia bosses across the country wanted Kennedy out of the way, believing that with JFK gone, Bobby's relentless pursuit of organized crime and corruption would end. The last group was the least organized but perhaps the most numerous—the right-wingers and racists who couldn't abide his liberalism and intellectualism and who were outraged by his unequivocal commitment to equal rights for all Americans.

There was little doubt that members of at least two of these groups had been following the president around the country, studying the rhythms and habits of his security detail in the hopes of finding weaknesses to exploit. Although the media had not reported the stories, attempts had been made to crash the Kennedy compound in Miami, and he had cut short a trip in Tampa because of a serious threat made on his life. After that, the focus shifted to Chicago and to Echevarria.

As for Dallas, I didn't believe we have, or will ever have, the full story. My opinion was that whoever was plotting the assassination trained their sights on Dallas once the Chicago attempt fell apart. I suspected that the responsible parties set up the agents on the president's protection detail by exploiting their reputed weaknesses for women and booze. Somehow, I theorized, they had managed to get the identification of one of those agents. I didn't believe that Oswald was a patsy, as some assassination researchers were claiming. There was evidence that made it likely that there were other assailants firing in Dealey Plaza that day who were probably unknown to Oswald, and that one of them fired the fatal shot from behind a fence in front of the presidential motorcade.

I firmly believed that the officer who confronted the unknown suspect behind the picket fence immediately after the assassination was indeed shown an authentic Secret Service commission book, the book that had been lost by, or taken from, an alcohol-impaired agent the night before. Further, I was convinced that the Secret Service leadership acted to conceal or at least obfuscate this fact by providing new commission books for all the agents in the Service. The Service has, of course, publicly denied this. Finally, it seems an inescapable conclusion that high officials in the U.S. government were—and perhaps some still are—well aware of the conspiracy or conspiracies that led to John Kennedy's assassination, and have concealed or altered supporting evidence.

In the final analysis, all that really mattered was that John Kennedy was gone. As the initial shock wore off, we all began to adjust to a new reality. Black Americans and others for whom the young president had represented so much hope felt the sting of his loss.

So as McLeod and I walked along Pennsylvania Avenue on May 17, I'd stopped at one of two conjoined telephone booths and told him that I was going to call my wife.

As I dialed the White House switchboard, McLeod entered the booth next to mine. I quickly suspected his actions when I noticed that I never heard the *ding* of the coin drop normally heard when a coin was inserted into a pay telephone. McLeod was not making a telephone call at all.

He had entered the booth to eavesdrop. I aborted the call, inserted another coin, and dialed the number to my home in Chicago. McLeod was silent in the booth next to mine.

"I know that you've heard the old saying that loose lips sink ships," Inspector McCann added now. "We have to protect ourselves and the Secret Service. We have to know that we can trust the agents who are working for us and that when the chips are down, they will stick together as a team."

"What are you talking about?" I demanded. "I am a team player. What have I done to make you say that I'm not—"

"Listen, Abe," McCann interrupted. "Kennedy is dead. We did our best to protect him, and it didn't work out. We are not going to stand by and let you bury our careers and destroy the Secret Service."

"So that's what this is about? Is that why I'm here? What have I done to destroy the Secret Service?"

McCann mopped his sweaty brow. "As I said, loose lips sink ships. That's the bottom line."

Agent Jordan tried a different tack. "Abe, would you answer a few questions for me on the polygraph machine? Martineau asked me to give you a test and—"

"Take a lie detector test? About what?"

"About some of the things Jones and Spagnoli said. It might help us clear up some of what Jones is saying."

"Jordan," I protested, "you above all know that polygraph examinations aren't reliable. They aren't permitted in a court because too much depends on the attitude of the polygraph operator. As far as I can see, you guys have already got a warrant for my arrest and believe that there is some truth to what Jones is saying. Jones will say anything that he is told to say in order to get out from under the case I have against him. No, I don't think I will take the test unless I have a chance to clear it with my attorney."

"Abe, you're still an agent, and we can order you to take the test," said McCann.

"You can order me, but I don't have to follow your order."

"Then we'll just fire you right now for insubordination and serve the warrant. We're not going to fuck around with you any longer."

There didn't seem to be any way out of this one. "Okay, I'll take a polygraph test, but I won't take it if Jordan is going to give it to me. He's been lying to me all day, and I think that some impartial administrator such as someone from John Reed and Associates over on Michigan Avenue should give the test. That's who the Chicago police use to examine their officers."

"We don't have time for that, Abe," Jordan said impatiently. "We need to get this done now. I'm just following orders and doing what I am told. I don't know whether or not there's anything to these accusations against you. I'm just doing what Marty and Torina tell me to do. I'm sorry that I lied to you, but I was just following orders."

"Okay, I'll take the test. But I'm not answering any questions about anything except the accusations. I want you to be clear on that."

THE POLYGRAPH ROOM must have been the only room in the building where the windows had been closed all day. The air was stale and dry and the heat was oppressive. I was sweating all over again, but when I asked to open a window, Agent Jordan got visibly annoyed.

"This will only take a minute," he said irritably. "I don't want to open a window because the room should be as quiet as possible." Jordan asked me if I knew how a polygraph machine worked. Even though I answered that I did, he proceeded to tell me anyway. He showed me the blood-pressure cuff and the leads into the machine, the electrodes that sensed chemical changes on the skin of my hands, and the needles that recorded my reactions during the test. Jordan clearly wanted to get on with the test, and flew off the handle again when I asked to go to the bathroom. I really didn't care, though; I just needed to breathe some fresh air.

When we got back, Agent Jordan slid a sheet of paper in front of me and asked me to sign it. It was a routine waiver stating that nobody had forced me to take the test. I signed, and we settled in for the examination.

"Now," Jordan began, "you trust me, don't you, Abe?"

"No. How could I possibly trust you after everything that has happened today? I have been lied to all day from Washington to Chicago. The Villa Park counterfeiting ring was a lie. The reason I was taken out of Secret Service school was a lie. Now you ask me whether I trust you. What kind of an idiot do you think I am?"

"I'm just doing my job, Abe. I know that we used a trick to get you here. I had nothing to do with that. I was just following orders from Marty and Inspector Torina. You know that we have worked together in the past. I wouldn't do anything to hurt you, and I don't have anything personal against you. You know that, don't you, Abe?"

"Why don't we have John Reed and Associates give this exam?" I asked again. "They're just around the corner. They are recognized experts in polygraph technology. They train polygraph operators from all over the world. I'm sure that if Martineau or Hanrahan called them, they would open up the office and—"

"Are you saying that I don't know what I'm doing?"

"No," I countered, "I'm not saying that at all. I'm saying that I'm being accused of some alleged criminal act by the Secret Service, and you are a supervisor in the Secret Service. It would be much better if an independent person gave me the test. John Reed and Associates gives polygraph examinations to members of the Chicago Police Department when they have a problem. The company is familiar with this kind of thing. That way, the examiner would have no interest in the results of the test one way or the other."

"We don't have time for that, Abe. All I want to do is ask a few questions and see where we go from there. Don't you trust me enough to answer these few questions? I'm not out to get you. I'm just doing what I'm told to do." Jordan seemed calmer now. "Now, let's get back to the questions. Is that okay with you?"

"I guess so. I still have my reservations about your giving me the test."

Agent Jordan began to ask me questions from a paper in front of him. "I'm going to ask you whether or not you gave Jones a piece of paper. Did you give Jones a piece of paper?"

"Did I give Jones a piece of paper about what?"

"Just answer the question yes or no," Jordan snapped.

"How can I answer a question yes or no when I don't know what piece of paper you're asking about? I gave Jones a copy of the search warrant when we found the counterfeiting plant in his house. I gave him a personal history form to fill out when he was arrested by me in 1962. I gave him a—"

"I'm not talking about those types of papers. I mean papers to be used in criminal activity between you and him."

"Then that's what you should say in the question. Show me the paper that you are asking about and I can tell you whether or not I gave it to him."

"I don't have the paper to show you right now," Jordan said. "Marty has it in his office."

"Well, how the hell can I answer a question about some paper that Mr. Martineau has somewhere in his office?" I didn't know whether to be terrified or just disgusted. "Why don't you go get the paper from Mr. Martineau and let me look at it? That's the only fair thing to do before asking me a question about some paper that Jones allegedly said that I gave to him."

"You don't have to tell me how to frame these questions, Abe," Jordan shot back. "Just answer them yes or no to the best of your ability. Either you gave him a paper to be used in a criminal activity or you didn't."

"Then the answer to the question is no."

"Did you ever eat at a McDonald's hamburger restaurant with Frank Jones?"

"I saw Frank Jones eating in a McDonald's on Sixty-ninth and Lafayette—"

"Just answer the question yes or no," Jordan hissed.

"I can't answer yes or no. Jones and I live in the same area of Chicago—"

"Try to answer yes or no."

It seemed that the only thing we were accomplishing was to crank up the tension. I sensed that I was into something deep here, but felt utterly helpless. I hadn't done a thing wrong, and here I was, trapped. I sat back in my chair and lit a cigarette, hoping to collect my thoughts, but Jordan snapped me back to reality. He tried to act sympathetic but also warned me that I needed to cooperate or he'd have to tell Martineau that I was refusing to take the test.

"Do you know a girl named Sandy Hafford?"

"I know of a girl named Sandy who's involved in Agent John Russell's bond case, but I do not know her." Sandy was to be a government witness against Spagnoli in an upcoming criminal trial.

"Just say yes or no." Jordan's voice rose again.

"I know of *a* Sandy, but I don't know if it's *that* Sandy. There's a difference."

"Well, for the record, you know Sandy Hafford."

"If you want to put it like that, I guess I know her, then."

"Have you ever lied to the state police?"

"Lied about what?"

"Anything you can think of," Jordan answered curtly.

"I don't see what the state police have to do with this."

"What I mean," Jordan explained, "is about something big, something involving a lot of money."

"No," I said emphatically, my temper rising again. "Look, I don't know what you guys are trying to pull, but I can tell you that it isn't going to work. You call me in here to take a polygraph test about some file and then you ask me about the state police and a girl named Sandy. You're going to pay for this someday, Jordan. You're going to—"

"Are you threatening me, Abe?"

"No, I'm not threatening you. I have better sense than that. I'm no fool."

Jordan tried to lower the tension in the room. "Let's both calm down, Abe. These are just questions we want answered." He relit the pipe he'd been fiddling with throughout the interview, filling the room with smoke.

"Do you have to smoke that thing?" I asked. "The tobacco

smells awful, and all of the windows and doors are closed. I can hardly breathe in here as it is."

Agent Jordan tapped out the tobacco, put the pipe in his pocket, and then questioned me for another hour with mostly simple, preliminary questions. Jordan suggested a break before starting in on the meat of the examination, and while he again denied my request for something to eat, we took a leisurely stroll together and found ourselves leaning on the railing overlooking the open central interior of the building. Jordan turned to me.

"Abe, I don't want to be personal, but how are your finances?"

"I'm in pretty good shape," I answered truthfully. "I'm not eating steak every night, but I'm living."

"You just bought a house, didn't you?"

"Yes. After eight years of saving and budgeting, my wife and I finally bought a little bungalow on the South Side of Chicago."

"Weren't you trying to go into business for yourself?" Jordan probed further.

"No. You must have your signals crossed. I'm not even thinking about going into business."

"Well," Jordan ventured, "I understand that you and Agent Cross were going into business together."

"That's not true. As far as I know, Agent Cross is going into the tavern business with a man named Taylor. Cross has been visiting different real estate companies, trying to find a good location." I looked at Jordan squarely. "I'm doing all right. I don't need the extra money."

Jordan walked me back into the hot, thick air of the examining room and carefully hooked me back up to the polygraph machine. When he finished setting up, he switched on the machine and started his interrogation.

"Are you Abraham Bolden?"

"Yes." I saw Jordan make a mark on the printout with his pencil.

"Did you give a piece of paper to Frank Jones?"

"No."

"Have you ever lied in an official report?"

"No."

"Did you attempt to sell a Secret Service file to Spagnoli for fifty thousand dollars?"

"No."

"Did you send Jones to Spagnoli's house?"

"No."

"Are you in Chicago, Illinois?"

"Yes."

"Do you trust me?"

"Yes."

"Are you telling the truth?"

Jordan paused and asked me to sit still for just a few minutes. He examined the printout from the machine for perhaps ten seconds. "You're lying, Abe," he blurted out. "Look, we can save a lot of time if you'll just say that you tried to sell the file. Anyone that looks at this chart can see that you are not being honest with me."

"I'm not lying, Jordan." I couldn't believe he was trying to pull this stuff with me. "You have to keep in mind that I've read Fred Inbau, too," I said, referring to the expert on such examinations, whom we both had studied. "I know the techniques of interrogation as well as you do, so don't try to pull any of those intimidating tactics on me. I know that I didn't sell any file to Jones or Spagnoli or anyone else."

"Will you take another test?" Jordan asked.

"Why not?" I answered wearily. "If these tests will clear up this mess, I'll take another one, but don't tell me that I'm lying after you look at the chart for less than a minute. I happen to know that even the most experienced polygraph examiner cannot look at a graph for one minute or less and come to an accurate conclusion." I asked again to have an impartial outsider administer the test, arguing that most experts agreed that the examiner's attitude significantly affected the interpretation of the test.

"Are you calling me incompetent, Abe?" Jordan snapped.

"I'm not calling you anything! I just feel that we need to have someone impartial like John Reed over on Michigan Avenue, or anyone not associated with the Secret Service, to give me the test. I think we would have a better chance at an unbiased reading of the results."

"Then you're saying that you don't trust me, huh?" Jordan continued, taking his pipe back out of his pocket.

"It's not that I don't trust you. The thing that puzzles me is the fact that you glance at the chart and right away you insult my intelligence and say that I'm lying. I'm trying to cooperate with you on this thing, but it seems that you are eager to trust Jones and are focusing your whole investigation on me. Like I told you, the last time I saw any piece of the Spagnoli file that you're claiming I sold to Jones was when I gave the copy of the summary report to Agent Conrad Cross, as I was instructed to do. Why don't you give Cross a test?"

"You said that you gave the onionskin copy of the report to Cross. When did you give him the onionskin copy of the report?"

"Look, Jordan," I said disgustedly, "I gave that onionskin to Agent Cross on the morning of May 8. Cross was sitting in his office, and I took him the onionskin copy of the report. I put it in his hands and told him that Agent John Russell wanted him to read the report and write a synopsis of the Spagnoli bond case."

"What did Cross do with the onionskin copy of the report?"

"Why don't you put him on the lie box here and ask him? I gave him the report like I was supposed to do."

"Have you seen the onionskin copy of the report since then, Abe?"

"No, I haven't. I can tell you this, though: On May 15, Agent

Russell asked me if I had finished my critique of the Spagnoli bond case. I told him that I had not written it yet. He asked me what I did with the onionskin copy of the report, and I told him that I had given it to Agent Cross, as he had instructed me to do."

Jordan wasn't ready to move on. "Why did you give the onionskin copy of the report to Agent Cross?"

"I just told you that I was instructed to do so."

"Who told you to give Cross the onionskin copy of the report?"

"Agent Russell gave me the onionskin copy of the report sometime back in April. When he handed me the report, he had written across the face of the onionskin that after I finished reading it, I should give it to Agent Cross. I didn't have time to read the report right away because of my own work requirements, and Agent Russell said that there was no emergency in submitting the critique. I read the onionskin copy of the report on May 8 and after reading it gave it to Agent Cross. Agent Russell has all of this information. Didn't you ask him about the report?" I asked.

"Well, we can't find the onionskin copy of the report," Jordan replied matter-of-factly. "Jones said that you had the onionskin copy of the report and that you offered to sell it to Spagnoli for fifty thousand dollars." On top of everything else, it was completely outside the scope of a polygraph examination for the examiner to be providing this kind of information.

"So Jones couldn't be lying," I said sarcastically. "You don't think that Jones would steal a report and try to frame an agent, huh? You don't think that Spagnoli or Art Rachael, another defendant in the Spagnoli counterfeiting case, could have stolen the report when they were in Cross' office on May 9 after we arrested them and brought them in? You haven't considered the possibility that Spagnoli and Jones are professional con men, counterfeiters, and known thieves, huh?"

"We have considered the possibilities, Abe. There are just too many things that Jones and Spagnoli told us that only agents knew. The only way they could have gotten the information was through an agent of this office."

"So you have excluded every other possibility without further investigation?"

"I think so," Agent Jordan said.

"So as it stands, I am accused of trying to sell an onionskin copy of the report that I gave to another agent as I was told to do. You are also accusing me of giving counterfeit money back to Jones when the records show that those bills were last in the possession of Mr. Martineau."

During the early stages of the interview, Jordan had mentioned that several of the counterfeit notes that had been seized by me in the Jones case were missing from the safe located in the office of the special agent in charge. When I reminded Jordan that Martineau and the acting assistant agent in charge, Stocks, were the only agents who had the combination to the safe, Jordan backed away from that line of questioning.

"Inspector McCann has accused me of not being a team player. It seems that all of your evidence against me—the bills, the report— was in reality in the hands of some other agent. That's strange. That's really, really a strange circle of coincidences."

"There's nothing strange, Abe."

It was now getting close to midnight, yet the heat in the room had not let up. Jordan, who appeared to be just as hungry and tired as I was, made some adjustments to the machine and began the second test, which was virtually identical to the first—the same set of questions and the same answers. When we were finished, Jordan came over and unhooked me from the polygraph. He tore off the long printout and left the room.

When the door burst open again, it was Martineau returning,

trailed by Inspectors McCann, Torina, and Hanrahan. They lined up in front of me, while another agent took up a position in the hallway, just outside the door to the room. Martineau, his white hair plastered down with sweat, stared down at me and said coldly: "Abe, I have a warrant to serve on you."

Chapter 8

Despite the hot, thick air in the room, despite the sweat soaking through my clothes, despite the scratching dryness in my mouth and throat, a chill rippled through my body.

Martineau read the particulars: "Here is a warrant issued by federal district Judge William J. Campbell at 2:00 P.M. on May 18, 1964. You are hereby being charged with conspiracy to sell a secret government file to Joseph Spagnoli."

I was twenty-nine years old, on the brink of thirty, the age at which my childhood vision would be realized. I could see it in Martineau's eyes and in the grim faces of the other men. The transition was near. My life as a Secret Service agent was over, done in by the Service itself. I felt dazed and had to fight back tears.

"You're making a mistake."

Inspector McCann asked me to empty my pockets and to surrender my Secret Service badge, and then Martineau handed me a document, saying, "This is for you from the chief."

From: SAIC Howard Anderson—Personnel
To: Special Agent Abraham W. Bolden
Subject: Suspension of Agent Bolden
Having been arrested on May 18, 1964, on a warrant issued at 2:00 P.M., you are hereby suspended, with pay for the period not to exceed five days.

The urge to scream and cry began to subside, and things started coming back into focus. It had all been arranged. The charge and the arrest had been foregone conclusions before I left Washington. They had spirited me back to Chicago, all the while intending to arrest me before the day was over. Clearly, they felt some urgency, but I couldn't say why. Other questions raced through my mind. How had Jones or Spagnoli ended up with the onionskin copy of the report I had given to Agent Cross? What did McCann mean by accusing me of not being a team player?

I asked for a phone book, so that I could call a lawyer, and found the listing for George Howard, an attorney who had been my fraternity brother at Lincoln University. It was 12:30 A.M., but I dialed his number.

"This is Bolden," I said when he picked up the phone. "I've been arrested."

"You're kidding," Howard said. "Who arrested you?"

I explained quickly that the Secret Service was charging me with trying to sell a government file. Martineau couldn't, or wouldn't, tell me where they were taking me for the night, so I asked Howard to call my wife to tell her what was happening. I asked if he would come the next morning to the federal commissioner's office to represent me, and bring my wife with him.

Howard was as reassuring as he could be. "I'll make sure that your wife is there. Don't worry about a thing."

Looking around the room, I saw that Special Agent John Russell, who had been at the center of the case Agent Jordan had questioned me about, had joined the other men in the room. Martineau got up and told me to follow Russell and wait with him in another office. Russell was the one who had written the report I was accused of trying to sell. Every agent in the office had been given an individual copy of Russell's report except Agent Cross and me.

Russell sat me down in the other office and left to get a camera so he could take my picture. He asked Agent Stocks, who had been lurking around, to keep an eye on me. When we were alone, I turned to Stocks, who had acted as if he had had it in for me from the day I arrived in the Chicago office. It was Stocks whom the special agent in charge had ordered to stop telling nigger jokes in my presence. Right now, his very presence sickened me.

"You're the one that's causing all of this trouble," I began. "You and Martineau sent me to see Jones, and now you're saying that my meetings with Jones were not official business."

Stocks ran his stubby fat fingers through his black hair and said, "Looks like you're in trouble now. I didn't send you to see anybody." When I saw a smile crease his pudgy face, I exploded.

"Listen, Stocks. I'm in trouble because of you, so you and Marty have won. You and your racist buddy Martineau have me right where you want me. Don't ask me any more questions about anything because I would have nothing to lose now if I tried to break your damned neck. I'd rather that you leave this room."

Agent Stocks merely smiled again and walked toward the door. He turned toward me, made a cartoonish face, and said with a snicker, "Y'all's da one dat's in trouble." Stokes stood there watching the door and the hallway, smirking and casually jingling the loose change in his pockets, until the others came back.

A short while later, Martineau asked me if I would take another polygraph exam, which I refused to do unless it was administered by someone outside the Service. When Martineau tried to tell me that they were only trying to help me, I blew up again.

"I don't know what you're trying to do or why you're doing it. All I know is that you bring me back to Chicago on a ruse and accuse me of trying to sell a file that I didn't have. I've been here for ten straight hours now without food. Jordan said that two of the counterfeit notes in the Jones case were missing. I turned those bills in to you with the Jones report. Something very strange is going on in this office, and I don't see any of it as being a help to me." The words came pouring out of me in an angry torrent.

Soon, Agents Stocks and Russell were escorting me to a Secret Service vehicle for the drive to the Wheaton County jail, where I would be held for the night. Unlike Stocks, Russell squirmed in his seat, obviously uneasy about having to participate in this process. Russell had always been more than civil, respectfully asking for and listening to my advice with his cases, and my arrest wasn't sitting well with him.

An officer buzzed us into the lockup and asked, "What do we have here?"

"This man is Abraham Bolden," Stocks blurted out. "He was a Secret Service agent. He's under arrest for trying to sell a Secret Service file."

Agent Russell cringed. He seemed both stunned and annoyed by Stocks' candor. "We don't want this to get out, though," he added quickly.

"We have a man that we want to lock up overnight," Russell explained to the next officer once we were inside. I could see that his eyes, already red with fatigue, were brimming with tears, which he dabbed at with a handkerchief. The officers methodically took me through the humiliating booking process that we had taken so many prisoners through in the past. They went through my possessions, fingerprinted me, and then led me to a room to take mug shots. As I stood there under the harsh lights, a blank white background behind me and the black-and-white identifying sign in my hands, I could see tears pouring down John Russell's cheeks. When the sergeant was done with the photographs, Russell walked up, sobbing openly without embarrassment, and put a comforting hand on my shoulder.

"Everything will be all right."

I could contain myself no longer. The dam that had been holding back my tension, grief, and fear all day simply burst. "It's okay,

John," I said, weeping. "None of this is your fault. I don't believe you had anything to do with this."

With the ugly business of getting me locked up concluded, Agent Stocks turned to the officer and said, "You won't need us anymore, will you, Sergeant?" I'll never forget the sight of the two agents walking off down the hallway. Russell's shoulders shook uncontrollably as he continued to cry aloud, while Stocks wrapped an arm around Russell's shoulder in an attempt to console him.

I HAD BEEN taught to play by the rules and had always taken those lessons to heart. I had dedicated most of my adult life to enforcing the rules as an officer of the law, even serving at the side of the president of the United States. Now I sat in the stillness of a jail cell at night with my mind racing as I tried to piece together the series of events that had brought me there. Scenes kept replaying themselves. There were the racist taunts and vicious jokes of the other agents on the White House detail; the memorandum denying me a hotel room in Palm Beach, and the ugly drawing of the disfigured Negro on the back; the squaring off with Henderson in the cottage at Hyannis Port; and finally, the inaction and utter breakdown of Secret Service protection as the bullets blew apart Kennedy's skull in Dealey Plaza. I suspected that all these events were connected to my undoing. Inspector McCann had been right about one thing: Kennedy was dead, and they could no longer count on my being a team player—if they ever had.

From my bunk, I could glimpse the light of morning and hear the sounds of traffic outside. I could even smell coffee, and now realized that I hadn't noticed an entire night passing. A cart came by with bad coffee and even worse sweet rolls, waking up my cellmate, a stringy-haired Southerner who had introduced himself as Smith and said he was from Kentucky. I had told Smith my name was Al Baker, an alias I had often used in undercover work. It was still early when a Du-Page County deputy sheriff came to unlock the cell.

"This way, Bolden," he ordered.

Smith raised his Styrofoam coffee cup in a mock toast and said, "See you, Baker. Everything will come out all right." His face split into a slightly demented smile and he added, "Hey, my name ain't Smith, either. Hope to see you again someday."

The deputy led me out to where Agents Stocks and Edward Tucker were waiting with a Secret Service car.

"What's going on, Abe?" Tucker asked. Tucker had been in Hyannis Port and had witnessed the incident between Harvey Henderson and me. It was Tucker who'd followed me outside to calm me down, and who went back in to confront Henderson about his comments. He took his job seriously and did it well. I started to explain how Frank Jones had accused me of trying to sell a government file.

Tucker interrupted. "That's absurd! I don't believe a word Jones says. Doesn't Martineau realize that Jones is probably out to get you?"

"We have more than just Jones," Stocks chimed in. "We have other evidence."

As we drove, I filled in some of the details of my arrest the night before. Tucker listened with a mixture of sadness and concern.

"Look, Abe, I don't know anything about this case. I was just sent to pick you up this morning. Tell me, who made the charge against you?" When he heard all the details of the allegations, as related to me by Martineau, he was incredulous.

"You mean they're taking the word of Spagnoli and Jones? You know, I remember when we tailed Arthur Rachael. We followed him to the South Side of Chicago, and he got off at Fifty-fifth Street and the Dan Ryan Expressway. How far does Jones live from there?"

"Jones lives about ten blocks from there," I answered. "Look, Tucker, I tried to tell Martineau and Inspector McCann that Jones said he knew Rachael and that Rachael's name had come up in my conversation with Jones on May 11. For some reason, everyone is choosing to believe Jones. I don't understand it, either."

MARTY MARTINEAU HAD instructed the two agents to bring me to the U.S. marshals' office on the eighth floor of Chicago's federal building. Perhaps I should have found comfort in the sight of the massive stone building, with its thick granite columns and ornate dome, representing a government committed to protecting the rights of its citizens. In that moment, though, it looked cold, imposing, and fearsome. Inside, we passed through the cavernous rotunda to the black wrought-iron doors of the elevator, where the operator greeted me.

"How're you doing, Bolden? I thought you were gone to school in Washington."

My voice was so shaky I could barely answer.

Martineau was waiting on the eighth floor and ushered me into a private office. Agent Tucker sat quietly by my side, staring blankly as if stunned by disbelief, until a sharply dressed marshal strode in.

"I've met you before, haven't I?" the marshal said to me with a smile when Martineau made the introductions.

"Probably so, sir," I said, offering my hand.

"I'm Marshal Tierney, and I'm sure that I've seen you here bringing in prisoners before. I'm sorry to meet you again under these awful conditions. I'll try to make your short stay here not too painful." Tierney arranged for me to be fingerprinted after the other prisoners picked up that day had all cleared out of the processing room. Even still, I remember scrubbing my hands hard when it was done, trying to remove every sign of my disgrace. Eventually, I found myself standing in front of the huge mahogany desk of the U.S. commissioner, whom I'd known for several years. I'd brought more defendants before this cheerful man in the previous four years than the entire rest of the Chicago office combined. On this day, he somberly carried out the requirements of his task.

"Are you Abraham Bolden?"

"Yes, sir."

"I have a complaint against you, charging you with violation of Section 201(c), Title 18, U.S.C. Now, I must warn you that you do not have to discuss this matter with anyone, and that anything that you say in this hearing may be used against you. Do you have money to afford counsel?"

"Yes, I do," I answered. "I have an attorney, but he is not here at the present time."

The commissioner looked to the side of the room and addressed the U.S. attorney, Charles Turner, who was standing against the wall.

"Are you representing the government in the Bolden case?" When Turner answered in the affirmative, the commissioner suggested they proceed with the discussion of bond even though my attorney was not present, and asked Turner if he had a recommendation.

"The government recommends a bond of twenty-five thousand dollars," Turner said.

The commissioner appeared irritated by the recommendation. He leaned forward in his chair and shook his head.

"No. I'm not going to hold this man under such a high bond. He is married and lives with his family in Chicago. A bond is only for the purpose of ensuring the appearance of the defendant. I have no reason to believe that this defendant will not abide by the will of the court."

"Your Honor," Turner protested, "the defendant is charged with a very serious crime. Under the circumstances, I don't feel that twenty-five thousand dollars is too high."

Making little effort to conceal his annoyance, the commissioner declared, "The defendant is hereby held under a twenty-five-hundred-dollar own-recognizance bond, and preliminary hearing is continued until May 21 at 2:00 P.M." He gathered up his papers to leave and handed me the bond to sign. Just as I finished signing, I heard a commotion at the door. In rushed my wife, her reddened eyes wide with disbelief. Behind her were my attorney, George Howard, my sister Cecelia, and my brother-in-law John Griffin.

My wife rushed up to me and with her lips very close to my ear said softly, "Everything is going to be all right. You were doing fine until Mr. Martineau came along. I knew that something was going to happen. I just felt it."

The commissioner filled my attorney in on what he'd missed, and made it clear that he wanted to make sure I was accommodated as much as possible. I was free to go. Howard, my old college friend, did what he could to relax me, telling me to get some rest and asking me to come discuss everything in his office later that evening. My wife and relatives took me home to our house on Sangamon Street. For the first time, I took a deep breath of relief as I stood in front of my own home, gazing at the green hedges and the young spruce trees in the front yard.

That evening, my wife and I climbed the steps to George Howard's second-floor office. The lawyer waved a copy of the *Chicago Sun-Times* at us and explained that the case had made headlines. The paper laid it out in detail. According to the news account, I had been arrested for attempting to sell a government file to Joseph Spagnoli. Spagnoli had told his story this way: He had been arrested on May 9 in connection with the counterfeiting of U.S. savings bonds. After the arrest, Frank Jones had visited Spagnoli's house and over several drinks told Spagnoli that he had a contact in the Secret Service and could deliver the file to Spagnoli for $50,000. Spagnoli claimed that on May 11, the day after Jones' visit, he called the Secret Service office and talked with the acting special agent in charge, Maurice Martineau, who told him that there was no truth to what he was saying. Martineau told Spagnoli that he was probably being conned. When Martineau failed to dispatch an agent to interview him, Spagnoli called a *Sun-Times* reporter, who came to the house to hear Spagnoli's story. The two called the Secret Service office on May 12 and again spoke to Martineau. This time, when Martineau realized that a reporter was interested, he agreed to meet with Spagnoli. Amazingly, the article identified me by name and address as the agent who stood accused and arrested by the Secret Service.

"They seem to be resting their entire case on the testimony of this guy Spagnoli," Howard observed. "Do you know him?"

"Yeah, I saw him down at the Secret Service office."

"Did you arrest him?"

"No, I didn't arrest him personally, but I was with a group of agents who arrested him on May 9."

Attorney Howard kept up his questioning. "Did you ever talk to Spagnoli?"

I went on to explain our encounter. "On May 8, I walked past Agent Thomas Strong, who was standing outside of his office. Spagnoli was seated in a chair next to Agent Cross' desk. Strong and Cross share an office. Agent Strong told me that he had to make a run to the washroom and asked me to watch Spagnoli until he returned."

"He asked you to watch Spagnoli?"

"Yes. I just stood inside the doorway leading into the office. Upon turning around and seeing me standing there, Spagnoli asked, 'Are you a Secret Service agent?' I told Spagnoli that I was an agent, and he said that he didn't know that they even had Negro agents in the government. Then Spagnoli said, 'FBI men ain't like these other cops out here. They don't take bribes like these other cops, do they?' "

"And what did you say?" Howard asked.

"I told him that there are thousands and thousands of FBI agents, and that there might be a few that weren't quite right."

That did not please Howard. "Why did you tell him that? Wouldn't it have been better for you just to ignore him?"

"Well, he caught me off guard. I didn't expect a question like that, so when he asked it, I just gave him my own opinion."

"Do you think that he was offering you a bribe? Why did you think that he would ask you a question like that?"

"No, he didn't offer me anything. Seeing what has happened so far with his charges against me and all, I think that what he was really asking was, if he were to claim that an FBI agent had tried to get some money out of him, would anyone believe him?"

"And what do you know about this file—where it is and who has it now?" Howard continued.

With careful questions, George Howard got the story out of me. Agent Russell had given me an onionskin copy of the report. He told me to read the report, write my comments on it, and pass it along to Agent Cross. On the morning of May 8, I handed it to Cross while he was seated at his desk and told him that Russell wanted him to comment on the report. I went back to work on my own cases, and when Agent Russell asked me about the report on May 13, I went to Cross and inquired about it. Cross told me that he had lost the report. He had read it and set it down on his desk, and then never saw the report again. On May 9, the day I stood in the doorway of Cross' office to keep an eye on Spagnoli, the desk looked clear, as if someone had just cleaned it. I didn't notice any report on the desk. I couldn't say if Cross had been in his office at all during the time that Spagnoli was there. Other agents used Cross' office to question Spagnoli while Cross worked in an office across the hall.

"So Spagnoli asked you about FBI agents while he was in the office where the report came up missing?"

"Yes."

"Okay." Howard nodded. "Now let's get to Jones. Where does he come into the picture? I want you to tell me the truth now. If you can't tell me the truth while your wife is in here, we can ask her to wait out in the reception area. I have to have the truth if I'm going to defend you. I don't want any surprises coming down the line during the hearing or the trial."

I could see that Howard was a thorough and meticulous lawyer. I explained how Jones had called the Secret Service office on May 11 and specifically requested that I be sent out to talk to him. Agent Stocks, who at that time was acting assistant special agent in charge of the Chicago office, told me about the call. At first, I refused to go meet with Jones. I had placed two cases against him and was concerned that meeting him without some sort of cover could be dangerous. I told Howard that Martineau had insisted that I meet with Jones or resign, and had accused me of trying to pick and choose my cases.

I gave Howard the details of my meeting with Jones on May 11. Jones had thumbed through the fishing guide and claimed to know Arthur Rachael. Jones and I had gone to the park and had subsequent conversations in which he pretended to be trying to help the Secret Service.

George Howard listened intently, taking detailed notes, until he was able to put together his own understanding of the situation. "From what I can make of this, Bolden, you were set up. The only question is who set you up and why. Jones has everything to gain by getting you in trouble with the office. Spagnoli could have stolen the file when he was in Cross' office, and may have had some prior association with Jones—they're both counterfeiters. The third problem is your relationships with Agent Stocks and Agent Martineau. Mr. Martineau could have killed this whole thing, but he chose to arrest you and end your career with the Secret Service. If either Stocks or Martineau acknowledged that they sent you to see Jones, then there is no criminal case. We could defend it as an assignment that went wrong, take the suspension or reprimand, and move on. However, as long as they deny that you had an official relationship with Jones on that day, what you have is a criminal conspiracy outside the knowledge of your supervisors."

By that time it was after 10:00 P.M., and Howard wrapped things up. He told us to go home and get some rest, and that he'd arrange for us to talk again before the hearing on the twenty-first.

George Howard was a slightly built man, but he cut a dashing figure. He was confident, sharp-witted, and eloquent, and anyone who saw this well-dressed young man with the big booming voice in action in the Cook County courts would remember him. Howard had worked hard to get where he was, driving a Chicago Transit Authority bus while he attended John Marshall Law School, where he finished near the top of his class. His record in state court was very good, but the fact was that he had very little experience handling criminal cases in federal court. With my limited resources, he was the best attorney I could afford, but I knew he would do everything he could for me.

Once Barbara and I got home, I peeled off the clothes I'd been wearing for two days and took a long, soothing shower.

"They came and searched all over the house Monday night," Barbara said as I crawled into bed. "They took my typewriter and a lot of papers from your files in the attic. The agents tried to take the Christmas card and picture that President Kennedy sent you, but I made them put it back in the attic. There were three or four Secret Service agents with some Chicago policemen, but they wouldn't tell me anything about what was going on." The intrusion had clearly troubled her. "They searched in here, too. When they finished, I went and looked in the drawer where I keep the extra house money. Four hundred-dollar bills were gone from the drawer where I kept them."

"Are you sure that the money was there?" I asked.

"I'm positive," she said adamantly. "I knew that you were going to school, so I drew out four hundred-dollar bills from the bank and put them in the top drawer right there. I put them on the right side of the drawer in a white envelope. They told me to leave the room while they were searching. I sat in the dining room. They were all over the place—the attic, the basement, and the back porch. As soon as they finished, I went straight to the drawer and looked for the envelope and it was not there."

"Maybe they took it to see if the bills were counterfeit," I suggested.

"No, I doubt it. With all of those Secret Service agents in the house, you know they don't have to take money to see if it's counterfeit. And why didn't they tell me they were taking it?" she asked, getting visibly more upset.

I did my best to calm Barbara down, and we agreed to bring it up with George Howard the next time we saw him.

Chapter 9

I SLEPT LITTLE that night, so I wasn't at my best when the door-bell rang at 7:00 A.M. Peeking out one of the front windows, I could see two men standing at the door. One was neatly dressed in a tailored brown suit and held a copy of the *Chicago Sun-Times* in his hand. The other, wearing overalls and a T-shirt, carried a huge video camera on his shoulder. I thought I could make out a third person sitting in a Channel 7 News van parked on the street. I opened the front door but kept the aluminum screen door closed between us.

"Mr. Bolden," the well-dressed man greeted me. The reporter's name was John Drury. "We are from Channel Seven News, and we want to talk to you about the story that's running in the newspapers today."

"I don't have anything to say to the press right now. I may have a comment later when I find out more about the charges against me."

"We are here to help you get your side of the story out," he continued. "Something is fishy about what has happened to you. We have talked to some other agents about you, and some of them feel that you are getting the shaft."

"What agents?" I asked.

"We can't name names, but when this story broke, we talked to some of our contacts. We know that you were very critical of the Secret Service over the Kennedy assassination and that you think that the Secret Service could have done more to protect Kennedy. We hear that from more than one source."

"Who told you that?" I asked again, this time more sharply.

"Why don't you let us in for a moment, or come on the porch where we can take a few pictures of you? I'll ask a few questions. If I ask something that you don't want to answer—"

"I can't let you in because my wife and children are asleep, and I wouldn't want to appear on television looking like this anyway," I said, cutting him off. "I would like for you to tell me who brought up the Kennedy thing. Yeah, I talked to some agents about testifying before the Warren Commission. I want to know how you found out."

"I can't tell you that, Abraham. All I can say is that it came from an agent that thinks a whole lot of you and thinks that you are getting a raw deal. But you have to get your own story out. The way it stands now, it looks bad for you. The public is seeing only one side of the issue."

"Why don't you take my telephone number and call me later today? I may talk with you after seeing my attorney." I wrote down the number and handed it to him.

"Thanks," the reporter said. "Now, don't talk to any of those other news guys who'll be coming around. We were here first, okay?"

"Okay."

About five minutes after that crew drove off, the doorbell rang again. This time I saw four men on the porch, two carrying video cameras. There were vans from two other Chicago television stations parked out front, and a man across the street pointing a video camera at the house. Again, the reporters told me they were there to get my side of the story. I referred them to George Howard and mentioned that I might have something to say at a later time.

Barbara met me in the hall as I walked back to the kitchen.

"Sure are a lot of people coming by here," she said.

"They want to interview me."

"I think you should let George do the talking. I think—"

"Hell, the Secret Service has blasted my name and address all over the newspapers and TV before they even got my side of anything. I don't believe Jones said anything to them. I think that the whole thing was set up to drum me out of the Service." Just talking about it to my wife made the anger rise inside me. "One reporter said that the Kennedy assassination might be the cause of my problems. He may be right for all I know."

"You need to settle down, Abraham," Barbara soothed. "Maybe you should get out of the house and go over to Cecelia's. That way they won't know where to find you."

"Naw, I'm not going to run and hide. I'm going to fight back. I'm not going to lie down and let them walk all over me," I fumed. "I'm going to call a news conference here at the house later today and give my side of the story. I'm not going to let them kick me in the balls."

I stormed into the kitchen and spread the reporters' business cards on top of the laundry hamper near the phone. I dialed each television station and left a message that I would be holding a news conference at my home at 2:00 P.M. I added that no photographic or video equipment would be allowed inside the house. Just before their expected arrival, I set up my own tape recorder under a table in the living room. As the reporters showed up, I ushered them all to the large circular couch, then sat myself down in a folding chair in front of them.

I began the conference by flatly denying that I had attempted to sell a government file to Spagnoli, as alleged by Frank Jones. Prodded by their questions, I gave them a rundown of my experience as a Pinkerton detective and as an Illinois state police officer.

"Do you think that race is a factor in this case?" one reporter asked.

"Yes," I answered without hesitating. I told them about the problems I'd had on the White House detail, both in Washington and in Hyannis Port. "It was an acting supervisor who told me that I was a nigger, was born a nigger, would die a nigger, and should act like one," I added emotionally.

A reporter asked, "Mr. Bolden, as I said earlier today when I talked to you on the porch, there is some talk about your being dissatisfied with how the Secret Service protected President Kennedy. Is that true? Do you think your attitude on the Kennedy matter has anything to do with your predicament?"

"I don't know who set me up or why. All I know is that my supervisors sent me to see Jones and now they are denying it. No, the Secret Service didn't respond properly when Kennedy was killed. I said it the day he was assassinated and have said it almost every day since." I grew increasingly emotional as I spoke. "This is nothing but a frame job. The agents around Kennedy didn't do their jobs because some of them were out nightclubbing and getting drunk the day before the assassination. Some of the agents who were in Dallas on the detail were nearly drunk while they guarded the president in Hyannis Port. They were hauling women around in Secret Service cars and drinking while on duty."

I was sweating heavily and breathing hard, having worked myself into a fit of anger. The idea that I could settle some scores at the Service now consumed me.

"I often said, to other agents and to personal friends, that someone needed to tell the truth about the lax protection the president received. I witnessed how the agency was covering up important investigations leading up to the day he was killed. I heard the rumors of the Secret Service identification that was lost or stolen in a Dallas strip club the night before the assassination. I heard that lie circulated by the Secret Service that Kennedy was partially responsible for his own death because he ordered that agents not ride on the running boards of his limousine. Prior to the assassination, I read no memorandum, received any official or unofficial directive, or heard any rumor advising agents not to ride on the running boards of the limousine."

The words were rushing breathlessly out of me now. "You won't find many agents in the Secret Service who believe that Oswald was not part of a conspiracy. You won't find many who believe that the agents in Dallas did their jobs, either. Even now, the agents in charge are running around trying to cover up for the agents who went out partying the night before Kennedy was killed. The irresponsible conduct of the agents in Dallas was the rule, not the exception, and there were several agents previously assigned to the detail who were concerned that Kennedy's life was jeopardized by the outlandish behavior and arrogant overconfidence of some of the agents on the White House detail.

"I was there when all of the Secret Service's identification books were secretly replaced by the Bureau of Printing and Engraving. In my own opinion, the replacement gives credibility to the whispered rumor that an agent had lost his identification or had it stolen from him."

By bringing this case against me, the Secret Service had unwittingly given me a national platform from which I could speak out about these issues. I wondered if they had considered the possibility that the press would be all over me. I thought that since I would be dead by the time I was thirty anyway, I had nothing to lose. I owed it to President Kennedy.

None of the reporters interrupted my tirade. When I was finished, I walked to the kitchen to get some water, then came back into the living room and announced, "The news conference is over."

The newsmen asked if I would be willing to go with them somewhere outside so they could get video of me saying some of the things I had just told them, and we made arrangements to meet near the expressway, not far from my house. They set up their cameras and interviewed me, and I repeated much of what I had said at my house. There weren't many questions about Spagnoli or Jones. The reporters seemed far more interested in my allegations regarding the conduct of the Secret Service—its shoddy protection of the president, and the drinking and carousing that had been publicly denied by Service supervisors. Even though the reporters pressed me, I refused to speculate about who might be trying to frame me.

I drove home, confident that now the public would hear my side of the story. As I passed the intersection of Seventy-ninth and Emerald, I noticed the real estate office on the corner, and realized that I had gone to that office with Agent Cross on the evening of May 11, a few hours after I had met with Frank Jones. Cross had explained to me that he wasn't satisfied with life as a Secret Service agent and wanted to open his own business, a nightclub, as soon as he could get the money together. He had a list of potentially available locations from this office, and had a private conversation with the owner while I waited near the entrance, in the Secret Service car. As we left, he told me that he would soon be able to open his own business. I don't know what he meant and don't want to speculate.

Later that evening, Barbara and I sat down to watch the six o'clock news. The Channel 7 team had told me that they thought they could get the story put together in time for the early news, and sure enough, it was the lead story.

"The Secret Service agent arrested on May 18 tells his side of the story," the anchorman announced. "Abraham Bolden was interviewed today and says that the case against him is a frame job. He accused the Secret Service of drinking while on duty and being lax in the protection of President Kennedy. Bolden stated that his efforts to tell the Warren Commission about the conduct of fellow Secret Service agents may be the reason that he was called out of Washington, D.C., and placed under arrest."

There I was on the screen in my cheap brown suit from Sears and Roebuck and my dark green Ray-Ban sunglasses, declaring open war on the United States Secret Service. It felt so much like a dream that I had to remind myself that it was really happening.

The newsman's voice was still echoing in the living room when the phone rang.

"Abraham. This is George Howard." There was no mistaking the irritation in his voice.

"Hello," I said calmly.

"Man, what the hell is going on?" Howard began. "I told you not to discuss this case with anyone. Now I just heard that you were on television discussing the case. If I'm going to defend you, we have to work together. I can't have you going in one direction and me going in another. Do you understand that?" Howard was insistent, and wanted it clear that he was taking charge of the situation. "Now, you have to understand that we have to defend against the charges against you no matter who you think is behind them or why. Don't say one word to anyone else. I mean it."

"Okay, George," I said apologetically. "I just wanted to get my side of the story out. That's all I was doing."

"Well, you may have done more harm than good. Don't talk to the press anymore unless I am with you. The hearing is tomorrow, and I will see you there. Keep quiet. Stay at home and get some rest. You're under a lot of stress and I can understand that, but don't say anything else to the press."

As soon as I hung up the phone, it rang again. This time I heard the soft, clear voice of my father, calling from East St. Louis.

"Abraham, are you all right? I just saw you on television down here about an hour ago on national news. Is everything all right up there?"

"Not really, Dad. Two men that I arrested are accusing me of trying to sell a government file to one of them." I tried to sound confident when I added, "There's nothing to the charges."

"Well, I think that you should quiet down and not talk so much.

You must have done something to step on somebody's toes. You be careful now, and don't talk so much," Dad ended in his fatherly tone. He hung up quietly, without waiting for an answer.

I left Barbara in the living room, scanning the channels on the television, looking for more coverage of our story. I was physically and emotionally spent, and took myself off to bed, desperate for the escape of a deep sleep.

GEORGE HOWARD SHOWED up at our house the next morning, May 21, to take us to the hearing in Commissioner C. S. Bentley's court.

"Man, that was some stunt you pulled yesterday," he greeted me. "Did you see the papers this morning?" He opened his briefcase and took out the *Sun-Times* and the *Chicago Tribune*. "You made the headlines in both of these," he said, handing the papers to me.

It seemed my statements had created a firestorm in the press. The Warren Commission was questioned about the findings concerning the performance of the Secret Service in Dallas on the day of Kennedy's assassination. J. Lee Rankin, counsel to the commission, stated to the press that the performance of the Service would be reevaluated in light of my accusations. *Newsweek* magazine was preparing a full-page story outlining all of my allegations about the Service's behavior. They had taken photos of Barbara and me as we left the commissioner's office. The Secret Service was suddenly on the defensive.

As George and I went through the articles, the phone rang. Barbara answered the phone and handed it to George. I watched his face as he listened to his secretary on the other end. When he was done, my attorney looked at me and said that the hearing was cancelled. The government had simply gone ahead and indicted me, rather than risk having the case thrown out in a preliminary hearing.

"There's nothing we can do now except prepare for trial," he said. As he went on to explain that the arraignment had been set for a week later, the doorbell rang.

I peeked out the window and recognized the neatly dressed, portly man standing at the door as Richard Walters, an occasional informant of mine. Walters was a card shark and a petty criminal who could neither read nor write. He had been an informant, although one of limited value, for the Secret Service since before I became an agent. In 1963, I'd sent Walters to Jones' home in an attempt to determine if Jones was still circulating counterfeit money. The investigation was discontinued when Jones became suspicious of Walters and reported to me that he had been approached by an old man looking for counterfeit money.

George asked who was at the door, and I told him. "Well, get rid of him," he said impatiently. "We have other matters to discuss."

I went out on the porch, where Walters was fidgeting nervously. Looking past him, I could see a young man sitting in a parked car and moving his head up and down periodically as if he was manipulating something in his lap.

"Who's that guy in the car?" I asked, nodding in the direction of the street.

"Oh, that's Louis," Walters answered. "He's all right. He's my nephew and he brought me over here."

Walters was obviously anxious. His lips quivered as he spoke, and he couldn't stop playing with his necktie.

"I came to pick up a piece," he said. "I need a piece to take care of Jones."

"What kind of piece are you talking about?" I asked.

"You know what I'm talking about. Jones needs to be taken care of for what he is doing to you. Give me a gun and I'll take care of him right now." Walters looked down at his feet as he shifted his weight from side to side.

"You stay away from Jones," I said firmly. "You stay far away from Jones."

"I'm just trying to help you, Abe," Walters pleaded, a little pathetically. It seemed to me he was almost about to cry.

George Howard was waiting inside the house. "What did he want?"

"He wanted me to give him a piece."

"A what?" Howard was clearly startled.

"A piece."

"A gun?"

"Yes. That's my understanding of what he was talking about. He said that he wanted to take care of Jones. I think he was wearing a wire transmitter. I think that the Secret Service or FBI sent him here to entrap me into some conspiracy to kill Jones. His behavior was very suspicious, and he was acting real nervous."

"They're really out to put you away, Abe," George said, shaking his head. "You have got to be very careful. The minute you do something like that, you're going away for a very long time, and you know it."

"I wouldn't give anyone a gun, George. I'm not that stupid. I told him to stay away from Jones."

"Okay. Don't let me down now." George stood up and gathered his things to leave. "This is a tough case, and I don't want you to complicate it any more than you already have. We'll be in Judge Perry's court on the 28th. In the meantime, I have to get busy drawing up the preliminary motions. I'll call you the day after the holiday if there are any changes."

George Howard walked out of the house, leaving Barbara and me to spend a tense, edgy Memorial Day weekend with our family, trying hard not to think too much about the hard road in front of us.

Chapter 10

ON THE MORNING of May 28, Barbara and I got our two older children ready for school, picked up the sitter to look after our youngest, Darren, and drove downtown, where we had arranged to meet George Howard in front of a restaurant. The three of us continued on to the courthouse together. George stopped as we were about to climb the courthouse steps, and warned me again not to say anything to anyone inside about the case.

"Let me do the talking and you keep quiet," he admonished.

Inside the building, reporters and cameramen crowded together in the large rotunda. Their harsh floodlights and persistent questions assaulted us as we made our way through to the elevators. George fielded a few of their queries but stopped anyone who addressed any questions directly to me with a curt "My client has no statement to make concerning this case at this time."

Upstairs, Secret Service agents lurked by the heavy wooden doors of the courtroom. George led us into Judge J. Sam Perry's court, past the cold and silent stares of Martineau, Jordan, Torina, and another agent named Louis Sims. The friendlier faces of friends and acquaintances who had come to show their support greeted me inside the courtroom. The judge opened the proceedings, which turned out to be brief and rather anticlimactic, given the tense drama of the moment. He asked if we wished to enter a plea.

"The defendant enters a plea of not guilty, Your Honor," George Howard said clearly and confidently. Judge Perry set a date

111

of June 12 to hear preliminary motions in the case, and we were done.

On June 12, the court heard Howard's motions. The judge denied our motion for a list of witnesses who were to appear in the trial. He did grant a motion for a list of witnesses to "any oral statements made by the defendant," and another for "a copy of questions put to the defendant and the results thereof during the polygraph test" that was administered by Agent Jordan. Judge Perry announced that the trial would begin in his court on July 6.

When that day came, we took our places at the long wooden defendant's table that stood to one side of the judge's bench. Across from us, at the prosecution table, sat U.S. attorneys Richard T. Sikes and Arthur Dunne. The courtroom doors swung open and a U.S. marshal led in a group of what seemed like two hundred or so prospective jurors. The judge explained the rules that would govern the voir dire, the jury selection process, and the lawyers began questioning the potential jurors one by one. Each side made a few peremptory challenges, and the judge excused some jurors himself for various reasons. Before I knew it, the clerk was swearing in twelve jurors and four alternates. I couldn't help but notice that the only nonwhite faces on the jury belonged to one Negro and one Mexican. Making it clear that he wanted to move the trial along as speedily as possible, Judge Perry asked the attorneys on both sides if they were prepared to go right into their opening statements.

No official transcript of the opening statement made by the government that day can be found. Neither do the official transcripts that do exist specifically identify the government attorney who made the opening statement on behalf of the government. According to defense attorney Howard's own opening statement, the government's opening statement was made by Richard Sikes. Sikes would have necessarily sought to convince the jury that the government was prepared to prove its charges against the defendant as outlined in the indictment by the grand jury on May 21, 1964. The indictment was of three counts charging that the defendant, Abraham W. Bolden, "being a public official, a United States Secret Service Agent of the Treasury Department did directly and indirectly corruptly ask, demand, exact, solicit, seek, and agree to receive a thing of value for himself, the sum of $50,000 in return for being influenced in his performance of an official act by disclosing matter and matters in violation of Section 201, Title 18, United States Code. The defendant did corruptly influence, obstruct and impede and endeavor to influence, obstruct and impede the due administration of justice in the prosecution of Case No. 64 CR 300, entitled *United States v. D'Antonio et al.*, in violation of Section 1503, Title 18, United States Code. And the defendant did unlawfully, willingly, and knowingly conspire, confederate and agree with Frank Jones, named as co-conspirator but not as a defendant herein, to commit offense against the United States Government in violation of Section 1503, Title 18, United States Code." The overt acts alleged were that "Bolden met Frank Jones on May 11, 1964, and gave Jones a piece of paper; on or about May 12, 1964, Jones went to 5301 West Quincy Street, Chicago, Illinois; on May 12, 1964, Bolden had a telephone conversation with Frank Jones; and on or about May 13, 1964, Bolden had a conversation with Frank Jones in violation of Section 371, Title 18, United States Code."

When the government finished its opening statement, it was George Howard's turn to pace in front of the jury. In a clear voice, he told the jurors that "defendant Abraham Bolden is not guilty of any crime against the United States. We will show that Bolden's meetings with Frank Jones were in furtherance of an investigation that was ongoing. My client did not give Jones any excerpt from a government file or ask Frank Jones to solicit a sum of money from Joseph Spagnoli." Howard closed by casting doubt on the men at the heart of the government's case. "We intend to show by evidence from the stand that Joseph Spagnoli has boasted of the number of times he has been arrested and never been convicted. We intend to show, not by speculation but by evidence, that these two men who are going to testify for the government are making a daring attempt to corrupt the United States government to save their own hides."

After the opening statements, Judge Perry called for a short recess before the government began presenting its case. George Howard and I walked out of the courtroom and stood with Barbara by the railing overlooking the rotunda.

"I'm going to give it my best shot," George told her. "We're up against it. They're going to try everything to convict your husband, 'and I'm going to try everything to see that he is found not guilty of these charges."

Acting Special Agent in Charge Martineau was called as the government's first witness. Maurice Martineau commanded everyone's attention as he strode to the front of the courtroom, his silver-white hair shining and his steely blue eyes darting behind horn-rimmed glasses. He neatly fit the image of the serious and responsible senior government agent, a man who knew his job and did it well. I knew that the jury would buy his act, but of course, this was the same man who had taunted me on so many occasions, who sent me on pointless errands to buy black Muslim newspapers just so he could yell at me when I objected, and who had thought the noose found hanging over my desk was no big deal.

Richard Sikes elicited the information he wanted from his witness. Martineau said that Spagnoli, arrested on May 9 and under indictment, had phoned on May 13. "Spagnoli told me that he had been approached in his home by a total stranger who was a colored guy calling himself 'Mr. Q.' He told me that Mr. Q told him that he had a connection in the Secret Service and that Spagnoli could buy the file in his bond case for the price of fifty thousand dollars. Spagnoli said that this Mr. Q told him that the Secret Service was going to have Sandra's hair dyed on the 12th of May." Martineau described how he had told Agent Russell about the call from Spagnoli.

During Mr. Martineau's testimony, I recalled that in several meetings at the Secret Service office, Russell informed us that in mid-April of 1964, Sandra Hafford was arrested by the Chicago police when she and a man named Vito Zaccagnini attempted to cash a series of counterfeit bonds at a bank in Chicago. The fraud was discovered when one of the cashiers in the bank noticed that another cashier was cashing another series of bonds bearing the identical name of the bond payee.

On May 7, Sandra Hafford came to the Secret Service office and was interviewed by Agent John Russell. Sandra had a close relationship with Spagnoli and testified on behalf of the government on May 8 before the Grand Jury in the *D'Antonio et al.* bond case. Spagnoli was a defendant in that case.

After testifying, she was placed in protective custody in the Conrad Hilton Hotel under the name of Mrs. Jay Lloyd Stocks. While in protective custody, Sandra decided to change the color of her hair. I do not know the reason that Sandra wanted to dye her hair and was only peripherally involved in the *D'Antonio* bond case.

It was alleged by the government that I schemed with Jones to give Spagnoli information about Sandra that would aid and abet her intimidation or murder.

"Bolden was sent away to Secret Service school on the 17th of May." Martineau continued, "On May 18, I saw Bolden in the United States Attorney's office at about 6:30 P.M. Present were Inspector McCann, Chief Inspector Torina, and the United States attorney Edward V. Hanrahan. At that time, I told Bolden that I had received information from Spagnoli that Spagnoli had been approached by Frank Jones, who offered to sell him the Spagnoli Secret Service bond file for fifty thousand dollars. I told Bolden that Spagnoli said Jones had given Spagnoli an excerpt from the file. I further told Bolden that

Jones was arrested and said that it was Bolden who had asked him to approach Spagnoli for the purpose of selling the Spagnoli file. At that point, I was interrupted by Bolden, who proclaimed that if we thought it was he who gave the excerpt to Jones, that he had a typewriter at home and that we were free to examine it and compare it to the excerpt. I hadn't mentioned that the excerpt was typewritten."

The anger surged up inside me. "That's a lie!" I hissed in George Howard's ear. "I never said that." I knew Judge Perry was watching me whispering my outrage to my lawyer, but I didn't care. "Nothing of the sort happened, George. I believe Marty set this whole thing up."

Judge Perry banged his gavel down hard and glared at me, and the jury followed his gaze. I'm sure everyone in the room knew that I believed that Martineau was lying.

Martineau kept going, unfazed. "Bolden told me that if he wanted to make a proposition of that kind to Spagnoli, that he would not have used Frank W. Jones; that he had many clever informants who could much more ably represent Mr. Bolden. I reviewed the daily reports of Agent Bolden for the days May 12 and May 13, and none of the reports reflect that Bolden was having contact with Frank Jones." Sikes had no more questions.

On cross-examination, George got Martineau to admit that he had helped arrange the elaborate ruse to bring me back from Secret Service school in Washington, but Martineau denied that he knew that I was the arresting officer in the Jones case. For that matter, he denied any knowledge at all of an official relationship between me and Jones.

"Are you denying that you have any knowledge of Bolden's contact with an investigation of Frank Jones?"

Martineau insisted that he had no knowledge of the Jones investigation or of my involvement with it.

George Howard turned his back on the witness box and walked back to the defense table, yanking his chair out in disgust. He was hog-tied. The judge and the prosecutors managed to slam shut every potential opening George could find. They would not let him mount a defense. Things didn't look good at all.

The government next called Frank Jones to the stand, and two Secret Service agents escorted him into the courtroom. Jones was a large man with very dark skin, and he looked uncomfortable in a neat suit and tie as he entered the room. Jones did not meet my gaze.

Under direct examination, Jones readily outlined his checkered past, admitting that he had been convicted of felony larceny in 1949 and convicted again, this time for writing bad checks, in 1954. "Abraham Bolden arrested me in 1962 on a charge of possession and passing of counterfeit money. I was indicted on that charge, and while still under indictment, Agent Bolden arrested me again in 1963 on a charge of manufacturing counterfeit money," he testified. "Those cases are still pending against me."

Jones next said that he was at home with his wife when "Bolden drove up in his car and parked across the street. I walked over to Bolden's car, got in, and Bolden told me that he had arrested Spagnoli for counterfeiting and that a great deal of money had been made by defendants in that case. Bolden said that Spagnoli wanted to know the whereabouts of a certain girl named Sandy. Bolden also had information about a prisoner who had been brought to Chicago on a writ and was going to testify against Spagnoli. Bolden said that this prisoner was at the Cook County jail."

I could see some of the jurors looking curiously back and forth between Jones and me as he told his story. "Bolden told me that he had a Secret Service file on the Spagnoli counterfeiting case and on the testimony of the witnesses. Bolden said that the file would be valuable to Spagnoli and that he would sell the file for fifty thousand dollars."

"And what happened next?" Dunne prodded.

You can't make a living as a con man and swindler, as Jones had done all his life, if you don't have a way of gaining people's trust. I could sense that the judge and some of the jurors were accepting Jones' story as absolute fact.

"Bolden told me that he wanted me to take a portion of the file to Spagnoli to prove that the rest of the file could be produced. He told me to give Spagnoli the information about Sandy and this prisoner in the county jail. Bolden said that Sandy was in a downtown hotel under the name of Stocks. Bolden then showed me some onionskin papers stapled together and another small piece of paper which was a portion of the same file which he handed to me. He took this typewritten piece of paper out of his briefcase and handed it to me."

Dunne walked over to the witness stand with a document in his hand. "I now show you government's Exhibit 6 for identification," he said, handing Jones a sloppily typed document alleged to be an excerpt from the summary report I was accused of trying to sell. "Is

Copied — 20 MAY 64   MN   AMD - Chgo
Photo Lab

It has been acertained that Spagnoli asked Vito Nitti, in presence of Zaccanini, if he wanted to use a greek name on some bonds and Vito Nitti said yes. Spagnli sais he would have Nickey (Identified as Pantoas) go with him . The next day at Spagnoli's house, Joe Spagnettl told Zaccanini that Nitti wanted to take his restaurant partner along. Spagnoli said he would make up indentification for Vito Nitti and Harvey. Spagnoli gave 8,000 in bonds to Nitti acording to Zaccagaini

Exhibit No.

this the paper that Bolden gave to you while the two of you were together on May 11, 1964?"

"Yes, it is," answered Jones after glancing briefly at the document.

Exhibit 6 was entered into evidence.

"Tell the jury what happened next."

During a break in Jones' testimony, Attorney Sikes walked over to the defense table and laid the plastic-covered exhibit in front of Howard.

My temper flared the instant I saw the document. "I've never seen this piece of paper before in my life. What the hell are they trying to pull? They know damn well that I wouldn't give anyone some crap—"

"Simmer down, Abraham," Howard warned. "They can hear you. You've got to control yourself."

"George, take a look at this paper," I insisted. "How could anyone believe that I would type something like this and try to pass it off as coming from an official document? The Secret Service knows that I didn't type this crap."

After the short recess, Jones continued to testify. "Bolden wrote the address of Spagnoli on the back of a fishing magazine that was on the front seat of his car," Jones continued. "The address was 5301 Quincy, in Chicago." He went on to describe his visit to Spagnoli's house the next day. "Spagnoli's mother answered the door. I told her that I needed to talk to Jones about the problem that he was having. A few minutes later, Spagnoli came out of the basement with two Caucasian men. I told Spagnoli that for a price, I was prepared to bring the whole file that the Secret Service had against him. I told him that I knew the whereabouts of Sandy, but Spagnoli said that he had no interest in Sandy. I showed him the paper that Bolden had given me and he asked me how much the file was going to cost. I told him that the man wanted fifty thousand dollars."

The government prosecutor, Dunne, kept drawing the story out of Frank Jones. "I went into the kitchen with Spagnoli and the two other men and we sat around the table drinking from a gin bottle and discussing other things. There was another young girl there who looked to be about twenty years old. Spagnoli told me that one of the men was Lou and that Lou had a beef against him for transporting marijuana. Lou asked me if I could have his case taken care of also, and I told him that I would look into the matter. I gave Spagnoli my home telephone number and told him to ask for Mr. Q whenever he wanted to talk with me."

"And did you subsequently meet with the defendant, Bolden, and have a conversation with him?" Dunne asked.

"Yes, I did," came the quick reply. "When I left Spagnoli's house, I called Bolden and told him to meet me at Marquette Road and Halsted Street. Bolden met me there in about an hour and we drove to a McDonald's restaurant on Seventy-first and Vincennes. Bolden told me that Sandy was having her hair dyed at 3:00 P.M. and that she would probably call Spagnoli sometime during the evening. Bolden told me to tell Spagnoli not to curse so much during his conversations with Sandra. I went back to Spagnoli's house and told him about Sandy's hair and the other information that Bolden had given me." Jones added that he had called me at my home to tell me he had delivered the message to Spagnoli.

"Did you have another conversation with the defendant after May 12?"

"Yes, I did," said Jones. "On the morning of May 13, I got a telephone call from Bolden. My wife answered the telephone and told me that Bolden wanted to talk to me. Bolden said that 'Spag called the boss,' and told me not to talk to him again. 'You don't know nothing,' Bolden said, and hung up the telephone."

Jones was winding up his testimony. "When I was arrested on May 18 by the Secret Service, I was getting into a green Secret Service car and noticed a magazine lying on the floor with the back cover missing."

Dunne walked purposefully to the prosecution table and picked up a magazine, which he handed to Jones, who could then finish, "This is the Phillips 66 fishing guide that I saw in Bolden's car on May 18. He wrote the address of Joseph Spagnoli on the back of this book."

Judge Perry again called for a short recess before cross-examination, adding, "I want to finish with this witness today and move this trial along." None of the jurors looked me in the eye as they filed back into the courtroom after recess, but I did notice that one of them smiled at the prosecutor Arthur Dunne. I took that as a bad omen.

George Howard agreed that Jones had done well under direct examination, coming off as a credible, successful professional rather than the career criminal that he was. "The dates and times of his meetings with you match almost perfectly with the times that you gave me when we discussed this case at my office," George said. "The only difference is that Jones says that the meetings were about one thing and you say that the meetings were about another. Of all the people to get to go up against you or to try to bring you down, why do you think they would use someone like Jones?"

"I'm not sure just how Jones came into the picture," I answered, a little annoyed by the question. "All I know is that Jones ups and calls me at home on May 10 and said that he wanted to talk to me. In mid-April, 1964, Jones called complaining about cameras and other printing equipment missing from his seized automobile. I investigated and found Jones' claims unfounded. I told him at that time that I was getting ready to go to Secret Service school and that I would try to get another agent to meet with him. As I told you at your office, Jones called Agent Stocks and told him that he wanted to talk to an agent about his case. When Stocks called me into his office,

I refused to meet with Jones, and Stocks complained to Martineau. Just like I said, Marty called me into his office and reamed my ass out, saying that Jones was my case and that I had to meet with him or quit. That's the only reason that I met with Jones, and that's the truth."

"So how do you explain Jones knowing all of those facts about Sandy and Spagnoli's address and all?" Howard asked.

"Spagnoli's address was in the newspapers. Everything that Jones has testified to was well known by all of the agents in the Secret Service office, including Agent Cross, who was the last one to have the report. I'm not saying that Jones didn't go to Spagnoli's house or that he didn't have something from the Secret Service that he either stole out of the Secret Service car when he was with me or got from another agent. All that I am telling you is that I never sent Jones to ask Spagnoli for anything. And that's the truth."

As the cross-examination began, Jones recounted how he was "arrested by the defendant in both 1962 and 1963."

"At any time after being arrested by the defendant, did you have conversations with him about assisting him in finding other members of the counterfeiting group?" Howard asked.

"I discussed it with Agent Bolden in 1963. That is the only time I ever discussed the two persons you have made mention of," he said, referring to Horace Foster and Princess.

Howard raised the question of Jones' obtaining money under false pretenses in a matter related to Alderman Chew. Jones was questioned concerning the allegation that Jones took money that had been collected for the Seventeenth Ward and converted that money to his own use. Jones steadfastly denied, under oath, Howard's contentions. Jones also denied, under oath, that he had gone into a hardware store and opened an account in Alderman Chew's name.

Howard resumed his questioning "Now, Mr. Jones, when the Secret Service arrested you, were you taken to the Secret Service office here in this building?"

"Yes, I was."

"And did you give a statement to the Secret Service?"

"Yes, I did."

"When you gave the statement to the Secret Service, you had in mind all the time framing Mr. Bolden, didn't you?" Howard asked, staring hard at Frank Jones.

Dunne was on his feet in an instant. "Objection, Your Honor. I ask that the question be stricken."

"Objection sustained," the judge said, and at Dunne's request he addressed my attorney. "That is not a proper question. Counsel is admonished not to follow that line of questioning again."

It was clear that George Howard had no friends in that court-room. Each time he poked a hole in Jones' testimony or that of any other government witness, the prosecutors would leap to their feet with objections, which were almost always sustained. They knew what they were doing, and set things up so that they were often pro-tected by the letter of the law. Even when they weren't, they clearly had a sympathetic judge on the bench. When we tried to get Jones to testify about his call to me on May 10 and his request to see me con-cerning a man named Horace Foster, Judge Perry was quick to insert himself into the trial as a third prosecutor. Howard asked Jones if he knew Horace Foster. Jones had already answered that he did when the government objected. Judge Perry promptly excused the jury and snapped at George Howard.

"What has this got to do with the cross-examination? This is far beyond the scope of cross-examination. I don't see the relationship—to going into this relationship in some other case."

George explained to the court that he intended to show that the conversations between Frank Jones and me after May 11 were all connected to the commitments that Jones had made to me to help find other people who were being sought by the Secret Service. "Mr. Jones testified that it was something about a file. I just want the ladies and gentlemen of the jury to hear both sides from this witness who is testifying."

Prohibited by Judge Perry from pursuing the Horace Foster question any further, however, Howard had to let the witness go. Good man that he was, George wouldn't let himself get discouraged, but these constant setbacks were wearing him down. The government's entire case rested on Jones, and we were blocked from implicating him or from pointing out the many untruths in his story. As he stepped down from the witness stand, Frank Jones looked at me and smirked. At least one of the jurors clearly saw this, and frowned.

AS THE TRIAL continued, the government called Myron Nason, a fingerprint examiner from a different branch of the Treasury Department. Nason testified that Frank Jones' fingerprints were definitely on a gin bottle (Exhibit 7) that had been introduced into evidence as proof of Jones' visit to the home of Spagnoli on May 11; however, when questioned as to whether or not he had found my fingerprints on Exhibit 6 (the alleged excerpt from the report), Nason first began his answer, "No, I didn't." Cutting his answer short, Nason quickly added that there were no latent fingerprints of any value on the exhibit, so he could not testify whether I had ever touched Exhibit 6.

During the cross-examination, George Howard asked if the witness had found other fingerprints on the gin bottle.

"Yes, I did. There were other fingerprint impressions there," Nason replied, shifting uncomfortably in the witness chair.

"Did you ever check Government's Exhibit Number 7 for Abraham Bolden's fingerprints?"

"No, sir, I did not," Nason replied candidly.

During Nason's elaborate testimony, which involved blown-up charts and fingerprint cards, there had been absolutely no finding that my fingerprints were found on any of the exhibits offered by the government. During the course of the trial, Howard raised a formal objection to Exhibits 6 and 7. "These objections are made for the reason that there is no competent evidence to show that the accused, Abraham Bolden, ever associated himself in any way with any of these items that are now sought to be placed into evidence."

"We take the position it is corroborative, and of course apparently Mr. Howard completely overlooked the testimony of Jones," Dunne countered.

The judge brought a quick end to the debate. "Well, it is a question of fact, for the jury to find, link by link. If the jury finds that Bolden was in no way associated with Frank Jones and Spagnoli, well, they will follow their own weight, but for what it's worth, the objection is to the weight and value and not to the admissibility, so therefore, the objection is overruled, and those exhibits are submitted and all other exhibits tendered are submitted."

Judge Perry's undermining of the defense case had grown almost comical. He had just told the jury, for all intents and purposes, that unless they found that there was no connection of any kind between Frank Jones and myself, they could consider me as a possible source of the evidence. It didn't matter if the connection was part of some criminal conspiracy or if it was completely legitimate. I'd just have to get up there and tell my side of the story, my word against his. If I hadn't known how my forefathers had confronted so many cruel and corrupt men hiding behind the badges and black robes of the law, I might have been surprised.

Having lost yet one more battle, Howard returned quietly to his chair, while Richard Sikes called his next witness, Jean Carpenter Jones.

The most damaging of the circumstantial witnesses, she was the common-law wife of Frank Jones. She testified that on May 11, she had received a call from a person identifying himself as Agent Bolden. She said that the man had said he wanted to talk to Frank Jones but that Jones was not home at the time. She went on to testify that the man had left a message that he wanted to talk to Jones and would come by the house on the morning of May 12.

She said that on May 12, she was home when "Agent Bolden came by the house and asked if Frank Jones was at home."

She told the jury that on May 13, she received a telephone call in which "I heard Bolden say that Frank should forget about everything and that they had called the boss and that Frank shouldn't talk to anybody." She went on to say, "Later during the week, I received calls from a person asking to speak to Mr. Q. I took his telephone number and wrote it down on a piece of paper near the telephone."

Howard's cross-examination of Jean Carpenter Jones was uneventful. He began questioning her about her behavior during the April 8, 1963, raid on their house in which Frank Jones was arrested. Despite vigorous objections from the government prosecutors and the judge's opinion that such conduct by the witness was "irrelevant," Howard got her to admit that during the raid she had rushed about the house, grabbed several sheets of counterfeit notes, and concealed them in her bosom until she was threatened with immediate jailing. Her attempt to conceal evidence had been presented to the U.S. attorney at that time; however, he'd declined to prosecute her.

THE NEXT WITNESS the government called was Joseph Spagnoli. Unlike Frank Jones, who had cleaned himself up for his appearance in court, Spagnoli wore an open-collared shirt and casual slacks, his black hair long. Under questioning by Richard Sikes, Spagnoli testified that he had been arrested by the Secret Service on May 9, 1964, and taken to the Service's office in Chicago, where he had a conversation with me. "I asked Bolden if Secret Service agents were like regular police." He said that when he'd asked me if agents took money, I told him that "out of fourteen thousand men, I imagine that some do."

Attorney Sikes then led Spagnoli through his testimony as to what occurred at his home on May 12, 1964. Spagnoli described how he was at his home when "a colored man came to my door and introduced himself as Mr. Q." He went on: "Mr. Q said that he wanted to talk to me about my case and he had some information that I would be interested in. I let him into the house and we went into the kitchen and sat around the table and had a few drinks of gin from a bottle. After he was there for a short while, Mr. Q showed me a slip of paper and said that it was a paragraph from my file that was in the Secret Service office. He told me that he wanted fifty thousand for the whole file."

Spagnoli appeared relaxed and unworried. "Later in the day, Mr. Q came back to my house and we rode around in the neighborhood. He said that Sandra was going to have her hair dyed at 3:00 P.M. If I wanted to kill her, I would have to get her quick. Mr. Q said that he could get hold of a badge to be used if I needed it. Mr. Q gave me his telephone number and told me to call him and say that 'cousin Joe is sick in the hospital' and he would call me back."

Prompted by Sikes, Spagnoli identified the appropriate exhibits, including the gin bottle and the alleged excerpt from the Secret Service file. Sikes asked what Spagnoli did after Jones left his house, all the while studying the jury for reactions to the testimony.

"On May 13, the next day, I called Mr. Martineau and told him that I had been offered my file from the Secret Service office for fifty thousand. The next day, May 14, I met Mr. Martineau in the parking lot of a supermarket and gave him the gin bottle and the slip of paper that Jones had given to me. On May 15, the Secret Service showed me some pictures while we were seated in the parking lot, and I picked out a man named Frank Jones as being the colored man who came to my house and tried to sell the excerpt. Later that day, I called the number that Jones had given me and asked for Mr. Q. The woman said that she didn't know anyone by the name of Mr. Q.

I told her that if she saw him to tell him that cousin Joe was sick in the hospital."

Done with his questioning, Sikes calmly sat down at the prosecution table, giving George Howard his turn with Spagnoli. George began by making sure the jury heard Spagnoli say that he hadn't been regularly employed in at least fifteen years, and at the present time his mother was supporting him and his two children.

"Now, Mr. Spagnoli," Howard said, "you say that you are indicted under case docketed as 64 CR 300 entitled *United States v. D'Antonio and others*. Now I ask you if the government or the Secret Service made any promises of immunity of any type for your testifying here?"

"No, because I didn't do any of those things. That's why. I don't need nothing. I didn't conspire with nobody. I don't have to have a deal," Spagnoli answered, becoming emotional and glancing quickly at the government attorneys.

"Nobody promised you any assistance in your indictment?"

"I don't need any assistance. I'm innocent of the charges," he said, waving his arms a bit wildly.

"That is not the question, Mr. Spagnoli. I am asking you if someone promised you something."

"Let his answer stand," the judge interrupted impatiently. "You have the answer. Let us just go on." The judge then addressed the jury: "He is not on trial, ladies and gentlemen, in that case here. That is a mere charge as far as you folks are concerned. The answer is there and it may stand. Now proceed."

"And while you were talking with this man in the Secret Service office, did he at any time offer to sell to you government materials for fifty thousand dollars?"

"No," Spagnoli answered restlessly.

"Did he offer at that time to place in your possession any files relative to your case?"

"No."

"Did he tell you at that time that he was going to have somebody get in touch with you about your case?" Howard continued.

"No."

"Did this man, Mr. Q, ever tell you that Abraham Bolden was the man that sent him to you?"

"No," Spagnoli answered.

"Now, when you say Mr. Q told you that this lady Sandy Hafford was going to be moved, that if you wanted to get her, you could get her, did Mr. Q say where they were going to move her to?"

"No."

"The only thing that this man Mr. Q said about Sandy was that they are going to dye her hair and move her at 3 o'clock, is that right?" Howard asked, pacing before the jury.

Spagnoli was clearly agitated and uncomfortable. "He said they were going to dye her hair at 3 o'clock, and move her at 9 o'clock that night, and if I wanted to get her, I would need a badge, because the one she'll let in is a Secret Service agent or an FBI agent, and I said, 'I don't want her. I'm not interested.'"

"Mr. Spagnoli, when these pictures were shown of this man, Mr. Q, when you identified him, did you have any trouble identifying him?"

"Objection, Your Honor," Sikes broke in.

While this was taking place, Dunne was muttering something about the killing of Sandra. Throughout the trial he had been making comments, favorable to the government and damaging to the defense, within earshot of the jury but not for official transcription.

"May it please the Court," Howard responded, remaining calm but clearly irritated, "if Mr. Dunne wants to make statements, I ask that he address them to this court instead of mumbling to the jury."

This time Judge Perry agreed with Howard and both overruled the objection and cautioned Dunne to address his statements to the court.

But we had no chance to turn this small success to any advantage. George continued his tough cross-examination, but Spagnoli stood by his story. Making matters worse, Spagnoli seemed to grow more confident, and so more flippant, as his testimony continued, as if he felt the judge and government attorneys were squarely in his corner. I wondered if his arrogant, disrespectful behavior toward my attorney might possibly work against the government's case. One of the jurors studied Spagnoli intently as Howard attempted to pin the witness down on a part of his testimony in relation to telephone calls that he had made to Frank Jones.

"Mr. Spagnoli, do you remember having called this man Mr. Q on the morning of May 15, 1964?" Howard asked, referring to Jones.

"I never talked to him at first," Spagnoli answered curtly.

"You did not call the number at 10 o'clock in the morning on May 15?"

"I don't remember the dates," answered Spagnoli impatiently. "When you come with them dates, I don't remember the dates. All I know is that I called the number."

"In the afternoon?" Howard pressed.

Spagnoli was clearly irritated by Howard's persistence and exploded. "Regardless, morning or afternoon, I talked to a woman over there. That's all I know," Spagnoli answered in a raised voice.

In the end, George got nowhere with Spagnoli, and wrapped up his questioning.

During a brief recess Howard and I stood outside the courtroom quietly discussing the testimony of Spagnoli when we heard the elevator open behind us and turned to see Agent John Russell get off, with Maurice Martineau right behind him. I pointed Russell out as they walked past, and said that I supposed he was going to be the government's next witness. Russell did not appear to be happy about what he was there to do. He looked down as he passed, but I could see the sadness in his face, and recalled how he had broken down in tears at the jail on the night of my arrest. Now he was about to take the stand against me.

Indeed, Sikes called Russell as the next government witness. Russell said that on April 28, 1964, he had prepared a summary report on the Joseph Spagnoli counterfeit bond case. He said that prior to Spagnoli's arrest, he "gave an onionskin copy of the report to Agent Bolden which I identified for Agents Bolden and Cross." On May 7, he continued, "I met a girl named Sandra Hafford in my office. Sandra had a close relationship with Spagnoli and testified on May 8 before the grand jury in the *D'Antonio et al.* bond case. Spagnoli is a defendant in that case."

Russell told the jury that at an office meeting on May 8, "Bolden was assigned to arrest a man named Arthur Rachael. The arrest was to take place on May 9. The arrests of Joseph Spagnoli and Arthur Rachael actually took place on the morning of May 9." On May 11, Russell explained, he went to the Conrad Hilton Hotel where Sandra Hafford was being concealed, asked her to phone Spagnoli, and taped their conversation. "Spagnoli used vile language and lots of curse words during the conversation. Sandra told me that she wanted to have her hair dyed red. Agent Noonan was to make the arrangements with a beautician to have Sandra's hair dyed the next day."

Russell had played the tape for all the agents in the Chicago office the next day, and we discussed whether we thought Spagnoli would harm the woman if he could. "Abraham Bolden spoke up in agreement with me that if given a chance, Spagnoli would probably try to kill Sandra," Russell asserted, adding that "after the meeting, I radioed Agent Noonan and told him to tell Sandra that I would be at the Conrad Hilton Hotel with a beautician at 3:00 P.M.

"On May 13, Special Agent in Charge Mr. Martineau called me into his office and told me that he had received a call from

Joseph Spagnoli. I left the office and went to the office of assistant U.S. attorney Richard Sikes and told him that Spagnoli had called the office. Bolden was nearby when I told Attorney Sikes of the telephone call."

Next, after determining that seven copies of the summary report had been distributed among the agents, Sikes asked, "Now, Mr. Russell, which copy is missing?"

"A copy which I identified for Agents Bolden and Cross," Russell answered.

The prosecutor picked up two pieces of paper from his table and handed them to Agent Russell. "I ask you to compare government's Exhibit 6-A with government's Exhibit 6 for identification. Have you examined them, Mr. Russell? Are they the same?"

"With the exception of the introductory words, and some misspellings, this is an exact excerpt from the fifteenth page of the summary report," Russell answered quietly.

Later during Russell's testimony, Howard and I examined the two exhibits together and confirmed that the wording was almost the same as what was contained in the summary report.

```
        Later, Zaccagnini stated that Spagnoli asked
Vito Nitti, in presence of Zaccagnini, if he wanted
to use a Greek name on some bonds and vito Nitti
said Yes. Spagnoli said he would have Mikey (Iden-
tified as Panteas) go with him. The next day at
Spagnoli's house Joe Spagnoli told Zaccagnini that
Nitti wanted to take his restaurant partner along.
Spagnoli said he would make up identification for
Vito Nitti and Harry Spagnoli gave $8,000 in bonds
to Nitti according to Zaccagnini.
```

"Your witness, Counsel," said the prosecutor.

During cross-examination, John Russell admitted that there was a rear entrance to the Secret Service office that was often left unguarded and unlocked. He confirmed that the door leading into the office was "often left ajar" and an unauthorized person could enter the office without being noticed. He further testified that while searching the home of Frank Jones after Jones' arrest on May 18, the Secret Service found Spagnoli's telephone number written in an address book near the telephone. In answer to Howard's question, Russell confirmed that the telephone number did not appear anywhere in the summary report.

"Did you ask Agent Bolden for the copy of the report that had been issued to him?" Howard asked.

"Yes, sir, I did."

"What did Mr. Bolden tell you he did with his report?"

"He stated he had given it to Cross," Russell replied.

"Did you have occasion to ask Agent Cross if, in fact, Agent Bolden had given him the report?" Howard asked

"No, at that time Agent Cross was not available and I was informed later that inquiry had been made of him and he did not have the report."

"Then, at the time Sandra Hafford's hair was changed, Agent Bolden was not the only agent in the office who knew this change was going to be made, was he?"

"No, sir. It was common knowledge," Agent Russell answered. His eyes darted quickly toward Sikes, who was leaning slightly forward in his chair as if he were about to object to the line of questioning. "The dyeing of Sandra's hair and the fact that she was secreted in the Conrad Hilton Hotel was common knowledge among the agents in the office."

"No further questions, Your Honor," George Howard announced, bringing the trial session to a close. I had previously explained to my attorney that the situation with Sandra Hafford had been discussed at a staff meeting on May 6. Near the end of April, Sandra had actually come into the Secret Service office and spoken with Agent Russell. We knew that over the weekend of May 1, a secretary from our office, June Marie Terpinas, had been dispatched by SAIC Martineau to stay with Sandra in the hotel after Sandra had called our office and said she was not only afraid of being alone there but also lonely. During that weekend, June had listened on another line when Sandra phoned Joseph Spagnoli and professed her love for him. It was Sandra, along with Vito Zaccagnini, both of whom had been arrested while trying to pass a series of counterfeit bonds at a Chicago bank, who had provided the information on the basis of which Russell had initiated the summary report now at the center of my case. In the May 6 meeting, all of the agents in the Chicago office were informed of Sandra's whereabouts, the name she was under, and the fact that she had contacted Joseph Spagnoli while in protective custody.

Chapter 11

WE ARRIVED AT court early enough the next morning to watch some of the jurors and attorneys file in. Judge Perry opened the session without delay, and the government called Agent Conrad Cross to the witness stand. Cross, looking like a young doctor in his dark gray suit, told the jury that he had been a Secret Service agent for about three years, prior to which he had worked as an agent for the Internal Revenue Service. He added that he and I had worked together on several occasions, including the time around May 14, 1964.

As Cross spoke, my attention was caught by a large brown-skinned woman opening the door to the courtroom and taking a seat in the spectator's gallery. I was stunned to see my mother, Ophelia, gazing at me. The hurt in her eyes belied the wide smile on her face. I also saw one of the jurors register that the woman who had just entered was my mother.

There was an eerie symbolism to my mother arriving at just that moment in the trial, while Conrad Cross was on the stand. Only a few months earlier, in February 1964, Cross and I had been dispatched to St. Louis, Missouri, as part of President Lyndon Johnson's protective detail. Johnson had come to St. Louis to make a speech at the Chase Hotel there. The day after the speech, Agent Cross accompanied me as I stopped by my parents' house in East St. Louis, just across the river in Illinois, before we drove back to Chicago. We sat for about an hour, chatting with my parents and one of my sisters. As Cross and I were getting into the car, my mother called me back into the house for a moment.

"That fellow you brought here," she began, "how long have you known him?"

"Aw, Mom, is that what you called me back in here for? He's my partner in Chicago. I work with him every day."

"Don't trust him," my mother warned through clenched teeth, waving a finger in my face. "He's a snake. The whole time he was here, he didn't look me in the eyes one time. I'm telling you, son, don't you trust him any further than you can see him."

At the time, I thought my mother had perhaps become a little paranoid and had formed the wrong opinion of Cross. Now, as I watched him fidget in the witness chair, it seemed more likely that my own opinion of him had been off the mark.

Sikes asked Cross if he had "received an onionskin copy of the summary report from Agent Bolden on or about May 8," and Cross answered that he had.

"And what, if anything, occurred at the time you received this material?" Sikes continued.

"On May 8, Bolden came into my office and laid the report on my desk and left the office. I glanced at it momentarily and then laid the report on my desk. I left the office and returned after being out of the office for about twenty-five minutes. When I walked back into the office, I noticed that the copy of the onionskin copy of the report was missing from my desk."

Then Agent Cross told the jury, "We were conducting investigations on the South Side of Chicago, and we were riding together, at which point Mr. Bolden said to me: 'What would you do if you had fifty thousand dollars?' I told Bolden that if I had that kind of money, I would buy a building and go into business for myself."

"That's a lie!" I hissed at Howard. I stared coldly at Cross, who looked away. "He's lying," I repeated, ignoring the stares of the judge and the jurors. My attorney shielded his mouth with his hand and whispered sharply, "Calm down." Judge Perry stared in our direction, as did Sikes, standing motionless by the witness box, as if waiting for the jurors to follow his gaze in our direction.

"Your witness, Counsel," he said somewhat smugly. As he sat back down at the prosecution table, Sikes and his co-counsel, Arthur Dunne, whispered and smiled knowingly to each other.

George Howard approached Cross in the witness box and said, "Agent Cross, you have testified that on or about May 8, the defendant came into your office and gave the onionskin copy of the report to you, is that correct?"

"Yes."

"And it is your testimony that you thumbed through the report, laid the report on your desk, and left the office, is that correct?"

"Yes."

"Was the defendant in the office when you left the office or when you returned some twenty-five minutes later?"

"No," answered Cross, "he was not."

"Did you ever see the defendant with the report after he gave it to you on May 8?" Howard asked, striding back and forth calmly in front of the jury, carefully framing each question.

"No, sir."

"When was the next time that you were asked about the report?" Howard asked.

"Around May 15, Michael Torina came to my office and asked me if I had the copy of the report and I told him that the report had been lost."

"After the report was lost in your office on May 8, did you ever look for the report?"

"No, I didn't," Cross maintained. "Inspector Michael Torina, Agent Bolden, and Agent John Russell asked me about the report, but I didn't look for it because I knew that I didn't have it."

"Even though you had previously placed the report on your desk?" Howard asked, shooting a meaningful look at the jury.

"Because I knew I didn't have it," Cross answered.

"Objection, Your Honor," boomed Richard Sikes for the prosecution. "Your Honor, I am going to object to these last two questions unless Counsel again makes representation that he intends to offer proof to prove the positive assertions implied in those questions."

"Objection sustained," Judge Perry declared, with a hint of annoyance. "The objection will be sustained and the questions and answers will be stricken unless there is positive proof made of the questions for which you are now laying foundation."

Howard changed his tack. "Now, Mr. Cross, you state that this statement was made on the 20th of May, 1964, and you signed it and you say that on or about May 11, 1964, in the afternoon, 'I was riding with Abraham Bolden in an official U.S. Secret Service car,' and you state that in essence that he said, 'What would you do if you had fifty thousand dollars? Is that right?"

"Yes, this was the conversation," Cross answered nonchalantly.

"And you stated that if you had [fifteen] thousand dollars, you would probably buy a building or go into some business or something. Was that your answer? Is that what you wrote?" Howard probed.

"That's right."

"Now, this statement was given—did you, Agent Cross, seek to buy a building on or about May 4, 1964?"

The prosecution knew that Howard was headed into Cross' dealings with the Dwyer Real Estate Company around the time that the file was lost in his office. The government had taken precautions to ensure that the Dwyer matter would not come before the jury.

"Objection," Sikes shouted.

"Objection sustained," said the judge, obviously disturbed by the question put to Agent Cross. "When I sustain an objection, Mr. Witness," the judge continued, "you don't have to answer."

"No further questions," said George Howard, and Cross was excused.

During the recess that followed, my mother came out to the balcony overlooking the rotunda and took me into her arms. She didn't plan on staying in Chicago, she explained; she just needed to see with her own eyes that I was all right. Barbara and I introduced her to George Howard.

"You take care of my son, Mr. Howard," she said. The tears in her eyes and the quiver in her voice brought the emotion up in me as well.

"He's going to be all right," George said. "I'm going to do my best."

After the recess, the government called June Marie Terpinas to the stand. Dressed in a prim white blouse and black skirt, the blond, blue-eyed secretary from our office nervously made her way to the stand. June testified that she had worked in the Secret Service office for about five years. On May 11, she said, "Bolden told me that Agent Russell would not tell him where Sandra Hafford was. I told Bolden that Hafford was in the Conrad Hilton Hotel under the name of Mrs. Jay Lloyd Stocks." She burst into tears as she told the jury that on May 13, she went into my office and listened to a tape playing in the next office of a recorded conversation between Sandra Hafford and Joseph Spagnoli. Working hard to compose herself, she went on to testify that she had been taking dictation from me on May 14 when I received a telephone call. "When Bolden hung up the telephone, he told me that his informant, Walt, had some information for him."

June was crying softly as prosecutor Arthur Dunne finished his direct examination and George Howard stood to approach the witness box.

"Mrs. Terpinas," George began, "you say that Mr. Bolden told you on the morning of May 11 that Agent Russell refused to tell him where they were keeping Sandra Hafford?"

"He said Agent—no, he didn't tell me that. He said he thought he was busy. I can't really remember."

"Mrs. Terpinas, did you know on May 11, 1964, that Mr. Bolden had been one of the arresting officers in the case involving *United States government versus D'Antonio and others*?"

"Yes," June answered softly.

"Mrs. Terpinas, do you know whether it was common knowledge in your office or not where Sandra Hafford was kept?"

"Well, it was common knowledge that she was an informant, but only a few knew where she was being kept."

Next Howard tried to get the secretary to confirm that I'd had previously had dealings with Frank Jones during the course of an investigation, but the prosecution objected, and the judge upheld those objections. With this important line of questioning blocked, Howard changed direction. "Now, Mrs. Terpinas, when you were in the hotel with Sandra Hafford on May 9, did you engage in conversation with her there?" he asked.

Again, Dunne was on his feet with an objection. "I do not know what the question is going to be or the answer is going to be, but I think we are pretty far afield."

The judge excused the jury while the matter was discussed further. The judge asked Howard the nature of his question, to which Howard replied, "I would like to ask her, Your Honor, if Miss Hafford told her on May 9 that she knew that Spagnoli had an inside contact in the Secret Service."

Dunne objected once again, stating that there was no evidence at all, with the exception of my own activities, that Spagnoli had a contact in the Secret Service.

After a brief discussion of the issue, the judge permitted Howard to bring out the fact that Sandra Hafford was afraid for her safety; however, in pressing the issue, Howard had inadvertently played right into the hands of the prosecution, and he knew it.

"No further questions, Your Honor." The frustration was evident in Howard's voice, and now, for the first time, his posture showed more discouragement than confidence. Judge Perry wasn't going to let him do his job the way he wanted to. The way he needed to.

The government's case against me was building. Jones and Spagnoli were well prepared for their testimony, which all matched up very neatly—much too neatly for anyone who was really paying attention. As we stood outside the courtroom during recess, two Secret Service agents got off the elevator, escorting Richard Walters, the man who had shown up at my house asking for a gun with which he could "take care" of Frank Jones. The agents, Jordan and Sims, could barely suppress their smirks. Walters, who used to say things like "I love you like a son, Abe" but who was there that day to help send me to prison, glanced fleetingly in my direction, but mostly kept his quivering gaze on the floor in front of him.

Sikes put Richard Walters on the stand after a recess and guided him through his story. Walters told the court that he could neither read nor write and had been an informant for the Secret Service for a number of years.

Walters testified that sometime in 1963, "Bolden sent me to tell Frank Jones that if he would play ball, Bolden would give his counterfeiting plates and Pontiac car back to him. At some other time, Bolden told me that we were all going to be rich because he had sent a man named Ed Jones to tell some fellow how to get rid of some checks and bonds for fifty or sixty thousand.

"Bolden told me that he had tried to use Jones as a stool pigeon," Walters said, "but Jones double-crossed him. Later, when Bolden came to see me, he told me that things were going bad at the office and that the G's had called everybody in the office except him. He said that Jones needed killing with a shotgun and that he had five hundred dollars for anyone who ups and kills Jones."

Later, during Howard's cross-examination, Walters said that "Bolden never mentioned a file or the name Spagnoli to me."

"Now, Mr. Walters," Howard continued, "did you give a statement to the Secret Service concerning your meetings with Agent Bolden?"

"Yes, I did."

"Did you read the statement before you signed it?"

"No, I can't read. They read the statement to me."

"In the statement," George pressed, "you said that Bolden 'said he would give me a shotgun to kill Frank Jones with,' is that correct?"

"Yes," Walters answered. "I said that. Bolden said Jones needed killing. He didn't give me no gun."

The cross-examination of Walters was very contentious. Walters could not recall any of the dates, times, or months pertaining to his testimony, often answering specific questions with, "I don't know. All I know is this is 1964; I don't remember what month I was out there . . . I don't know what time it was." The judge and Dunne often interrupted the questioning in an attempt to clarify Walter's answers for the jury.

"No further questions," said George Howard.

Richard Walters slowly climbed down from the witness box and dragged himself toward the courtroom doors, a Secret Service agent on either side of him. He turned for a moment and looked back at me with sadness in his eyes. I knew this experience had been painful for him, but he had been helpless at the hands of the manipulative government agents and attorneys. In that moment, I forgave the old man.

RICHARD JORDAN SEEMED always to be in a hurry, and today was no different. He scurried up to the witness stand. As he raised his hand to take the oath, he glared at me. Sikes drew the necessary information out of him. On May 18, Jordan said, "I was alone with Bolden in the United States attorney's office. Bolden told me that Jones had ample opportunity to steal the file from Bolden's car and that he and Cross had seen Jones at McDonald's hamburger stand on May 11, 1964. Bolden further said that Jones was in his car on May 11, and could have stolen the report then."

Jordan told the jury that he'd interviewed me in the Secret Service office in preparation for a polygraph test. "I asked Bolden when was the first time he knew the agents were going to have Sandra Hafford's hair dyed. Bolden said that he didn't know that and that I was the first one to tell him that. A few minutes later, Bolden said, 'I didn't even know that she was going to have her hair dyed red.'

"When I asked Bolden who had said anything about red hair, Bolden told me that I did," Jordan testified. "Actually, I hadn't mentioned the color at all."

George Howard didn't get much out of Agent Jordan except to have him confirm that he was part of the scheme to mislead me into coming back to Chicago for a nonexistent counterfeiting investigation. Jordan testified that he was carrying out direct orders from his superiors when he took part in that deception.

The situation looked bleak as the court session ended. "It was a rough day," said Howard. "They're coming at you with both barrels, and the judge is helping them all he can. This is the toughest case I've ever had to deal with."

"I see what their strategy is, George," I offered. "They're mixing truth with lies. I never said anything to Martineau about a typewriter, or about Sandra's red hair to Jordan. They are injecting those allegations for the obvious effect they're having on the jury. They're making it seem that I was trying to conceal something, and that I didn't have the control not to blurt out statements against my own interest."

"It's a dirty game, Abe. They're putting words in your mouth, and the judge is letting them. We need access to the Secret Service's case files to show that Martineau had official knowledge that you were working on the Jones case." Howard had already filed a motion about those documents, but it had been turned down. "I would like to go into the Court of Appeals and file a writ for those case files, but that's going to cost more money and time, and the judge would probably be against holding up the trial so that the appeal can be heard."

"I don't see how we can prove anything unless I take the stand."

The next day, the government called a series of witnesses who substantiated parts of the story they had already created. One Secret Service agent, John Sokoll, confirmed that Spagnoli had identified Frank Jones from a photograph, and that he interviewed Spagnoli and heard Spagnoli say that Jones had come to his house and tried to sell him an excerpt of a report. Mary E. Myers, from the Illinois Bell Telephone Company, verified that a phone number found in Jones' possession belonged to Spagnoli. Louis Calvin Hall, Richard Walters' nephew, confirmed that Richard Walters had had a conversation with me on the front porch of my house.

Howard rose and approached the bench, where he was met by Sikes and Dunne. He announced that he intended to move for a directed verdict, and Judge Perry had the jury removed from the courtroom, so that the arguments could be made outside of their presence.

"Your Honor," Howard said firmly, "at this time on behalf of the defense we move for a direct acquittal, the reason for this being that there has been no evidence in this case that will show that the defendant has committed any of the acts that were set forth in the indictment. Statements have been made, but all of the statements, all of the evidence that has been introduced here, does not in any way show that Mr. Bolden is guilty of having committed the acts of which he has been accused." One could almost hear the confidence returning to Howard's voice as he made his impassioned plea before the court.

"The motion is denied and the defendant directed to proceed, if he elects, with the defense. Do you elect to call your defendant, or what?" the judge said impatiently.

I would have to go on the stand. In many arguments during the trial, Howard had represented that he would offer affirmative proof that contradicted the testimony of several government witnesses. I was the only person who could offer that proof to the court.

Howard told me that I would be the first witness after the recess. "The main thing you have to do," he admonished, "is keep your cool. Just tell the truth as you have told it to me, and let me direct the questioning. You're going to have to be careful and not become angry during cross-examination. They're going to try to make you angry and inflame you on the stand. You know how to testify, so be at your best, and I think that we will come out of this all right."

I was thinking about more than just the verdict. "George, I think that I should tell the jury what I really believe this is all about. I told you what Inspector McCann said about me not being a team player. Jordan testified that we were alone all of the time, so that shows they are trying to cover something up. He didn't want McCann's name to come up. Somehow they knew that I tried to call J. Lee Rankin [chief counsel for the Warren Commission] through the White House switchboard. I think—"

"Abe, do you realize what you're saying? If you do that, even if we win this case, you're not going to be able to reclaim your job in the Secret Service," Howard advised.

"I'm not worried about ever going back into the Secret Service, George. I just think—"

"We have to defend against Jones' testimony," Howard insisted. "How are we ever going to prove anything about what happened in Dallas? You weren't in Dallas. You have a chance to win this case as it stands now, and I don't want you to complicate things more than necessary. Judge Perry isn't going to admit anything about Kennedy or what happened in Dallas into evidence in your trial. The only thing that you would accomplish by bringing Kennedy into this is to put your life and the lives of your wife and children in jeopardy. You're dealing with people who killed the president on the street in broad daylight. You have to think about the effect of what you want to do on your family." My attorney was not only adamant but also more than a little upset.

I had worked hard trying to keep my nerves in check as I prepared to make my case. Many nights my mind raced as I tried to make some sense of all the fantastical testimony and to get some kind of grip on the many conflicting emotions inside me. When I thought about the end of my career as a trusted and valued agent of the federal government, I felt both anger and a wistful sadness. Here I was about to defend myself against accusations made by the very same bad guys I had been chasing all those years. And yet I found I had no bitterness, or even any real anger, toward Frank Jones and Joseph Spagnoli. They were my accusers, to be sure, but they weren't the brains behind any of it. Jones was facing his third conviction and the likelihood of a life sentence, and I was sure he was just doing whatever he thought he had to do in order to save himself. I knew I probably would have done the same thing. No, the real villains were my own colleagues and peers at the Secret Service. The agents themselves— sworn to uphold and enforce the laws of the country, as I was—had engineered this masterly plot and made it possible.

After the short recess, George Howard announced: "The defense calls the defendant, Abraham Bolden, Your Honor."

I was no stranger to the witness box, having testified countless times in criminal cases on behalf of the Secret Service. But speaking in my own defense was something entirely new. I sat tall and straight and met the gaze of the jurors as Howard began his questioning.

I was able to tell them about my childhood in East St. Louis. "After graduating from high school, I attended Lincoln University in

Jefferson City, Missouri, graduating cum laude, and ranked third in a graduation class of ninety-five students." I told them about my brief stint as a music teacher before becoming the first Negro agent for the Pinkerton National Detective Agency, and then spending four years with the Illinois state police, until finally taking a position as an agent for the United States Secret Service in October 1960.

"And as a member of the Secret Service, did you have an occasion to protect the president of the United States?" Howard asked.

I described my meeting with Kennedy at McCormick Place, where he had personally asked if I would like to be on the White House detail, and how I subsequently became the first black American to be honored with that assignment.

"Mr. Bolden, tell the jury how you met Frank Jones and came into contact with him."

"In 1961, I began to take up a surveillance of Frank Jones, who was suspected of passing counterfeit five- and ten-dollar bills. Following a lengthy investigation, I placed Jones under arrest in 1962 on a charge of passing counterfeit currency. Jones was indicted, but the indictment was dismissed by the United States attorney. I continued to keep Jones under surveillance until April of 1963, when I again arrested Jones at his home at 6649 Lowe Street in Chicago, Illinois. During his arrest, we found a printing press and sheets of uncut counterfeit notes. There were also printing inks similar in color to that used to print U.S. currency. We also seized a plate used to make counterfeit notes. That case is still pending in federal district court."

Howard asked me if I'd had other conversations with Jones after his arrest.

"Between 1962 and 1963, I had many conversations with Jones. These conversations continued even after his arrest and indictment in 1963. I continued to see Jones occasionally. I recall that in April of 1964, Jones called me at the office and told me that some cameras had been removed from his automobile at the time of his arrest on April 5,

1963. I looked into the matter and found that Jones' allegations were unfounded. I discussed Jones' allegation with Acting Special Agent in Charge Martineau, who told me that Jones was just trying to get out from under the charges against him."

"When was the next time you heard from Jones?"

"Jones called me at my home on May 10 and told me that he was interested in assisting the Secret Service in locating three other people who were involved in the counterfeiting ring with him. I told Jones that I was going away to Secret Service school in about a week, so he would have to work with someone else. I told him that he would have to call the Secret Service office and they would assign some other agent to work with him on the case."

"And what happened after that?" Howard asked.

"Monday morning, the 11th of May, I went into the office at around 7 o'clock. At about 9:00 A.M., the Assistant Special Agent in Charge, J. Stocks, called me into his office and told me that he had just received a telephone call from Frank Jones, and Jones wanted to talk to me about his case. I told Stocks that I didn't have time to fool around with Jones, as I was trying to get my case files up to date before I left for Secret Service school. Stocks went into Mr. Martineau's office and told him that Jones wanted to give the Secret Service some information and that I was refusing to go talk to Jones. Mr. Martineau told me that Jones was my case and I had to go talk to Jones, as no one else was available. After talking to Mr. Martineau, I called Jones and set up a meeting with him at his house.

"I drove to Jones' home on Lowe Street and from there Jones and I went to a park located at Marquette Road and Racine Street. During the drive, Jones looked at a fishing book that I had lying on the front seat of the car. He mentioned that the Secret Service had made a big bust over the weekend and asked me if I was involved in the arrest. Jones noticed that one of the addresses that I had written on the back of the fishing guide on May 8 was the same address as one of the men in the newspaper article. When Jones tried to go into more details concerning the names on the back of the book, I took the book out of his hands and tore off the back page."

"Why did you do that?"

"Because the information was no longer needed," I answered. "I had written the addresses of two of the suspects on the back of the book when I was about to drive to Melrose Park in order to participate in the arrests of Spagnoli and a man named Arthur Rachael."

"What did Jones say to you when the two of you were together?" Howard continued.

"Jones told me that he was an old man and was afraid of going back to the penitentiary. He told me that he wanted to help the Secret Service clear up some of the loose ends in his case if I could promise him that he would not go to the penitentiary." I described to the jury how Jones told me he would get in touch with a man called Slim, who had taught him how to make counterfeit plates.

"The next day, Jones called me and told me that he had made contact with Slim and that he needed to see me as soon as possible. I met Jones, and we drove to a McDonald's hamburger stand on Seventy-first and Vincennes. Jones said that he had met with a man named Horace Foster and that Foster told him that Slim was still dealing in counterfeit money. I thought that Jones was giving me the runaround, so on May 13, I avoided contact with him. When he continued to call the office looking for me, I told Jones over the telephone that the case was over as far as I was concerned. I told him that I was leaving for Washington and would have no more time to follow up his leads."

Next I explained that Agent Russell had given me an onionskin copy of a summary report and told me to give it to Agent Cross after I had finished with it. "I gave it to Agent Cross as instructed. When I left his office, Cross was seated at his desk reading the report. On May 15, Russell asked me about the whereabouts of the report and I told him that I gave the report to Agent Cross like he told me to do."

Then I told the jury about the lies I had been told by the agents who brought me back from Washington to Chicago. "When I was in the U.S. attorney's office, Mr. Martineau asked me if I had a typewriter at home, and I told him yes. He then asked me if they could check it to see if it matched the typed excerpt and I told him that 'you can check it if you let me call my attorney.'" I could see that I had the jury's rapt attention.

Under Howard's questioning, I denied that I had asked June Terpinas the whereabouts of Sandra Hafford and that she had ever told me where Sandra was located. I confirmed that I had met with Richard Walters after he called the office and asked me to meet him on May 14. I agreed that Walters was truthful when he testified that I told him that I had tried to use Jones as a "stool pigeon" and that Jones double-crossed me and tried to set me up. "I never told Walters that I had five hundred dollars for anyone who killed Jones," I said emphatically.

Arthur Dunne, one of the government attorneys, sat at his table throughout my testimony, doing everything he could to let the jury know what he thought of my testimony. Judges cannot allow attorneys to denigrate a witness' testimony by making faces or vocalizations, and yet Arthur Dunne twiddled his pencil, shook his head, rolled his eyes, and winced in mock pain at anything I said that didn't conform to the story they were putting into the jurors' heads. Judge Perry never said a word.

After about two hours on the stand, I was done with direct examination. Having given it his best, George Howard quietly said, "No further questions, Your Honor."

Judge Perry ordered a brief recess before I would be delivered into the hands of Sikes and Dunne. When I walked back into the courtroom to retake the stand, I saw the two government attorneys at their table, deep in conversation with Agent Louis Sims, who had been acting as the liaison between the Secret Service and the U.S. attorney's office. Sims leaned in close and covered his mouth as he spoke to the prosecutors. I had never thought much of the guy. He seemed to spend his whole time in the office sitting behind his tidy desk, writing in a notebook and sucking on his pipe. In the entire time we'd worked together in that office I couldn't recall him cracking one serious case, and yet none of the agents in charge ever pressured him to do more, as they did with even the most productive agents in the office. When the rest of us were running around in the icy Chicago winter, chasing down bad guys, Sims sat hunched over his notebook, filling his office with smoke. I knew Sims had been in army intelligence, and many times I wondered if he was even a Secret Service agent at all. Perhaps he was with one of the other government agencies whose offices were in the same building, such as the CIA. There were plenty of reasons to suspect that Sims' assignments somehow went beyond the usual work of the Secret Service.

Sims and the lawyers wrapped things up, and Judge Perry called court back into session. I readied myself as Arthur Dunne approached the witness box. His first line of attack was to ask about the two jobs I'd had after college, teaching music and writing background music for a small movie studio. He produced a copy of my security clearance application for the Secret Service and asked if those employers were included on the application, which of course they were not. I tried to explain that not only had I worked at those jobs just a few short weeks but also Fred Backstrom, the agent who had advised me on my application, had told me to list only significant employers. Dunne cut me off and told me to answer with only yes or no, while the judge shot down George Howard's objections before he even finished saying them, allowing Dunne's assertion that I had "lied" on my application to linger in the air.

I held my ground during cross-examination, never wavering from my direct testimony. I sensed that I had impressed the jury with my testimony, and that they found my explanation of my dealings with Frank Jones to be credible

In an attempt to discredit my contention that I was brought to the White House detail as a result of my conversation with President Kennedy, Dunne produced a document, date-stamped April 18, 1961, allegedly informing me that I was to serve on the White House detail. I had never seen the document and so testified. The document named several other agents who were to report to the detail with me. The fact of the matter is that, to my knowledge, none of the agents listed on the "memorandum" had reported to the White House detail with me, as the document claimed. I knew right away that the document was a fake, backdated so as to deprive me of the credit and historical fact of having been appointed to the White House detail at the recommendation of President Kennedy. Dunne found no weaknesses to exploit and so had to shift gears, which he did very skillfully and effectively. He positioned himself in front of the jury box and in a loud, theatrical voice opened his new line of questioning.

"Mr. Martineau lied when he said that you told him that he could check your typewriter, didn't he?"

"Yes, he did," I answered.

"And June Terpinas lied when she said that you asked her Sandra's whereabouts, didn't she?"

"Yes, she did."

"And Conrad Cross lied when he said that you talked to him about what he would do with fifty thousand dollars, didn't he?" Dunne twisted his face into a mocking sneer for the jury to see.

"Yes, he did."

The government lawyer went down the list of his witnesses, asking me to confirm that each one had lied. He knew what he was doing. The government had built its case on a complex and subtle mixture of fact and fiction. As Dunne went through the case, he only asked me about the untrue things that witnesses had said. Had they all lied? Yes, of course they had. And yet by getting me to repeat endlessly that each one had lied, it could only have made me look like the liar in the jury's eyes.

When he finished, I managed to say that yes, they all had lied. "And I will prove it," I added.

Dunne had no more questions. The trial was almost finished, save for a few character witnesses, the government's rebuttal, and the closing arguments. Then would come the judge's instructions to the jury before the deliberations would begin. As we went down in the elevator, George seemed encouraged and did his best to offer some hope.

"I think you came through the cross-examination fine," he said.

"I did my best," I said wearily. "I just didn't know how to handle it when Dunne started calling out all of those witnesses and asking me if they lied. It looked bad for me, I think."

Barbara interrupted. "Well, you told the truth, didn't you?"

"Yes."

"Then that's all that matters."

He turned to Barbara and told her that she'd take the stand next as a character witness.

"The questions that I will ask will not be about the case, because you don't know anything about the case except what you have heard from Mr. Bolden and in the courtroom. So don't be afraid that I'm going to ask you something that you can't answer," he said with compassion. "They're trying to make your husband look like he's lying about everything, especially his teaching music in St. Louis. I want to clear that up before the jury."

"Oh, I'm not afraid," Barbara said emphatically. "You can ask me what you want to. I know what my husband went through with the Secret Service and how they mistreated him in Hyannis Port and here. I know all about it."

All eyes were fixed on Barbara when she took the stand. Beautiful and dignified, her features were, oddly, a mixture of Jackie Kennedy and the great singer Lena Horne. She told the jury that she had been my wife for almost ten years. Howard kept his questioning short, concentrating upon Barbara's knowledge of my employment teaching music.

Watching her take the stand in my defense and doing her best to help me in my times of trouble brought tears to my eyes. God had truly blessed me with a great wife and mother to my children. The government knew better than to cross-examine her, and when Barbara rose from the witness chair, she walked straight to the defense table, where she placed her hand over mine and kissed me on the side of my face. Everyone in the room watched her walk regally to her seat in the gallery.

Judge Perry adjourned the trial for the day. Outside the courtroom, George Howard gushed to Barbara about her compelling presence on the stand. "They were really impressed, and if Abraham wins this case, it will be because of you."

Barbara's composure was an important example for me.

Chapter 12

BEFORE THE JURY was brought into the courtroom, the lawyers argued in front of Judge Perry regarding his charge to the jury. Again, the judge showed his determination to bring in a guilty verdict by the prejudicial language he wanted to use in his instructions, but for once George Howard was able to keep the judge in check. The attorneys agreed on these final matters, and the jury filed into the courtroom for the final phase of the trial.

Richard Sikes began his closing statement by reciting the charges against me. He told the jury that the government had proved its case "one hundred percent" and that the combined testimony of the government witnesses "leaves no other conclusion than that Agent Bolden conspired with Frank Jones to sell a government file to Joseph Spagnoli. There's no other explanation as to how Jones had the information." He added that each time Jones and I had met, I gave him some more information about the Spagnoli case. His voice thick with disdain, he added it all up for the jury. "When Spagnoli called Mr. Martineau on the 13th, who was it that heard about the call? It was Bolden. The minute that Bolden heard that Spagnoli had just called on May 13, he called Frank Jones and warned him.

"And when Bolden was arrested by the Secret Service and Martineau asked him about the excerpt, what did Bolden say? I'll tell you what he said. Bolden blurted out, 'If you believe I did it, you can check my typewriter.' And when he was back in the Secret Service office, under questioning by Agent Jordan, what does Bolden say when asked about the dyeing of Sandra's hair? 'I didn't even know that they were going to dye her hair red,' Bolden blurted. Who said anything about red?

"The government has met its burden," Sikes concluded. "I request that you return a verdict of guilty on all three counts." (In addition to the main charge concerning the sale of the file, there was an obstruction-of-justice charge and a conspiracy charge.)

One could easily believe that Richard Sikes honed his courtroom theatrics by watching lawyers in movies, but George Howard seemed to be infused with the spirits of the Sunday preachers from the black churches of America. When his turn came, he stood slowly and walked to the jury box, where he placed both hands on the railing and turned his eyes toward heaven.

"Cain slew his brother, Abel," Howard began. "He slew Abel because he was jealous of Abel's relationship with God, not because Abel was guilty of anything. Agent Bolden was given the summary report by Agent Russell and instructed to read the report and give it to Agent Cross. What does my client do? He reads the report and does what he was instructed to do. He gave it to Agent Cross, and Agent Cross has admitted that he received the report. The report has not been found. Jones is the only person who says that my client had something that looked like the report, but my client's fingerprints aren't on any of the evidence that the government presented in this trial." The attorney's voice rang clearly through the courtroom.

"My client spoke directly to Joseph Spagnoli at the Secret Service office, and Spagnoli testified that Bolden didn't ask him for one dime. Who was it that asked Spagnoli for money? It was the felon, Frank Jones, who my client arrested for committing crimes against the government and who was awaiting trial on a case brought against him by my client. My client denies that he heard that Spagnoli called the Secret Service on the 13th of May, as testified to by Agent Russell.

"Bolden's calls and meeting with Frank Jones were requested by Jones and were official business. They were the result of Bolden's attempts to round up other members of Jones' counterfeiting group," Howard explained. "My client did not seek out any of the people who testified against him during this trial. Don't you find it rather strange that the witnesses that testified against him during the trial all called my client and asked him to meet them at a particular time and place? Don't you find it rather coincidental that this case was started by Jones' call to Agent Bolden the next day after Spagnoli was arrested and the report was stolen or lost from the Secret Service office? Walters' testimony was the result of Walters' call and a request for a meeting with Agent Bolden; Spagnoli's conversation with Agent Bolden in the Secret Service office was the result of Agent Bolden being sent into the office where Bolden was asked a question by Spagnoli; and the alleged conversation that Agent Bolden had with Agent Cross was the result of Agent Cross' request to work cases with Agent Bolden on the day of the conversation."

My lawyer was hitting his stride, and his voice rose and fell dramatically. I could see a couple of the jurors react physically to his presentation, giving that quick shudder and shrug of the shoulders I had seen so many times in church when the preacher's message and delivery combine to strike a nerve in the congregation.

Howard closed with an impassioned, steady refrain, his voice swelling. "When Jones tells you that this agent—who was a stellar agent until these charges were placed against him—solicited a bribe or engaged in a criminal conspiracy with him, don't you believe it. When his supervisors tell you that this experienced agent blurted out damaging statements after they had denied him counsel and food during questioning, don't you believe it."

Howard concluded his summation and sat down next to me. As he wiped the sweat from his face, he turned to me and said, "That's the best I could do. I gave it my best shot."

Of course, that was not the last word. Arthur Dunne got up to offer his rebuttal, which in comparison to Howard's stirring oration felt weak and mean-spirited. "How many agents are lying in some alley dead because of turncoats like Abraham Bolden? He is nothing but a Benedict Arnold. He was an agent, but was untrustworthy. Did Bolden prove that any of the witnesses were liars? No, he didn't! Bolden is the only liar."

And that was that. Judge Perry called a recess, after which he gave his charge to the jury. He explained the difference between direct evidence and circumstantial evidence, told them that they were the "trier of the facts," and that in order to convict, they "must find the defendant guilty beyond a reasonable doubt." The jurors rose and marched solemnly into the jury room, the door clicking shut behind them.

It is virtually impossible to describe what it feels like to sit waiting for a jury's verdict when you are the defendant. The volatile combination of fear, anger, supplication and utter helplessness brought on physical sensations unlike any I had ever felt. Pressure built up in the back of my neck and worked its way down into my belly. I felt tightness in my gut, and could feel the blood pulsing and rushing through my body. The weakness in my knees made me afraid to stand. Unexpected groans and sighs formed in my chest and involuntarily forced themselves up and out through my throat.

Secret Service agents paced near doors, obviously anticipating a quick verdict, but after two hours, there was no verdict, and it was approaching 5:00 P.M., when the courts normally closed. Judge Perry called in the jury and asked them if they were close to a verdict.

"No, we are not," answered the tall, middle-aged white man serving as jury foreman, and the judge excused everyone for dinner. Sitting in the courtroom after dinner, there was a moment when the muffled voices of the jurors could be heard through the door of their chamber. I distinctly heard a woman shouting, "He said that he gave that report to another agent and that agent said that he received the report. Show me how he is guilty of giving someone something that he did not have." Then I heard another woman with what seemed to be a Hispanic accent declaring, "You can't take my vote away from me." It seemed like I had at least two jurors pulling for me.

I asked George Howard if he had heard the same thing, and he immediately put a finger to his lips to quiet me. "Shhh. Don't let anyone know that you heard that. Yeah, I heard what she said, and that's a good sign for you, but I think that we should move away from sitting so close to the door. Someone might get the idea that we are trying to illegally influence the jury." We moved out to the corridor to continue our vigil.

At about 8:00 P.M., Judge Perry called the jury back into the courtroom and again asked if they were close to a verdict.

"No, we are not, Your Honor," the foreman replied again, this time shooting a glance in the direction of two jurors, a distinguished looking African American woman and a Hispanic woman who appeared to be wiping tears from her eyes. The judge announced that he intended to sequester the jury in a hotel overnight so that they could continue deliberating the next day, a Saturday. By lunchtime on Saturday, they had been at it for a combined six hours or more, with no conclusion in sight. The lawyers agreed to let the judge ask the jury specifically where they stood.

"We are eleven to one for conviction," the foreman announced, again looking at the two women. I had watched the black woman and seen the disdain in her face while she listened to Cross and Martineau spout their lies. I'm not sure how, but she seemed to sense the trial was a sham.

Another hour of fruitless deliberation passed after lunch, until Judge Perry asked the lawyers if either side objected to his reading of the Allen charge, a statement made by a judge to a jury that is deadlocked, encouraging them to reach agreement on a verdict. The government attorneys voiced their assent, but Howard strenuously objected to the charge being given. "This might, in my opinion, give the jurors the impression that the court would like for them to vote one way or the other just to get it over with . . . and that certain words here would induce some of the jurors to vote merely because someone else is doing so."

Howard's objection was summarily noted and overruled by the judge, who after calling a brief recess delivered the Allen charge as prepared and presented to the judge by prosecutor Richard Sikes.

"Ladies and gentlemen of the jury," Judge Perry began, "in a large proportion of cases absolute certainty cannot be expected. Although the verdict must be the verdict of each individual juror and not a mere acquiescence in the conclusions of others, yet you should examine the questions submitted with proper regard and deference for the opinions of each other, and you should listen to each other's opinions with a disposition to be convinced. It is your duty to decide the case if you can conscientiously do so. If a much larger number of jurors favor conviction, a dissenting juror should consider the reasonableness of his doubt when it makes no impression upon the minds of other jurors, equally intelligent and impartial, and who have heard the same evidence. If upon the other hand, the majority favors acquittal, the minority should ask themselves whether they might not reasonably doubt the correctness of their judgment.

"If you should fail to agree on a verdict, the case must be retried, and that is very expensive for the government. It is very expensive for the defendant. It takes time. Any future jury must be selected in the same manner and from the same source as you have been chosen, and there is no reason to believe that the case would ever be submitted to twelve men and women more competent to decide it, or that the case can be tried any better or more exhaustively than it has been here, or that more or clearer evidence could be produced."

Now, suddenly, Judge Perry rose from his seat. He stood behind his bench and raised his arms as if to make some kind of benediction.

"Ladies and gentlemen of the jury," he said, scowling. "I will now exercise a prerogative that I have as a judge that I seldom exercise. I will express to you and comment upon the evidence. In my opinion, the evidence sustains a verdict of guilty on counts one, two, and three of the indictment." His face grew red and his breath came hard and fast, as if he were exerting himself. The judge then went on to tell the jury that they could disagree with him if they chose to do so.

"Now, with that in mind, ladies and gentlemen, you may now retire and reconsider the evidence in light of this court's instructions," the judge concluded.

I turned quickly to George Howard to ask what was going on, but Judge Perry glowered at us, his face contorted with rage. It was clear to every soul in that courtroom that this federal district judge wanted me convicted. He sent the jury back into their room, from which we could hear shouting, and even some crying, for the next hour, until they returned and the foreman once again announced that they were still deadlocked, eleven to one for conviction. The lone holdout, Mrs. Anna B. Hightower, sat still and quiet, her jaw clenched and her arms folded across her chest. The jury foreman told the judge that the party who was holding out for a not-guilty verdict "definitely will not change her mind."

The judge was obviously disappointed at the decision, and without the usual formality of asking the government attorneys whether or not the case would be retried, said: "Ladies and gentlemen of the jury, I thank you for your services here, and now that the foreman has stated that the juror has definitely stated that she will not change her mind, I have no recourse left except to declare a mistrial. I now discharge the jury with my appreciation for your services. Now, the case is again set for Monday, August 3, for trial. I will start—call another jury and set it on that day for trial, unless somebody can convince me that there is some tremendous hardship involved. All right, the court now stands adjourned. Thank you very much."

Outside the courtroom, we were blinded by the glare of television lights. Sikes and Dunne were already giving interviews when George Howard caught the attention of the reporters.

"Judge Perry brought the jury out after it had deliberated for some time and made a statement that 'the evidence sustains a verdict of guilty.' That statement was highly prejudicial to my client, and a reversible error," he said forcefully, meaning that the Court of Appeals would more than likely have reversed the decision of the jury and ordered a retrial if I had been convicted. Howard positioned himself to shield Barbara and me from the press as we made our way to the elevator and out of the building. He left us with a strong warning not to give any interviews to the press.

Later that evening, we sat down to watch the news. Mrs. Hightower, the jury holdout, neatly dressed and speaking with the diction of a well-educated woman, ably defended her stance. "They have nothing on that agent, as far as I could see. The whole thing seems like a made-up case to me. I sat there through the whole trial, and his race had nothing to do with how I voted. I went by the evidence as it was presented by the government, and they did not prove their case beyond a reasonable doubt. He did as he was told to do with the report, and nobody showed me that he ever had any report to sell," she said adamantly. "I'm not going to take the word of two confessed criminals over the word of that agent."

Attorneys Sikes and Dunne filled the screen next. Richard Sikes told the reporter that the government would have had a conviction had it not been for the "Negro woman" juror. "She has a son who is an agent with the Internal Revenue Service," he made sure to add.

The next interview astonished me. There was Judge Perry himself, dressed in his black robes and sitting comfortably in his chambers, chatting for the cameras. The reporter asked if it was unusual for a trial judge to express an opinion concerning the defendant's guilt to a deliberating jury.

"I didn't say the defendant was guilty," Judge Perry answered. "I said that the evidence showed that the defendant was guilty." He elaborated, arguing that instructing the jury regarding what the evidence shows wasn't the same as expressing his personal opinion of the case.

The reporter pressed him. "You said that in your opinion, the evidence showed that the defendant is guilty. Even though you told the jury that they could disagree with your opinion, weren't you usurping the duty and purpose of the jury and thereby becoming a juror in the case yourself?"

"No, I was not," Judge Perry insisted. "As a federal judge, I have the prerogative to comment upon the evidence to the jury, and I exercised that prerogative. It was not my personal opinion of his guilt that I expressed, but it was my opinion of what the evidence showed."

"Well, Your Honor, respectfully, I don't see the difference in the two when it comes to the influence that you have as a federal judge over the minds of the jurors," the reporter said. "Is that prerogative used often in the Seventh Circuit?"

"No, it is not, but we do have that prerogative whenever we deem it necessary to apply."

As soon as the interview ended I phoned George Howard and started railing about Judge Perry.

"Yeah, I saw him, too," Howard said. "I'm preparing motions for a change of venue and a substitute judge. I'm also filing a motion for a continuance, which will probably be heard in a week or so."

I was filled with indignation. "We really do need another judge. Did you see the look on his face when he was talking to the jury? Man, if he had had a gun, he would have shot me right there. He's a racist to the bone. I wonder how many times he has used that prerogative in trials where the defendant was white. I bet—"

"Hold it, Bolden," Howard interrupted. "There you go again. If you say something like that to the press, the judge is going to hold you in contempt. I know that you are upset, but you have to watch what you say, and let me handle it."

"I understand, George. It's just that we don't have a chance at all if we have to fight the judge and the U.S. attorneys and the Secret Service, too. They wouldn't do this to a white agent, and you know it."

"We have to fight this legally, and I'm getting the motions ready at this very moment." Then Howard and I talked about the things we needed to do to prepare for the retrial.

I hung up the phone and exhaled long and slowly, for what seemed like the first time in days. I was tired to the bone, but I knew I'd need strength. My ordeal hadn't ended that day. It had barely begun.

Chapter 13

I TOOK ADVANTAGE of a couple of nice sunny days after the trial to decompress and to get our house back in order. But the second trial loomed, and we had a lot to do. I needed to find that young man I had talked to on the morning of May 9 as I was headed to Melrose Park to arrest Arthur Rachael and Joseph Spagnoli. He had seen the addresses on the back of the fishing guide before I talked to Frank Jones. Jones had testified that I had written the name, while he watched, for the purpose of sending him to see Spagnoli, but this young man could help us prove that Jones had lied under oath. I also needed to confirm Agent Cross' relationship with the real estate agency, and that he had been dealing with them around the same time he lost the report.

On July 21, I put on a suit and tie and visited the Dwyer Real Estate Company, which was just around the corner from my home. I explained to the secretary there, a young black woman, that I was on trial in federal district court and that one of the issues in the trial was whether or not Agent Conrad Cross had visited their company, and if so, what business had been conducted.

"Yes, I remember you coming in with him," she answered politely. "You're that agent who is on trial, who used to be with President Kennedy, aren't you? I'll see what I have on file."

She went back to her desk for a few moments before returning with an index card with the name "Conrad Cross" written across the top.

"I think this is what you're looking for." The notations on the card were perfectly clear, showing that Cross had visited the office on the morning of May 11, 1964, and inquired about a tavern for rent. The card indicated that Cross wanted to take over a tavern somewhere between Seventy-ninth and Sixty-third Streets in Chicago.

"I need a copy of this," I told the secretary.

"I can't do that," she said. "I can't give you a copy of our records unless the owner, Mr. Dwyer, says it's okay. He's not here now, but he should be back later in the day. You should stop back by later this evening, and as soon as he comes in, I can give you a call if he says that it's all right."

"Okay, but don't let anything happen to that card. Here's my attorney's telephone number," I added, writing the number down for her. "You probably will hear something from my attorney. Thanks a lot for your help."

I went straight home and phoned George Howard, excitedly telling him the great news. Howard acknowledged what a good break it was for us, but he wasn't pleased that I hadn't gotten a copy of the card. He urged me to go back and try to convince her to give me a copy, saying he'd get a subpoena if he had to, but would prefer to have Dwyer provide the evidence of his own accord. I realized he was right and immediately raced back to the real estate office.

The secretary rose from her desk and greeted me. I sensed something different in the office and looked around. Behind the counter was a door leading into a small office. When I first visited, that door had been open, and the office had been dark. Now the door was closed, and there appeared to be a light on inside the office. I was trained to notice that kind of thing.

"Hi. You remember me?" I asked. I reminded her of what we had discussed previously, and asked if she had spoken to Dwyer. She told me that Dwyer had indeed been in the office and that she had discussed the matter with him.

"He took the card with him," she said. "He was in the office for a few minutes, but he had to leave again. I gave him your message."

I knew immediately that something wasn't right. "I hope he doesn't let anything happen to that card. It will be very important to my trial."

I paced disgustedly outside the office. I was sure someone was in that office behind the secretary's desk, and most likely it was Dwyer. Why would he be hiding from me? I looked up and down the block until my eye settled on a used-tire store, where I happened to know the owner a little. I made my way to the store and pushed open the heavy wooden door of the entrance. Les, the owner, came out and greeted me.

"Hey, Abe, man, I've been thinking about you." Les wiped the sweat from his face with a shop rag. "I heard about what's been happening to you, and I intended to call George and see how you were doing."

"Les," I began, "the real estate company down the street has some valuable information that could help me in my trial. I was wondering if I could stand here inside your shop and see if I can see the owner of the company when he comes in. I think he is ducking me."

Les quickly agreed and set me up in a comfortable spot with a good view of the real estate office—that is, as comfortable as the pounding vibrations of the air compressor and the acrid smell of hot rubber would allow. He even gave me a cold drink. My only real problem, it occurred to me, was that I had never met Dwyer. I had seen him only once, from a distance, while he chatted with Conrad Cross. The only real image I had of him was of a small African American man.

Suddenly I saw a familiar car pull up and park next to the real estate office. It was one of the vehicles from the Chicago Secret Service office. I went to the window to get a better view and saw Agent Louis Sims and another agent, who from my vantage point looked

like Richard Jordan, get out of the car and go into the real estate office. They stayed inside the office for about an hour before getting
back into their car and speeding away. I understood, in that moment,
that the Secret Service was either following me or tapping my phone,
possibly both. One way or another, they knew about my conversation with the secretary at Dwyer's company.

I walked back across the street and into the office. Clearly, the
secretary was surprised to see me again, and started talking nervously
before I asked her anything.

"Mr. Dwyer still isn't here. We're getting ready to close now, so
you can check back some other time."

I didn't call George Howard until the next day. I explained everything that had happened, and offered my opinion that the Secret Service was either threatening potential witnesses or otherwise trying to
discourage them from testifying on my behalf.

"They can't do that," Howard said angrily. "That's a criminal
offense, if we can prove that's what they were doing."

"Well, that's one hell of a coincidence that the minute I find that
card on Agent Cross at the real estate office, two agents visit that office the same day."

"I agree that it looks like something underhanded is going on,
but Dwyer isn't under subpoena yet, so technically, he's not a government or a defense witness," Howard explained. "I probably won't
issue a subpoena until after the trial starts, so as not to tip our hand
as to what we plan to do. You can back off for now. Don't go over
there again. We don't want to scare him off."

Later that afternoon, I drove over to the service station at Fifty-
ninth and Morgan Streets. I had been there the day before and
learned that Eddie, the young man I was looking for, would be working the second shift. He was expecting me.

"Hi," Eddie greeted me. "I remember you. I still have that guide
you gave me."

"That's what I'm here to talk about, Eddie. Do you remember how it was that I gave you the fishing guide? I mean, do you remember how you happened to ask for the guide?"

"Yeah," Eddie answered, "I remember that you bought some gas here and I saw a fishing guide lying on the front seat of your car. I picked it up through the window while you were out of the car buying cigarettes."

"Did you notice anything about the fishing guide when you first looked at it?"

"Yeah, I remember that I asked you if I could have the book, and you told me that you made some notes on the back. I remember looking on the cover and seeing some addresses written on the book."

"And what else do you remember?" I continued.

"Well, you reached around and got another book from the backseat and gave it to me. Is that what you're talking about?"

"Yes." I asked Eddie if he would testify in court to what he had just said, and he consented easily.

On Monday, July 27, George Howard went before Judge Perry to file a motion for a continuance. I went with him into court that day. Richard Sikes was there, representing the government. Howard based his request on the fact that the judge's widely publicized comments about the case and about me would make it very difficult to find an impartial jury. He also advised the court that he had several other cases coming to trial in the Cook County court, to which he needed to devote some of his time and attention.

Sikes didn't have any argument to make against the continuance, but he didn't really need one. He merely said that a continuance was unnecessary, and then sat back and waited for Judge Perry to agree with him. Sure enough, Judge Perry denied the motion, and declared that the trial would begin as scheduled, on August 3.

Outside the courtroom, Howard explained that he had also filed a motion with the clerk of the court for a substitution of judge. "The motion should be on Judge Perry's desk soon, so keep in contact with me. I think that it will be heard before the week is out."

Neither Howard nor I felt much better about the upcoming trial than we did about the first. We both knew that the government had made sure to stack the deck in its favor. We would have a tough time mounting our defense, especially if Judge Perry was on the bench again.

"We need to win that motion, George," I said, almost pleading. "We won't have a chance at all if Judge Perry presides over the trial again."

"Don't worry, Abe," Howard soothed. "The judge has already said that he formed an opinion about your case, and what he said to the jury makes it almost a one hundred percent chance that he'll recuse himself from another trial."

"He's not going to recuse himself, George. I looked into his eyes at the time he declared the mistrial. He is not going to give us another judge."

"The only other option is to go directly into the Seventh Circuit Court of Appeals, but they can't rule on anything that hasn't been heard by the lower court. We would have to be prepared to go right from Judge Perry's courtroom to the Court of Appeals for an emergency hearing," Howard said heatedly. "Do you have enough money to do that? It will cost quite a bit to print up and file the briefs. We are looking at another two thousand to three thousand dollars on top of what our expenses already are. And that's before we even get into the second trial."

"I can't get my hands on any more money," I answered ruefully. "I've already borrowed from my family. I don't have that much equity in my house, so that's out. We just have to push hard for the change of judge. I guess that's all we can do."

"Come on, Abe, you know that I'm doing the best that I can for you." Howard put his hand on my shoulder. "I'll file the motion, and hopefully we'll get a new judge and things will turn out differently." He tried hard to cheer me up, but I couldn't relax. All I knew was that I didn't trust Judge Perry one bit, and for now, my fate was in his hands.

A few days later, on Thursday, Howard called and told me that Judge Perry would be hearing our motion the next morning. I was restless and agitated all night, pacing the floors of my house, replaying the trial and everything that had led up to it over and over in my head. The government to which I had given nothing but my very best had me at its mercy, and for a crime I hadn't committed—a crime that, in fact, had never even happened. I knew that Judge Perry would deny our request the next day. There was no question. As I paced in the dark, imagining the moment when he would issue his final judgment, a crazy thought flashed through my mind. The defendant's table in Judge Perry's courtroom stood a very short distance from the judge's bench. No problem at all for someone who was good with a handgun, someone who had shot a perfect score on the combat course in Treasury school and who had qualified as an expert on the U.S. Customs Department firing range. All it would take would be six quick pulls on the trigger. I couldn't miss.

I walked silently to our bedroom closet and reached up to the high overhead shelf. My hand found the holster that held my personal Colt .38 weapon. Keeping the gun down by my side, I went to the dresser and opened the drawer where I kept the bullets. Just as I pulled the drawer open, Barbara stirred in bed.

"What are you doing, Abraham?"

"Oh, just getting ready for today."

Barbara fell back to sleep. Taking six bullets out of the box in the drawer, I walked out to the dining room, loaded the gun, and clicked the cylinder shut. I slipped the gun into my briefcase, pulled the zipper closed, and went back to bed.

All night, I felt haunted. I imagined the terrible reality of what I was contemplating. At the same time, my memory flashed back to a day a few years earlier when a young man had leaped to his death from the sixth floor of the federal building while I was at work there. I could still hear the flapping and fluttering of his clothes as he fell. At the time, I couldn't imagine any problem so intractable that I would choose to destroy myself, but now I stood ready to do just that. Certainly, I would have the chance to put a bullet in my own head after shooting the judge—and if I didn't, surely someone else would—but I came to see that it would not have been the end of things. When I finally got out of bed and began to get ready for the day, I stood staring at my reflection in the bathroom mirror, and realized I was not a man who could bring such horror down on his wife, his children, and his children's children. I exhaled and felt the muscles of my body relax. Violence would not be my release. I had to keep faith, to remain a believer in the power of the truth.

We were in for a surprise the next morning in court. It turned out that the chief judge of the district was not sitting that summer, and so who should we see on the bench hearing emergency motions from a series of lawyers in various cases but our own Judge Perry.

George Howard was his usual eloquent self. "Your Honor, this petition is submitted respectfully. It is submitted with the understanding and appreciation of the great latitude that the federal judges have in commenting on the evidence, but it is the opinion of the defendant and defense counsel that when the court expressed an opinion on the ultimate issues, that is, as to the innocence or guilt of the defendant in this cause, we fear that because of this that we cannot receive a fair and impartial trial in this courtroom."

"Did you get one the last time?" the judge asked.

"Yes, sir," Howard answered to my surprise. "I think that the court was completely fair all the way through in the trial. There was no indication at all, and we certainly do not make an objection to that, but it is because of the comment, Your Honor, that we feel we cannot get a fair trial."

Howard went on to describe the statements Judge Perry had made to the jury regarding his belief that I was guilty, and how those comments had been made public through the media. He asked that the court grant a substitution of judge and that the case be transferred to the presiding judge for the district court for reassignment. When Judge Perry turned to the government attorneys for a response, Richard Sikes argued that the motion had not been filed in a timely manner, and that the motion had not included certification of counsel.

The judge agreed: "The motion is denied and the case is set." Certification of counsel is a sworn statement by counsel that the motion is filed in good faith and not for purposes of delay.

We'd never had a chance. I would never receive a fair trial before Judge Perry, and the government attorneys knew it. They were counting on it. I couldn't help but think of Emmett Till and the "fair" trial he got before a mob bashed in his skull, shot him full of holes, and threw him into the Tallahatchie River. As far as Sikes, Dunne, Judge Perry, and who knew how many others were concerned, I had committed a crime, all right. Maybe not the crime I was accused of, but the crime of speaking out about laxity and unprofessional behavior of the Secret Service, especially of the presidential detail around the time of Kennedy's assassination.

Howard was outraged, though he tried to assure me that things were still okay, and that even if Judge Perry did hear my case a second time, it could surely be reversed on appeal.

For a moment, I felt I knew better than he did. "They're not worried about any appeal, George. They want my black butt now, any way they can get it. If they have to go outside the law to convict me, they will. You've seen that already."

Howard knew I was right, but he encouraged me to keep chasing down the guy from the real estate company. "We're going to need everyone that we can get. They're playing real dirty now."

When Barbara and I got home, I flopped down on the couch. As

I set my briefcase down next to me and felt the unusual heft of it, I suddenly realized that I had never taken the gun out of it. Luckily, I had left the briefcase in the trunk of the car when we went into court, but I shuddered as I imagined what would have happened if anyone had discovered I had brought a loaded Colt .38 service revolver to court. Given that they were already pulling out all the stops to put me behind bars, that surely would have been the end of me. I had believed that even though he didn't know it, Judge Perry had survived a close call. But now I saw that the lucky survivor that day was me.

JURY SELECTION FOR the retrial began on the morning of August 3, 1964. As with the first trial, it was agreed that the judge would do all the questioning, but what seemed different this time was the makeup of the jury pool. They were overwhelmingly white, with only a few blacks or Hispanics in the group. I suspected that the government attorneys had somehow had the opportunity to scan the list of jurors prior to that day. That suspicion was reinforced when Arthur Dunne challenged one of the potential jurors on the grounds that he had been convicted of a felony in the past. The man denied the accusation, and it came out that Dunne's information was incorrect; in fact, it pertained to someone with a different address and different birth date. The government excused the man anyway. He was black.

The government could use their peremptory challenges to eliminate African Americans as prospective jurors, always citing some clever but ultimately hollow rationale. The jurors were mostly from suburban areas around the city, rather than the South Side, like me. George Howard found the potential African American jurors acceptable, but they were either eliminated by the prosecution or released from consideration by Judge Perry himself.

By that afternoon, twelve white faces sat staring at me from the jury box.

Off the record, Judge Perry asked: "Are there any objections to the impaneling of this jury?"

"We have no objections, Your Honor," said Sikes.

All eyes turned to Howard, who rose from his seat and said, to my utter astonishment, "We have no objections, Your Honor."

Later, he explained himself to me. "The color of the jury doesn't make any difference, Abe. I've seen black jurors convict black defendants and white juries find them not guilty. I have faith in the American judicial system, and I believe that given all of the facts of this case, any jury is going to find you not guilty."

I wasn't buying it. "Do you think for one minute that a white juror would have stood up for me like Mrs. Hightower did?"

Howard didn't like me challenging him. I saw a vein beginning to bulge on the side of his forehead. Even in college, I'd known it was a sign that his blood was rising.

"You need to come off that black-and-white thing, Abe," he snapped. "Let me handle your defense. You have to have confidence in me. We have just as much of a chance before this jury as we did before the last jury."

"Yeah, but the one vote that saved my black ass was black, and I don't believe we're going to get a fair trial with Judge Perry hearing the case before an all-white jury. That's just my honest opinion."

"Well, you have your opinion and I have mine, so let's leave it at that, and put on the best defense against the indictment that we can."

I took my leave of Howard, knowing that even if my confidence was weakening, there wasn't a thing I could do about it. I didn't have any more money. I couldn't add another attorney to my defense team. I knew that if I tried to replace Howard, the judge had the authority to determine that the move was a delaying tactic, and thus could overrule it. It was within his power to revoke my bond, lock me up, and reappoint Howard to represent me. Fighting any move the judge or the government might make would mean more money. I realized that I was out of options and had to play the hand I'd been dealt. It was not a winning hand, and the game wasn't being played by the rules. I trusted George to do his best, and I knew that he believed fully in me, but I could not help worrying that he was overmatched in this case.

When opening statements began on August 4, it struck me right away that the government attorneys seemed even more confident than they had the first time around. Sikes stood before his all-white jury and in a very relaxed tone laid out the government's case against me. As he spoke, I saw his partner, Arthur Dunne, give a little smile and wink at one of the female jurors.

George Howard held his own. His dapper appearance and articulate presentation seemed to captivate the jury. He not only denied the government's charges but said he would show that the entire case had been concocted by the counterfeiters Frank Jones and Joseph Spagnoli. Howard had an uphill battle in front of him, but he was going to give it everything he had. During the recess that followed, I heard many spectators congratulate Howard on his impassioned opening, and I thought I detected looks of concern on the faces of Sikes and Dunne.

The government first called Agent John Russell to the stand, who testified to the same facts as he had at the first trial. The only exception was his statement that I had testified in the first trial that I'd heard that Spagnoli had called Martineau on May 13. I had been a private detective, a state police officer, and an agent of the United States Secret Service and was no stranger to the basic rules of criminal procedure. I knew that Russell's describing my previous testimony contained in a transcript of a previous trial was hearsay evidence— absolutely inadmissible, and grounds for an immediate mistrial. I turned to look at Howard, who made a cursory objection. The judge looked down at Howard from his bench, and the government lawyers turned to watch him, too, but he made no vigorous move to press the issue and use it as a point on appeal.

This was the first sign that, despite his fiery opening statement, the fire had gone out of Howard. Maybe he had lost confidence in himself or the case. Maybe he didn't think we could overcome the powerful forces opposing us. Maybe he was worried about his own professional future, knowing how much he stood to lose if he angered an influential federal judge. Howard did not cross-examine Russell as aggressively as he had in the first trial. I knew that some of Russell's testimony was untrue, such as his statement that I had been nearby when he told Richard Sikes that Spagnoli called Martineau at the office, but I didn't believe Russell was out to get me. I just think his recollection was off. Nor did I believe that he would offer hearsay testimony about what I might have said in the first trial unless the government attorneys had instructed him to do so.

The same disregard for the rules of criminal procedure surfaced again during the testimony of Special Agent Myron Weinstein, who told the jury, "Bolden testified in July 1964, at his first trial, that he placed the name and address of Spagnoli on the back of government's Exhibit 9 [the fishing guide] and that he said he later ripped off the cover." It didn't even matter if Weinstein's testimony was accurate or not. Every lawyer in the courtroom, and of course the judge, knew that such hearsay evidence was not only inadmissible but grounds for an immediate mistrial. Judge Perry had both the authority and the duty to warn the prosecution about illegal third-party hearsay evidence. A judge must ensure that every defendant before him is tried within the established rules of criminal procedure. I can only assume Judge Perry's determination to see me convicted outweighed his commitment to his legal duty. He said nothing. When Howard, too, kept silent regarding Weinstein's improper testimony, I realized my fate was sealed. An all-white suburban jury and a judge who saw nothing wrong with telling the jury how to vote were bad enough. Now my own attorney seemed to have forgotten the basic rules of criminal procedure. My conviction seemed certain.

Throughout the second trial, Judge Perry rode Howard very hard. He left no doubt that he intended to play hardball. Howard had even less leeway than he'd had the first time. One exchange illustrated the judge's attitude particularly well. At one point during Frank Jones' testimony, it seemed that Howard had trapped him in a blatant contradiction. In the first trial, my lawyer had shown Jones a copy of the statement Jones gave the Secret Service after his "arrest" on May 15, 1964. The statement contradicted the testimony Jones was giving from the witness stand at the time. When Howard asked him if he had signed the contradictory statement, Jones dodged the question by saying, "I can't answer the question because I can't see the signature without my glasses." Thus he failed to verify his signature on the statement.

Now, in the second trial, Jones testified that he had not been wearing his glasses when he met me in front of his house on May 11, but that "Bolden wrote Spagnoli's address on the back of the fishing guide and I read the address from the back of the guide." So this witness who'd said he couldn't read his own signature on his own statement without his reading glasses claimed to have read much smaller writing on the back of the fishing guide, also without his glasses.

Howard pounced on the obvious contradiction. "On July 6, 1964, I tried to show you your signature, which was written in big letters, and you said that you couldn't see it without your glasses."

Arthur Dunne leaped to his feet as if shot from a cannon. "Objection, Your Honor!"

Judge Perry scowled irritably and immediately sustained the objection.

"Now, Counsel, again, you have the record there. If you want to ask what questions were there, let us go back and ask them just like they are in the record. You have a transcript. Counsel is admonished to not follow that procedure anymore. When you wish to ask an impeaching question, go back to the record and ask it correctly."

Howard continued his cross-examination of Frank Jones, finding more and more inconsistencies. With Jones' testimony on the verge of unraveling, Judge Perry called a recess, excused the jury, and at the behest of Arthur Dunne lectured Howard on proper procedure for cross-examination.

Judge Perry reminded Howard again that he must go back to the record when asking impeaching questions, and not rely on his memory. "I ask you not to do that again. You are going to bring that up again, and Counsel is going to raise it, and it is going to bring forth an admonishment that may not be helpful to your client." His voice heavy with meaning and condescension, he added, "You owe it to your client not to do that anymore. Do you hear me?"

"Yes, sir," came my lawyer's meek reply.

"All right," Judge Perry continued. "Let us remember that. Otherwise, I am not going to take any action while this case is pending." He did, however, turn to the two prosecuting attorneys and offered, "If you gentlemen wish to take action—there is nothing that warrants any action—but if things develop here that you just heard outside of the presence of the jury and anything will be continued until a later time, until after this case is over, but now we are going to stop that practice. It is not going to be done now. Do you know what I mean?"

The words may have been roundabout, but we knew what he was implying. There was no mistaking the threat to George Howard. Judge Perry was signaling to the government lawyers that they could consider bringing charges or complaints against Howard if he kept up that kind of scrappy defense.

"Mr. Jones," Howard continued, "did I ask you if you were acquainted with a man named Alderman Charles Chew? And (on July 6, 1964) did you answer that question by saying, 'Yes, I do know Alderman Chew'?"

"Objection, Your Honor," Arthur Dunne shouted. "I will ask for a hearing out of the presence of the jury." Dunne waved his hands in the air in a display of exasperation.

The judge excused the jury from the room so that the lawyers could debate the admissibility of this line of questioning. As soon as they had left, George Howard made his case.

Howard argued, "I have a copy of the arrest record and conviction of Frank Jones where Alderman Chew and another man signed the complaint. I have the judge's name who convicted him." Clearly Jones had committed blatant perjury on July 6.

"We object, Your Honor," Dunne pronounced theatrically. "If soliciting an ad is a felony, perhaps we are practicing in the wrong court. I ask that Counsel be admonished in the presence of the jury, in light of his conduct, because we went through the same thing. I made a statement prior to this case beginning and I think, Your Honor, we are completely in line with respect to that."

Judge Perry wasted no time. "The law is very clear. You can show a record of a felony, but not a misdemeanor. It cannot be shown. That is the law in the district, and there is no question about it. It is the law in the State of Illinois with respect to defendants. It is the law in respect to witnesses also. That's all there is to it." The trial judge sustained the government's objection and instructed Howard not to go into the matter in front of the jury, which he then called back into the courtroom.

ON THE MORNING of the second day of the retrial, I paid another visit to the Dwyer Real Estate Company, hoping to talk Dwyer into producing the document concerning Agent Cross, and appearing as a witness. The secretary recognized me immediately and rose to meet me at the counter.

"Did you have a chance to talk to Mr. Dwyer?" I asked.

"Yes, I did, but he's not here now."

"The trial has started. I need to know if he is willing to come to court and testify as to his transactions with Agent Cross."

She seemed nervous. "Mr. Dwyer isn't in town."

"Where is he? Did he leave the card?"

"Mr. Dwyer went to the Bahamas on a vacation and won't be back until the final week of August," the secretary said. "He took the card with him."

I didn't need to hear another word. Whether he was really in the Bahamas or not, the Secret Service had gotten to Dwyer and through either persuasion or intimidation had made certain that neither his testimony nor his evidence would be available to me. When I recounted the visit to Howard that afternoon at the courthouse, he was disgusted but not despairing. He said he'd issue a subpoena and let the U.S. marshals find Dwyer.

I wasn't so sure. "He's going to stay hidden during the rest of the trial," I said. "If he doesn't want to testify, I don't think we can force him. Forget about him. I'm not going to kiss his black ass to get him to testify. He's afraid of the government, just like most people are. I knew when I saw Agents Sims and Jordan come out of that real estate company that something was up. Someday I'll see that Jordan gets what he deserves—"

"Now hold it, Abe," Howard interrupted. "Don't go threatening agents."

"They're going to find me guilty, George. There's just no way they won't . . . this all-white jury before Judge Perry. No way."

THE GOVERNMENT RESTED its case less than a week later, and we began our defense. George Howard called Eddie Miller, the service station employee who had noticed the names and addresses on the back of the fishing guide two days before Frank Jones claimed I had written the address in his presence. Howard wanted Eddie to tell the jury about our meeting on May 9 at the service station.

"On May 9, I saw Mr. Bolden at the gas station where I work, at 855 West Fifty-ninth Street. Bolden drove a green Plymouth into the station, and while he was paying for cigarettes, I noticed a Phillips 66 Fishing Guide with some writing on the back cover lying on a seat in Bolden's car."

Howard asked Eddie about the conversation we had had regarding the names on the back of the fishing guide, and the government objected. With the jury watching, the judge tore into Howard.

"That's what he is objecting to, the hearsay evidence outside the presence of any representative of the government. This is just a conversation that took place between him and Mr. Bolden," the judge interrupted angrily, concluding, "If we put that kind of evidence as a defense, there would be no end of the defense of how many people you talk to and told you were innocent or something else."

Stunned by the apparent double standard operating in the trial, Howard pleaded with the judge. If all such conversations were to be excluded as evidence, he argued, "then we wouldn't have had Joseph Spagnoli on the stand, and we wouldn't have had—"

"Now just a second," Judge Perry shouted. "We are not going into a lengthy argument of the case here. The agency has already established before that evidence came in. I will excuse the jury and we will hear what your ground is. We will excuse the jury to the jury room, but this is no time to castigate the court about its past rulings." Judge Perry waved a finger at Howard as the astonished jury looked on.

When the jury was out of the room, the judge continued his tirade. "Mr. Howard, you will reserve your arguments about the past rulings of this court for the Court of Appeals, and not for the jury. Do you understand that? If you don't like the decision here, that is proper up there, but not here."

Any first-year law student could understand that Judge Perry had turned the trial into a sham. He never missed a chance to make

Howard look like a villain or a buffoon in the jury's eyes. Judge Perry blocked every move we tried to make, but gave the government the widest possible latitude, both inside and outside the law. Prevented from mounting a proper defense, our only hope was that someday one of the witnesses would crack and all the lies would be exposed. I knew in my heart that I was watching a kind of lynching—my lynching. Judge Perry's black robe didn't fool me. It might as well have been the hooded white robe of a Klansman.

The rest of the second trial proceded much as the first had. I neither added nor changed anything in my own testimony, although Arthur Dunne did everything he could to make me look like a liar. In his closing statement, of course, Dunne spoke at length about the integrity and honesty of his two key witnesses, Spagnoli and Jones, both of whom were under federal indictment. He saved his ridicule for me.

"Ladies and gentlemen," said Dunne, "you believe that testimony under oath—I hope, I pray—except when a person has been proven under oath to be a liar. Who has been proven to be a liar? Abraham Bolden." He turned and glared at me. "You may not believe this, but did Mr. Howard once prove any of our witnesses was lying? Not once, ladies and gentlemen. They may not be the most respectable people in the world, but they are certainly not liars. You saw them on the stand, every one of them."

When George Howard rose to deliver his closing statement, he looked to me like a beaten man. He spoke with eloquence and even some passion, but his presentation never rose to the level of the first trial. I had the sense that he was rushing through, anxious for the trial to be over, and looking back on it now, I'm not sure I blame him. It must have been so difficult for him, defending an old friend and fraternity brother against such unfair odds. Howard had been threatened and disrespected—at times all but humiliated—by the combined efforts of a federal judge and two government prosecutors. And I couldn't forget that Howard had more to worry about than just winning my case; he had to protect his right and ability to go on practicing law in the United States courts.

Around noon on August 11, after denying our motion for a directed verdict of not guilty, the judge charged the jury and sent them off to deliberate. I had expected a quick verdict, given everything the judge had done to ensure my conviction, but by the end of the afternoon, the jury still hadn't finished. Barbara and George and I could only pace the corridors and wait. Around 3:00 P.M., a few Secret Service agents stood in the hallway, just outside the jury room, making conversation with the two government attorneys, Sikes and Dunne. We all watched as Arthur Dunne positioned himself just in front of the closed door of the jury room.

"He knows he's guilty," Dunne said in a voice loud enough for everyone nearby to hear him. "I don't see why he's putting the government through all of this trouble." His audience of Secret Service agents all smiled broadly.

Howard immediately stiffened. "He's trying to talk to the jury through the door. He realized that his voice can be heard inside the jury room. That's jury tampering."

Just at that moment, the court clerk came out and announced that Judge Perry was about to take the bench. I sensed that my time was up, that I was about to hear the harsh judgment of this bogus court, but it turned out that the jury had not finished deliberating, and the judge wanted to arrange for their dinner. The three of us also went out for a quick dinner, although food was the last thing on my mind. Howard tried to reassure me that the jury still being out was a good sign, but I couldn't get myself to believe it.

We returned to the courthouse and waited. As the hours passed, looks of concern appeared on the faces of the prosecutors and Secret Service agents, who must also have anticipated a quick verdict. Howard just kept telling me, "In this situation, no news is good news." Finally, at about 5:30 P.M., the judge called the opposing attorneys into the courtroom, where the attorneys assembled in front of his bench.

"It's been a long day, and it is getting late. I'm tired, and I'm going to close the courtroom for tonight and go home and get some sleep. We will meet back here tomorrow morning at 9:00 A.M. and the jury will continue its deliberations at that time. If there are no objections, the jury will seal its verdict until the attorneys can be gathered and the verdict can be read in open court. I'm going to close the courtroom now, and I will advise the jury of my decision." Perry instructed Arthur Dunne to see that the courtroom was emptied.

Dunne motioned to George and me, gathered up the spectators remaining in the gallery, and then escorted us all out of the courtroom. Martineau, Sims, Jordan, and Torina followed, taking an elevator to the Secret Service office on the fourth floor. The rest of us went down in the elevator with Arthur Dunne, who ushered us out of the building and then remained inside. I remember watching Dunne walk back toward the elevators as the heavy glass doors to the courthouse were locked behind us by the uniformed guard.

"What's going on, George?" I asked anxiously. "They've locked us out of the courtroom and the jury is still deliberating. The Secret Service agents and government attorneys are still inside the building. We're standing outside, and I don't know what's going on in there."

Howard didn't seem alarmed. "The judge said that he was going to release the jury until tomorrow morning. They aren't going to do any more deliberating tonight," he said. "The jury will give a sealed verdict if they reach a verdict before we arrive in the morning. That's what the judge ordered."

"They're not going to reach a verdict before I get here in the morning. I don't like the idea of having the judge say anything to the jury when we can't hear what he is saying. You know what happened in the last trial. Now he is locked up inside this building with nothing but government agents, prosecuting attorneys, and an all-white jury. He can say anything that he wants to say, and there's nobody in there—"

"Look, Abe, the court is closed for tonight. There won't be any more deliberating until tomorrow. The judge is going home, and the jury can't deliberate without the judge being there," he repeated impatiently.

"Then why didn't he say what he had to say to us in front of the jury? How come he didn't bring the jury in?"

"Abe," Howard replied, "the man is a federal judge and he can run his courtroom any way he wants to. He can—"

"Well, who is going to release the jury tonight, and when is he going to release them?" I snapped.

"Judge Perry will release them."

"I don't trust Judge Perry to do anything or say anything to that jury when we are not in the courtroom. The building is full of government agents. Everybody in that building now is against me and hoping for my conviction. Judge Perry maneuvered us into a position so that he could tamper with this jury like he did the last one without us hearing what he is telling them. I have a constitutional right to be in that courtroom while the jury is deliberating."

"I'll meet you here at 9:00 A.M. tomorrow," Howard said coldly as he turned and headed home.

As Barbara and I walked toward the parking lot, I let loose. "It's a done deal. I'm as good as convicted right now. There is no way that Judge Perry will let that jury find me other than guilty."

A few moments later, as we were driving home and I was scanning the radio for any news about the trial, we heard a news reporter announce a special bulletin.

"There has been a verdict in the Bolden trial. The jury has just reached a verdict in the trial of Secret Service agent Abraham Bolden," the newscaster said. "The verdict was sealed and will be read in court tomorrow morning at 9 o'clock. The judge has released the jury until tomorrow morning."

I was not surprised. "That's what I was saying," I shouted at Barbara. "The judge didn't go home. He stayed in the courtroom. He flat-out lied to us when he said that the jury would stop deliberating for the night. He lied so that he could get us out of the courtroom and do his thing with the jury behind our backs. He tampered with the jury, I'm sure."

"There's nothing you can do about it now," Barbara said sadly. "Control yourself. Don't go in there tomorrow exploding if they find you guilty."

"I need to do more than explode."

Another tormented and sleepless night passed. I fielded calls from my sister and brother, offering their love and support and vowing to be with me in court for the reading of the verdict. I went over and over it in my mind. Judge Perry had clearly manipulated the situation so that he could be alone with the jury. That fact was not in dispute. Nothing he had said made sense. Why did he need to make a provision for a sealed verdict if the jury had stopped deliberating for the night? Of course, there was no court reporter present, and no transcript exists of what went on in that courthouse after we were shown out, but I have no doubt that the legal process was horribly corrupted that night.

The next day, August 12, brought no surprises. Everything unfolded according to the government's well-planned script, although to me it all seemed utterly surreal. The room was crowded with onlookers. The relaxed confidence of the government lawyers and the many Secret Service agents present suggested their certainty about the verdict. When Judge Perry ordered me to stand and hear the judgment, two marshals appeared and took up positions just behind me. The clerk unsealed the envelope and on the judge's cue began to read.

"We, the jury, find the defendant Abraham Bolden guilty of count one of the indictment. We, the jury, find the defendant Abraham Bolden guilty of count two of the indictment. We, the jury, find the defendant Abraham Bolden guilty of count three of the indictment."

There had never been any doubt.

Judge Perry explained that he felt no need for any further reports or hearings before passing sentence, but did offer George Howard the chance to make a statement. My attorney took the opportunity to remind the court of my spotless record and years of dedicated service, and argued that I deserved a sentence of probation, but Judge Perry looked like a man whose mind was already made up. Then he asked if I wished to make a statement.

I stood and told the court that in my years as a private detective, state police officer, and Secret Service agent, I had always tried to do my best. With my voice beginning to crack and Howard tugging lightly at my sleeve, I forged ahead, declaring that all of my actions had always been in the best interest of the government. As I spoke, my emotions suddenly burst through to the surface. "Have mercy," I pleaded, bursting into tears. "In the name of God, have mercy." I sobbed openly before the court.

"That's the first sign of repentance that you've shown," Judge Perry said bitterly. "You committed perjury in this court and have brought shame upon the Secret Service. I hereby sentence you to the custody of the U.S. attorney general for a period of six years on count one and five years each on counts two and three. The sentences are to run concurrently." Of course, there was no evidence of perjury, nor was any perjury charge ever filed against me, but Judge Perry managed to slip in that reference to make me look even worse in the eyes of the press and the public.

Despite the government's request that I be immediately incarcerated, the judge declared that I would remain free on bail pending any appeal. He set a hearing date of September 4 for post-trial motions.

"All rise," intoned the clerk. "The court now stands in recess."

The Secret Service had its conviction, but I didn't think for a moment that it was over. The trial was but the first phase in what would be a long ordeal. Putting me in jail would not be enough. I had no doubt they'd try to discredit me further if they could, to destroy any last bit of respect or credibility I might have had.

Chapter 14

BEFORE THE VERDICT, my father had given me some words of warning that now helped me focus on some immediate priorities. "The government has several ways to get you," he said. "If they convict you, they will send you to prison, or they will send you into financial ruin. You will lose everything trying to fight them and stay out of prison. Either way, you'll be a broken man when they finish with you."

Indeed, a week or two after the conviction, I received a registered letter from the chief of the Secret Service formally notifying me that I had been terminated as an agent of the government. The letter included information on claiming the roughly $6,000 that I had contributed to the government retirement program in the four years of my employment there. I was going to need that money, and more.

Neither Barbara nor I had a job now. In addition to the ongoing expenses for our home and family, we needed to finance the upcoming appeal. For starters, I went straight to the unemployment office, hoping to draw compensation while I looked for a job. I waited for hours and hours like everyone else, but when I finally got to see a case worker, a thickset, middle-aged black woman, she told me there wasn't much she'd be able to do for me.

"You haven't had any salaried income other than the government job within the last four years, and government salary does not qualify you for unemployment compensation," she explained.

"Just thought I would check," I muttered as I got up to leave.

"Not so fast," the woman said. "I know who you are, and I have followed your case all through the summer. You got a bad deal. I can't guarantee you any unemployment check because, as I said, you do not qualify, but I'm going to issue you an unemployment card anyway. That way, I can send you out on some of the job interviews that come across my desk. I'm going to help you try to find something to do."

I was extremely grateful and got myself registered, but I knew that I couldn't wait around for the unemployment office to find me work. I pored over the help-wanted sections of all the Chicago newspapers. In those days, it was still the best way to hunt for a job, especially because I could easily scan all the available positions, whether or not they matched my specific experience or qualifications. One ad I answered came from Alpha Engineering, which was seeking a temporary draftsman. Knowing a little about drafting and lettering, I went downtown and applied for the job. It went well, but my style of lettering wasn't what they needed. Thinking fast, I recommended Barbara, who I knew could letter almost as neatly as a typewriter.

The next morning, she went down and landed the job. It didn't pay all that well, and we had no way of knowing how long the temporary position would last, but it was something, and it felt like a tremendous lucky break. I would be around to watch the children while she worked. Soon after, my brother-in-law helped me find work as a skip tracer for a tire company, tracking down people who were behind in their payments. This was exactly the kind of investigative work I was good at, and a lot of it was phone work that I could do from home, but I'd have to work as an independent, receiving a commission of half of any money recovered from delinquent accounts. I made less than a hundred dollars in each of the first couple of weeks.

Bills were coming due. By January, my retirement check from the government still hadn't arrived, and the attorney and legal printer needed payment. I was learning that with a client like me, people wanted payment up front, in case I ended up in prison with no source of income.

As I approached my thirtieth birthday that cold January, I began to despair. We could just about put food on the table, but we had nothing to spare.

"It looks like I'm going to have to drop the appeal," I said to Barbara one night. "If I go away, at least there won't be the expense of me eating and driving the car. I think you and the children can get better support if I'm not here."

"I'm not going on aid or anything like that," Barbara responded defiantly. "I think that you should stay out as long as you can."

"I need at least three thousand dollars to go to the appellate court. We don't have the money. My retirement won't be here until later."

"What we can do, Abe," she argued, "is borrow money against your retirement check. Before you go and tell them to lock you up, we can talk to the people at the bank and see what they say. I wouldn't turn myself in to anybody. What you need to do is have faith and pray."

Incredibly, the doorbell rang at that very moment, and on the porch I found a deliveryman with a package. It was heavy, and the sender's name on the outside of the box had been smudged so badly in transit that it was unreadable, though I could see that it came from Massachusetts. I set the package on the floor and tore it open.

"It looks like a typewriter," I said to Barbara. "Who would send me a typewriter? Maybe it's a trick by the government. You know, that faked excerpt was typed. Maybe this is the typewriter that it was typed on and someone is trying to set me up."

Sure enough, inside the box was a brand-new Olympia manual typewriter in a case. Attached to the typewriter was a hand-printed note that read simply, "You should type your story." It was signed

"Bill." His address and telephone number were neatly printed below his name. When I went to throw out the shipping box, I found an envelope, the contents of which surprised me even more: a check for $2,100, signed by a William R. Wagnet. I had never heard that name before.

"This is really weird," I said to Barbara. "Here we are, talking about needing money or going to jail, and out of the blue this check comes right to my door from somebody I don't know."

"You said that you were reading the Bible and trying to see what to do. God knows what to do," Barbara answered. The check covered our legal costs and our other bills for the month. Maybe Barbara was right.

After discarding the wrappings, I telephoned Mr. Wagnet and thanked him over and over for the check. I found out that he was an elderly man living in Massachusetts who had followed my case closely.

I turned thirty on January 19, 1965. All that day, I couldn't stop thinking about the dream I had when I was young, in which I saw myself lying trapped in a steel box with a small glass window. Through the window I could see a young woman standing with three small children, a vision that now made perfect sense to me. The image haunted me, even as we sat eating cake and ice cream with the children, listening to Barbara sing "Happy Birthday" in her beautiful soprano voice. I went to bed that night pondering that check, a strange but very timely birthday present from Massachusetts, and wondering where the next miracle might come from.

The next day, the telephone woke me as I was slumbering in the easy chair. It was Ray Smith, the attorney who was handling my appeal, having taken over from George Howard. I could hear the excitement in his voice.

"Something has happened in Judge Perry's courtroom that you should be real happy about, Abe. Spagnoli has just admitted that he committed perjury against you in your trials," Smith said. "I was in the federal building when all hell broke loose. I need to talk to you as soon as I can, so that we will be on the same page about this."

"Wait a minute," I said incredulously. "Are you saying Spagnoli admitted that he lied? When did that happen?"

"Just now. He was on the stand in Judge Perry's court in his own trial, and all of a sudden he told the court that he'd committed perjury in your trial. He accused Sikes of telling him to commit perjury. He had some document with him that he said Sikes gave him for the purpose of committing perjury in your case. I don't have all the details yet; it just happened an hour ago," Smith explained. "The press is outside the courtroom right now, and Judge Perry has called a recess. The reporters have already talked to me about Spagnoli's admission and are asking me to comment, but I don't have enough information about what was said on the record. The reporters are saying that Spagnoli outright admitted that he lied in your case."

"Man, that's really something." I couldn't believe what I was hearing. "So what do I do now?"

"I'm going back to the clerk of the court in a few minutes and order up an immediate copy of the transcript of the proceedings for today and a copy of the document that Spagnoli said that he got from the U.S. attorney's office. I want to see exactly what Spagnoli said to the court. In the meantime, I want to talk to you Friday. Don't discuss this case with anyone outside of your family."

"I know the press is going to be coming out here tomorrow," I said.

"Don't give any interviews to anyone, Abe. Don't say anything! Tell them to see me. Better still, don't answer the door if they come to your house. I have filed the notice of appeal already, and this case is officially out of Judge Perry's hands. I don't want you to say anything that will tilt the advantage away from you at this point." I promised to keep my mouth shut, and we agreed to meet at Smith's office that Friday.

When Barbara came home from work, I was near bursting with the news, and at first she was overflowing with joy.

"Does this mean that you're free now?" she asked.

"No, not yet. The case is filed in the Court of Appeals right now. I don't know how Smith is going to handle this. I think that we are going to have to go back to Judge Perry and ask for a new trial."

Barbara's smile quickly faded. "Judge Perry won't give you another trial. He did everything to get you convicted, and I doubt if he will free you no matter what Spagnoli or anybody else says."

I needed to remain optimistic, but I could hear the weary hopelessness in Barbara's voice every time we talked about the case. Judge Perry had unmanned George Howard and me during the trials, and I hated him for it, but at that moment I needed Barbara to remind me where things stood. I also had to think about the additional money that any new motions were going to require, money that we didn't have.

That night, we sat riveted by the news coverage, and thumbed through the local papers. We found an article in the *Chicago American* newspaper in which assistant U.S. attorney Robert J. Collins had been interviewed just after Spagnoli's bombshell admission.

"I can make no comment while the current trial is being held," Collins had told the reporter. He said that Spagnoli's statement would be evaluated, and if the perjury occurred as he had testified, there was a chance that the case against me would be dismissed. "I assure you that there will be a full investigation at its conclusion." Collins refused to comment on Spagnoli's assertion that Sikes had told him to lie. "Sikes, a government prosecutor in the case against Spagnoli and the others, was in court and heard the perjury admission. When questioned by the reporters outside of court, he repeatedly became indignant and repeatedly answered, 'No comment whatsoever' . . . Bolden's attorney, Raymond J. Smith, a former United States attorney who resigned to enter private practice, immediately asked for a transcript of the Spagnoli comments."

I flipped through the television dial, catching pieces of the story on other channels, but didn't learn anything more. I knew I should have felt massive, cathartic relief, but I was still apprehensive. I had been through enough that I couldn't believe this could end quickly or easily.

Ray Smith was the picture of confidence when I saw him at his office that Friday. He believed we could get the case thrown out of court, and told me he was preparing to go before the Seventh Circuit Court of Appeals with a petition to remand the case back to Judge Perry, with an order for a new trial.

"With the information that I have been able to get so far, I think that we have a good chance to get this case thrown out," Smith said. "Spagnoli said that Sikes told him what to say in your case and that a lot of it was perjury. I was able to get a copy of the exhibit from Spagnoli's trial." The paper that Smith handed me was an outline of the testimony that Spagnoli had given in both my trials.

JOINT EXHIBIT 36

"That's Sikes' handwriting on the left side and Spagnoli's on the right side," Smith told me.

"How did he get this?"

"He told the court that he took it."

"Took it? You mean that he said that he took this paper from the U.S. attorney's office without them knowing about it?" I recalled that I had tried to tell the Secret Service that Spagnoli could have pilfered the excerpt I was accused of selling from somewhere in our office when he was being interviewed by Agent Tom Strong after his arrest.

"Yep, he said he took it, right before Judge Perry." Smith gave me some pages of the unofficial transcript he had procured from the court reporter, and said I could read them in the office but couldn't take them with me. I made myself comfortable and started to read.

The transcripts told a remarkable story. It seemed that at the time he made his admissions, Spagnoli was under questioning by his own attorney, Frank Oliver, a savvy veteran of the Chicago courts who was known around the Secret Service office as a mob mouthpiece. Richard Sikes, now prosecuting Spagnoli instead of using him to prosecute me, had attacked Spagnoli's character and credibility by demonstrating that he had been untruthful when he testified in his own trial that he was supported by his mother, plus some part-time construction work. This matched Spagnoli's testimony in my trial almost exactly, but it no longer suited Sikes' purposes. Now he needed to show that Spagnoli's income came mainly from counterfeiting and gambling. This obviously contradicted Spagnoli's earlier testimony in my trials, which Sikes had not challenged at the time.

On redirect, Oliver asked Spagnoli if he had ever committed perjury in a federal criminal trial in the past, and Spagnoli acknowledged that he had. They then produced a piece of paper that had been torn out of a legal pad, and had it marked as an exhibit. Spagnoli testified that he had been in Sikes' office when Sikes drew up the document.

"What was the purpose that he gave you for writing up such a document?" Oliver asked.

"So I would remember what to say in the Bolden trial," Spagnoli answered.

The record showed that Sikes leaped to his feet and objected, but got nowhere. Judge Perry allowed Oliver to rebut the accusations about Spagnoli's credibility.

Oliver continued, "After he wrote it up, did he give it to you?"

"No."

At this point, Judge Perry interrupted and asked Spagnoli directly, "How did you come into possession of it, if he did not give it to you?"

"I took it."

"What was the purpose of your studying the document?" Oliver now asked.

"To remember the lies in there," Spagnoli answered bluntly.

Standing in front of the stunned onlookers in the courtroom, Oliver pointed at the document in his hand and kept probing. "Mr. Spagnoli, I call your attention to certain dates enumerated on this exhibit. I call your particular attention to the fourth line down, a date, Wednesday, May 13. Do you see the notation that follows that Wednesday, May 13, 'Call from Martineau'?" Did that call occur on that day?"

"No."

Just reading it made me shout out loud, "Dammit!" Finally, the facts that I knew to be true were coming to the surface.

When Oliver moved on and began asking if Spagnoli had ever given testimony contrary to the testimony he gave in this case that he gambled for a living, Richard Sikes strenuously objected on the grounds that Oliver was "impeaching his own witness."

At first Judge Perry sustained the objection, stating that he had no intention of trying another, previous case during Spagnoli's trial. He felt it was enough that Spagnoli had admitted giving false evidence, and did not want to go into any more specifics about it. Oliver sparred with Judge Perry as he tried different approaches, until finally getting him to reverse the ruling and allow the line of questioning.

Spagnoli testified that in preparation for my trial, the U.S. attorneys had told him not to admit that his main income came from gambling and to maintain that he was supported by his mother.

"And was that true or false?" Oliver demanded.

"That was false," said Spagnoli.

"And who suggested that you give such testimony?"

"Attorney Sikes."

"And did he say why he wanted you to so testify?" Oliver pressed.

"Because I would look good in the eyes of the jury."

Judge Perry interrupted Oliver's examination several times, trying unsuccessfully to derail Spagnoli's revelations. When Oliver was done, Judge Perry began to question the witness from the bench.

"Just wait a minute. I want to ask the witness: Did I understand you to say a while ago, when you had that document in front of you, that it was to enable you to remember lies?" Judge Perry asked.

"Yes, sir," said Spagnoli.

"Are you telling this court now that under oath you lied in the Bolden trial?"

"Yes, sir."

"You committed perjury then?"

"Yes, sir."

"In what respect did you commit perjury?"

Spagnoli testified that he had committed perjury "on dates and his employment." He added, "That's all I can remember right now."

On January 21, 1965, the special agent in charge of the Chicago Secret Service sent a memorandum to the chief of the Secret Service in Washington, D.C., confirming that on January 20, Spagnoli "stated that the testimony given by him in the Bolden trial had been perjured and that Spagnoli further states that he had given the perjured testimony relative to his émployment and income at the direction of assistant U.S. attorney Richard T. Sikes." The memorandum noted that Spagnoli's testimony resulted in television, radio, and newspaper publicity and that I had appeared on television stating that I would seek a retrial.

Ray Smith talked excitedly about how he felt sure the case would now be overturned. But Smith was new to this case, and he was white. I respected Smith but wondered if he knew how serious our disadvantage was. He had been a prosecutor himself and probably couldn't fathom how deeply corrupt the system was, at least in this case. I could see only gloom, although I chose not to share that with Smith. For instance, one thing that I hadn't seen anywhere in the transcript was any mention of the judge, the prosecutors, or anyone else threatening any legal ramifications for Spagnoli's self-confessed perjury. I saw the whole case through the eyes of a black defendant— my eyes—in a white judicial system where nothing was guaranteed and nothing was as it seemed. This was America in the early 1960s, the country where three Freedom Riders had been kidnapped and murdered in Mississippi and where four little black girls had been blown up in their church in Alabama. Racial tension boiled over in every corner of the country, much more so since the assassination of John Kennedy, which many black Americans felt was connected to his vehement stance against racism.

In the last week of January, Ray Smith called, sounding very upbeat.

"I just left the Court of Appeals," he said. "I filed a motion to have the case sent back to Judge Perry with an order of retrial."

"I hope we get the retrial," I said, "but whatever happens, I don't want to be retried before him again."

"We have to take one step at a time, Abe. First, we get the case remanded back to Judge Perry, and then we see what else we will have to do before the retrial." It occurred to me that the complicated rules and procedures of our legal system worked against the interest of justice as often as they helped carry it out.

As soon as I hung up with Smith, the phone rang again. Barbara answered and shouted from the other room that George Howard was on the line.

"Abe, I just hung up from talking to Spagnoli." Howard sounded excited. "He was pissed because he had just found out that the government dismissed your case against Frank Jones today. He told me that he and Jones got together and fixed up the case against you."

"What? He admitted that to you?"

"Yeah, and that's not all," Howard laughed. "He told me that he stole that excerpt out of the Secret Service office and that he was going to blow up the government case against you by revealing how he and Jones fixed it with the help of Sikes and the Secret Service. He said that he would name names."

"Did he say who in the Secret Service helped him fix up the case?"

"No. I told him to get in contact with your new attorney, Ray Smith. I tried to call Smith at his office before I called you, but he was out. In the meantime, I'm going to make out a sworn affidavit about my conversation with him and get it over to Smith as soon as possible, probably tomorrow."

"Man, this is really something."

"Abe, I know you have another appeal attorney on the case now, but I'm going to advise you as a friend and fraternity brother. If Spagnoli tries to talk to you, don't say anything to him without the presence of your attorney. This could get real nasty, and there is no telling how high up in the government this case will go when Spagnoli talks. So be very careful," Howard cautioned, "because you could wind up in the alley in back of your house with a bullet in your head. These people don't give a damn about you. You know what I'm talking about."

"Yeah. Thanks, George."

I hung up the phone and looked across the table at Barbara. "Spagnoli called George and admitted that he stole the file out of the Secret Service office," I said, tears gathering in my eyes. "He told George that he was going to name the people who helped him and Jones set me up."

"What are they going to do about it?" Barbara asked bitterly. "He already admitted that the day after your birthday last week, and they still haven't done anything to him about it."

I tried to reassure her, reminding her that these things take time, but it wasn't easy, since I had so little confidence myself anymore.

"I hope it ends soon," Barbara said, sounding more resigned than hopeful. "I hope it ends soon."

IN MID-FEBRUARY 1965, the Court of Appeals ordered the case back to Judge Perry but did not order a new trial. Ray Smith outlined his immediate strategy.

"I am going to file a motion for a new trial before Judge Perry, and he will probably set the case for hearing within the next two weeks or so. I talked to Howard, and he gave me his affidavit about the conversation that he had with Spagnoli. I'm going to include that in our motion for a new trial. I've already talked to Frank Oliver, and I'm going to make a certified copy of Exhibit 36 and have it ready for the hearing. Attorney James Ward is helping me with the appeal. You remember Ward, don't you?"

"I had a couple of forged-check cases with him when he was an assistant U.S. attorney," I answered.

"Well, he's assisting me at no cost to you. He doesn't like the way you are being treated and has volunteered to help us through the appeal. I'm optimistic, Abe. I think that we have a good chance of having a retrial of this case."

Smith rang off, saying he'd let me know as soon as he had a date for the hearing before Judge Perry.

ON A COOL, wet, wintry day in early March, I showed up at the new Dirksen Federal Building for the hearing. The featureless glass-and-steel high-rise now housed the federal courts in Chicago, having replaced the stately old granite courthouse with its ornate dome and massive pillars. I stepped into the elevator to go upstairs, and just before the doors closed, a young man darted in. I had been in law enforcement long enough to be able to spot another cop, even one in plainclothes. I figured this guy for either an FBI or Secret Service agent, and my instincts told me he was following me. That didn't surprise me. I had been hearing suspicious clicks and hums on my telephone line for months, but by that point I no longer cared. I knew I had nothing to hide.

Inside the courtroom, my attorneys, Smith and Ward, plus Richard Sikes for the government, took up their places in front of Judge Perry. Ray Smith opened the proceedings by advising the court that we were seeking a new trial based upon newly discovered evidence that had been obtained subsequent to the conviction. He said that in light of Spagnoli's admission that he committed perjury in a federal criminal trial "before Your Honor," a new trial was necessary to correct the unfairness of a trial that hinged on perjured testimony.

"Yes, but Spagnoli did not say that he lied about many of the facts that he testified to," Perry responded.

"Your Honor, if you will recall the proceeding, it was Your Honor who stopped Mr. Spagnoli from going into detail about the perjured testimony. I believe the record will show that this court ruled that no further inquiry could be made as to the extent of the perjury while Mr. Spagnoli was testifying at his own trial. If I can refer you to the rec—"

"I'm familiar with the facts, Counsel," Judge Perry interrupted. "I was there at both trials, and saw the witnesses and heard them testify."

Ray Smith argued that the court "should conduct a hearing in which Mr. Spagnoli and other witnesses can be subpoenaed and called to the stand and placed under oath once again." Smith spoke with the confidence of someone who believed in the obvious truth of his argument. "We need a hearing where this court can determine what the facts of this case really are."

"I will decide whether or not a hearing is necessary," Judge Perry replied a bit testily. "I know so much about this case. If a hearing is necessary, I will give him one."

James Ward rose at this point and got the judge's attention. "Your Honor, if there is a hearing to be held in this matter, which we hope there will be, there will need to be subpoenas issued for several witnesses. I wonder how we may arrange for that to be done so that prior to the hearing date, we may have arranged for our subpoenas."

"I'm going to docket this case for March 22, at 9:00 A.M.," declared Judge Perry. "I will only hear oral arguments that day. Then I will decide on that day if there is a hearing to be held. If there is a hearing to be held, we will fix it immediately."

"Your Honor," said Smith, "Attorney Sikes has filed an affidavit in opposition to this motion with the clerk of the court. Nowhere in his affidavit does he once deny the testimony of Mr. Spagnoli that Spagnoli committed perjury in the Bolden trial. The affidavit filed by Attorney Sikes states that during the two-week period between Bolden's first and second trials, Spagnoli was having trouble remembering the exact dates of occurrences in the Bolden trial. His affidavit says that Spagnoli could not relate the dates to the days of the week, specify times within those days, or describe what occurred at those times on those days and dates. I find it doubtful that Spagnoli could not remember anything about his testimony in such a short period of time, necessitating Attorney Sikes to draw up Exhibit 36, which Spagnoli testified that he stole from the U.S. attorney's office."

"Your Honor," Sikes interrupted, "Counsel is arguing the case now. I thought that Your Honor just ruled that this case would be argued on the 22nd of March if a hearing was necessary."

"Yes, that is correct," answered the judge. "We will recess this case now and will docket it for March 22. At that time, as I have said, if a hearing is necessary, I will hold a hearing."

As we left the courthouse, Smith tried to appear unfazed, but by the frown on his face I could see how annoyed he was. "I'll keep in touch with you, Abe. I was sure that Judge Perry would at least assure us of a hearing so that we can put Spagnoli under oath again and hear what he has to say."

I knew in my bones that we were wasting our time in front of Judge Perry, but I kept my mouth shut. He wasn't about to allow any evidence in open court that might support my innocence. Now we had to follow the rules and procedures, and sit there meekly and watch him steer my fate.

Three weeks later, on the 22nd, Judge Perry seemed all but indifferent to Smith's and Ward's oral arguments, nor did he care that Sikes made no effort of any kind to deny Spagnoli's charge that Sikes had told him to commit perjury. Sikes argued that Spagnoli had suffered a loss of memory sometime around July 29, 1964, in the period between my two trials, and that in order for Spagnoli to "refresh his memory," they had recovered his previous testimony from various sources and reduced it to a written document (Exhibit 36). At one point, it was brought up that when he testified in my trial, Spagnoli had vehemently denied that he had been made any promises in exchange for his testimony, but now Spagnoli was alleging that Sikes had indeed made him a promise before my trial.

Sikes responded to the challenge, claiming that all he'd told Spagnoli was that information about his cooperation "would be brought to the attention of the sentencing judge in his own case, should the time for sentencing ever arrive, and I further told him, and it appears in the record, that he was fortunate that the same judge that is hearing the Bolden case will be hearing his case."

In addition, Spagnoli had testified that he committed perjury when he testified that he called Martineau on May 13, and in his own trial, Spagnoli testified that Sikes was aware of the fact that he was committing perjury when he testified to the May 13 date. Nowhere in Sikes' affidavit did he once deny that he told Spagnoli to lie about any of that.

"Your Honor," said Smith, "Attorney Sikes has not denied any of the allegations of Joseph Spagnoli as outlined in defendant's motion for a new trial based upon newly discovered evidence. Under those circumstances, the defendant should be given a new trial where the perjured testimony can be challenged before a jury. The defendant has been denied a fair and impartial trial by statements made to the jury by Your Honor and by the many instances of perjured testimony contained in the record."

"I have heard all of the evidence that I need to hear," replied Judge Perry. "We will continue this motion until March 25, and then I will be prepared to enter a decision in this matter."

"This case is continued until March 25 at 10:00 A.M.," Judge Perry continued, obviously in no mood for further discussion. "I will only hear oral arguments that day. Then I will decide on that day if a hearing is to be held. If there is a hearing to be held, we will fix it immediately." The Honorable J. Sam Perry banged his gavel down hard.

Ray Smith had never seen anything like it. "Did you see that?" he asked as we left the court. "Sikes stood there and so much as admitted that he knew that Spagnoli lied in your trial. I thought surely that Judge Perry would grant our motion today, especially after the way Sikes acted in court."

"I don't think that we'll get anywhere with Judge Perry," I said disgustedly, stating what to me was obvious. "He's been against me all through the trials, and now that he sees the whole thing was a setup, he's not going to admit that he made a mistake about the case." I left my lawyer shaking his head in bewilderment, and headed home in a light rain, feeling that we had come so close but were still so far away.

IN THE FEW days before we were due back in court, my govern-ment retirement check came. Nearly all of the money was already earmarked for court costs and lawyers' fees. As it was, Ray Smith was making next to nothing on this case, and I wanted to be sure he got what was coming to him. Barbara was lucky to still have drafting work, but things were getting tighter, and I needed to find steady work. I felt like the world was closing in on me.

The courtroom was mostly full of lawyers on March 25. Ray Smith and Richard Sikes sat watching and waiting while other lawyers argued motions in other trials before the court. When our turn came, Smith approached the bench, apparently still under the impression that Judge Perry intended to listen to reasonable argu-ments in my case.

"Your Honor, prior to making a decision and the entry of a final order here, the defendant would request that since Your Honor was the judge in the D'Antonio case," the counterfeiting case in which Spagnoli was a defendant, "you take into consideration that portion of the transcript in the D'Antonio case that Mr. Sikes referred to the other day when he was talking about the time of the Spagnoli sen-tencing. He called to your attention exactly what was told to Spag-noli about his cooperation in the Bolden case."

But Judge Perry was done. He told Smith that he had taken into consideration every statement made by both attorneys and was about to enter a decision on the motion for a new trial by way of written opinion containing his findings of fact and conclusions of law.

"I am going to enter them here because I am convinced that Bolden had a fair trial," Judge Perry declared. "Bolden had two fair trials and there is no question about his guilt. There is no reason for another trial. With that in mind, the new findings of fact are now entered."

Ray Smith squeezed the sides of the lectern with his hands to calm himself. "Your Honor," he began cautiously, "so that we may be clear on this, in addition to denying the new trial, you are also denying the defendant a hearing in which evidence can be presented?"

"I am denying a hearing because it is unnecessary," Judge Perry answered sharply. "I know so much about the facts. Had one of the trials been before another judge, even there I would be able to examine the transcripts, but all three of the trials were before me, and I am very familiar with them in this instance."

"And are you denying a hearing in which we could call and subpoena witnesses, such as prosecutors?" Smith continued, shooting a glance in Sikes' direction.

"Absolutely," the judge shot back. "I am denying that because it is entirely unnecessary. It is just another roadblock as far as this court is concerned." There it was. Without one iota of testimony or offering of proof, Judge Perry ruled that Spagnoli's admission of perjury in a federal trial was nothing more than, in his words, "a plot by the witness Spagnoli to discredit the United States of America in the administration of justice."

It's hard to describe the rage I felt. A plot? Could anybody believe that Joseph Spagnoli would admit to committing perjury in a federal trial as part of a scheme to free me? And what about Richard Sikes, who never once contested Spagnoli's claims? He was in on it, too? He'd let the record stand that he met with Spagnoli at the Secret

Service office between my two trials, and that he told Spagnoli that the Service knew he was innocent of the counterfeiting charges, as Spagnoli claimed he had. Sikes would admit to criminal misconduct just so I could stay out of jail?

There was a plot, all right—a scheme to lock me away—and Judge Perry appeared to be in on it. Whether it was the Secret Service he was protecting or his own judicial conduct, he had no intention of overturning my conviction. At no point in his testimony did Joseph Spagnoli give a specific time or date for his meeting with Sikes. Yet the following statement appears in Perry's findings of fact:

> That this court expressly finds that on the date upon which Joseph Spagnoli stated that he met Assistant United States Attorney Sikes at the offices of the United States Secret Service and had been informed by Assistant Unites States Attorney Sikes that he was not guilty of the charges in the *D'Antonio* case, Assistant United States Attorney Sikes was on trial before the court in another case in Freeport, Illinois, Western Division of the Northern District of Illinois.

In one sentence, Judge Perry furnished an unsworn alibi for Sikes, and also acknowledged that a witness before him in a federal criminal trial had knowingly committed perjury, a crime for which neither Judge Perry nor anyone else made him answer. Judge Perry's findings of fact were more like his twists of fact. At one point, he wrote that "the witness Joseph Spagnoli did not recant the substance of his testimony with respect to his meetings and conversations with Frank Jones and the receipt of the information from the Secret Service file in the case of *United States v. D'Antonio et al.*" Of course he hadn't recanted: when Oliver had asked Spagnoli to give a full accounting of his perjury in my trial, so that he might "purge himself of any impropriety," Judge Perry had quickly shut down the testimony, forbidding Spagnoli from providing any substantive detail. "He [Spagnoli] says his evidence was false in another case," Judge Perry had ruled. "We are not going into what it was." Judge Perry even went so far as to claim that "I told Mr. Oliver not to go into that subject matter and he worked up a scheme to get it in by the back door on redirect, so as to let it appear that he himself was not in contempt of court."

Ray Smith was finally getting the picture. He had heard of Judge Perry's statements about my guilt in the first trial and about his locking us out of the courthouse while the jury deliberated in the second. Now he listened as Judge Perry manipulated the facts surrounding Spagnoli's admissions to prevent us from using them in support of my innocence.

"I can't see how the circuit Court of Appeals could do anything but reverse Judge Perry," a stunned Smith said as we left the federal building.

"We're really fighting Judge Perry now, aren't we?" I asked.

"How do you mean, Abe?"

"Well, I'm not a lawyer, but as I understand it, we now have to show that Judge Perry abused his discretion as a sitting judge, don't we?"

"Yeah, that's right. I think we can show that happened in many instances in your case," Smith answered.

"The judge has filed his findings of fact and conclusions of law, and unless they contain glaring indiscretions, aren't they almost impossible to overturn? These judges are members of the same legal organizations, visit each other's homes, and go to conferences, parties, and banquets with each other. When push comes to shove, they're going to stick up for one another," I said.

Smith seemed irritated by my questions and by my cynicism.

"Let me handle it," he said sharply. "I'll take care of it, and we will come out all right."

Again I found that I couldn't share my lawyer's confidence. The Seventh Circuit Court of Appeals had a reputation for being fairly tough, reversing very few of the cases sent to them for review. Smith had already filed portions of the appeal, and now the only thing we could do was wait until the time came for oral arguments. At least I could turn my attention to finding some work.

Chapter 15

BY OCTOBER 1965, when our case came before the United States Court of Appeals, Ray Smith had grown even more convinced that we would prevail. He and I had met several times since the hearing before Judge Perry, and he had mapped out his plan of action. When I arrived back in court at the federal building for oral arguments in the appeal, Ray Smith was already there, with James Ward again seated beside him. The government had sent a young lawyer named John Powers Crowley, who had shown himself to be skillful and successful in appeals courts. The Honorable Chief Judge John Hastings presided. Circuit Judges Winfred Knoch and Luther Swygert made up the rest of the panel. All were senior jurists, white men in late middle age. Earlier Ray Smith had told me that he hoped not to have to argue before either Hastings or Swygert, both conservative Republicans.

As the appellants, we opened the proceedings. Smith vigorously attacked both the credibility of Joseph Spagnoli and the prejudicial conduct of Judge Perry, arguing that denying me a new trial before a different judge after Judge Perry had told the jury his opinion about my guilt had violated my right to due process. But it was Smith's allegation that Richard Sikes had suborned perjury from Joseph Spagnoli that really got the judges' attention.

"I noticed that you raised the issue of government-solicited perjury in your brief," said Judge Hastings with apparent irritation. "Are you saying that you charge the government attorney with knowingly soliciting perjury in a federal criminal trial?"

"Your Honor, we raised this issue of Spagnoli's perjury in the arguments for a new trial in the court below. Attorney Sikes has filed affidavits denying some of the points that we have raised on appeal, but he has been mysteriously silent on this issue of assisting and aiding Spagnoli's perjury in the trial below," Smith responded.

Judge Swygert challenged Smith immediately. "Are you standing there and telling this panel that you believe that the government solicited perjury in a federal criminal trial?"

"I'm not telling this court what I believe or what I do not believe," answered Smith, holding his ground. "I am telling this court that the accusation was made under oath by Joseph Spagnoli, and the assertion is a matter of record in the *D'Antonio* trial below. I am further advising this honorable court that Attorney Sikes has been given the opportunity on at least two occasions to answer to the accusation, but he has failed to do so. There is no denial of the assertion by Joseph Spagnoli anywhere in the record, and to this day, the accusation remains unanswered by anyone in the government prosecutor's office. We feel—"

"These are very serious charges," interrupted Chief Judge Hastings. "These charges could land someone in prison, and I am going to get to the bottom of this now. We are going to suspend these arguments in this case at this time, and we will summon Attorney Sikes before this court. Attorney Crowley, you will let the U.S. attorney know that Attorney Sikes must appear before this court immediately, so that we may clear up this matter once and for all." Crowley rose and quickly left the room. A few short minutes later, he returned with Richard Sikes and Edward Hanrahan, all out of breath from having rushed to the courtroom.

Judge Hastings summoned Sikes to the podium. "Attorney Sikes, we are hearing arguments in *United States vs. Abraham Bolden*. I am sure you are familiar with the details of that case, are you not?"

"Yes, I am, Your Honor." Sikes seemed to lack his usual bravado.

"Well, it has been brought to this court's attention, during the oral arguments of the case, that one of the witnesses against the defendant has accused you of soliciting perjured testimony that was given in the trial. I called you here so that you may personally answer the accusation. The counsel for this defendant has stated in his brief, and during oral argument, that you have failed to answer this serious question that reflects negatively on the United States government." Hastings dramatically emphasized this last piece. "Now I ask you, did you solicit perjured testimony by one witness, Joseph Spagnoli, in any of the Bolden trials in the court below?"

Sikes shifted his weight from one foot to another nervously. "Your Honor, I want to say—"

"That question can be answered yes or no," Hastings interrupted. "Either you did or you did not. This question needs to be answered now so that this court can make a fair ruling concerning this issue on appeal. I ask the question again: did you solicit perjured testimony by Joseph Spagnoli in any of the Bolden trials before the court of District Judge J. Sam Perry?"

Sikes swallowed hard. He glanced over his shoulder at his colleagues Crowley and Hanrahan.

"Your Honor," he finally answered, "I refuse to answer that question on the grounds that my answer might tend to incriminate me."

"You are refusing to answer on the grounds of self-incrimination?" the chief judge asked in a loud voice.

"Yes, sir, Your Honor," said Sikes, lowering his eyes.

"Very well, then. We will look into this matter, and depending on what this court finds, someone might go to prison. We are going to get to the bottom of this," Hastings declared to the shocked spectators in the courtroom. He turned to Attorney Smith and asked, "Based upon the allegations of Joseph Spagnoli, do you think that the assistant government attorney should be prosecuted and incarcerated?"

Smith was taken aback by the question. "Your Honor, such a decision is for this court—"

"I'm asking you what you think we should do in this case," shot back Hastings. "I'm asking you as an officer of the court and a member of the bar."

"Your Honor, I have no recommendations as to the actions that this honorable court should exercise. This court is well aware of the seriousness of the allegations made under oath by witness Spagnoli. My client has been unlawfully convicted of a crime in the court below and the government attorney has refused to answer the allegations made by the witness. At the least, this case should be referred back to the court below for a retrial of the issues."

"So you have no opinion as to the course that we should take as to the government attorney?"

"No, sir."

"Very well. We will proceed with the argument of this case."

Crowley took over the podium and impressively presented the government's arguments, never once mentioning the issue of Spagnoli's perjury. He closed by declaring that I had received a fair trial in every instance before Judge Perry, and asking the appeals court to affirm my conviction.

On the way out of the courtroom, the many attorneys in attendance came up to us, all of them excited about our apparent triumph. For a federal prosecutor to take the Fifth in such circumstances was unprecedented.

"You guys got it made," one lawyer said. "Your case is as good as reversed. I can't see how the court could do anything else with what I've just seen happen in there."

Another attorney clapped Ray Smith on the shoulder and said, "I sure wish that my case was as sure a reversal as your client's case is. You can start preparing for a new trial."

Just then, a loud voice cut through the din in the corridor outside the courtroom. "Attorney Smith."

I looked up to see U.S. attorney Edward Hanrahan walking hurriedly toward us. He and Smith moved a bit off to the side for a private—and, from the look of it, none too friendly—chat. Hanrahan, with a scowl on his face, seemed to be lecturing Smith, shaking a finger in Smith's face as he spoke. When Hanrahan was done talking with Smith, he stalked off, and Smith walked slowly back toward me, frowning.

"That son of a gun just threatened me," he said under his breath. "He actually threatened me. I've never had anything like that happen to me before."

Ray Smith had just had his baptism in my case. For me, I once again found myself with nothing to do but wait for the appeals panel to hand down their decision.

It had been somewhat comforting to hear the encouraging reactions of all those seasoned courthouse veterans after the oral arguments for the appeal, but even at the time, I saw Sikes' refusal to answer the court as both good news and bad news for me. The good news was that it made clear to the court that Spagnoli's accusations had some kind of merit and were more than just some scheme to get me off the hook. The bad news was that now my going free, or even getting a new trial, would be tied to some kind of official reprimand of Sikes for assisting perjury in a federal criminal trial. If it ruled in my favor, the court would have to voice its official condemnation of Sikes; any such finding would trigger investigations by the bar association or judicial oversight committee and would surely end the career of a budding young white lawyer in the Justice Department. In the early winter of 1965, I couldn't see those three conservative white justices ruining the career of a promising young lawyer by overturning the conviction on a charge of judicial misconduct.

A week before Christmas, Attorney Smith called. His grim tone of voice immediately told me everything I needed to know.

"I just got word from the Court of Appeals that they affirmed your conviction."

"You've got to be kidding," I blurted out, even though I knew he wasn't.

"I don't see how they could have confirmed your conviction in spite of Attorney Sikes taking the Fifth Amendment during the argument, but they did. They didn't even comment on some of the constitutional issues that we raised."

Smith had been one of those who assumed a reversal by the Court of Appeals was inevitable. "I'm going to ask that the full panel of nine judges hear this appeal," he asserted. Smith was ready to keep fighting, and Barbara, as she later told me, was prepared to fight it all the way to the Supreme Court if necessary. "I'll start preparing the petition for a hearing en banc. In the meantime, I'll run off a copy of the decision by the court and give it to you when you come to my office." We agreed to get together just after the holidays. A few days into January 1966, I went down to Smith's office to read the decision.

I was not naive, and I understood that reasonable people can differ in their interpretations. I also realized that the law is not absolute—that in the end, the laws as written will mean whatever judges say they mean, or whatever a clever lawyer can convince a jury they mean. In this situation, we didn't need the appeals court to dismiss all the charges or completely exonerate me. We only needed them to say that there were enough irregularities in my trials, or that sufficient new evidence had surfaced, to put the fairness of the verdicts in doubt, and thus warrant a new trial, with an impartial judge, where all the evidence could be heard in open court.

The appeals court opinion brilliantly danced around all the substantive issues and all the constitutional questions Smith had raised in his brief and in his oral argument. Maybe we were just deluding ourselves and no improprieties had ever occurred. Maybe the appeals court just didn't feel the two trials had been unfair enough to waste time and money on a third trial. Maybe the judges just couldn't believe that some of their own had done anything so obviously corrupt. Whatever the reason, the court chose to leave matters as they stood.

Most glaring was the omission of any mention of Sikes having taken the Fifth during oral arguments and refusing to ever answer Spagnoli's charges directly. Referring to Spagnoli's charge that Sikes had told him to lie about his source of income in my trial, so that he might "look good before the jury," the Court of Appeals wrote that "Spagnoli's livelihood was clearly a collateral matter bearing upon his credibility. His credibility, in turn, had been adequately put before the jury. We do not believe that the jury's overall appraisal of this witness would have been substantially affected by the knowledge that he was being 'less than forthright' concerning his source of income."

As for Spagnoli's admission that he had perjured himself at the request of the government with respect to Martineau, the court found that "the record amply supports the district judge's finding that the conflicting evidence with reference to the specific date of that contact was thoroughly explored at the *Bolden* trial."

They found that neither Judge Perry's statement to the first jury that he believed the evidence sustained a verdict of guilty, nor the refusal to grant a change of judge after that statement showed that the judge had a "personal bias." Citing a prior ruling, the appeals court wrote, "Trial Judges are invariably called upon to conduct impartial trials despite whatever opinion they may have. We cannot see how the exercise of that discretion in one trial, without more, could necessarily result in prejudice against an accused in a second trial."

Further, the appeals panel found that "prior to the second trial, defense counsel moved for a substitution of judges on the grounds of prejudice. The motion was denied. The defendant says that the motion should have been granted, that since the judge had expressed an opinion of guilt, an impartial trial before the same judge was impossible. The defendant, significantly, cites no authority for his proposition. Nor do we find any merit in it." Our appeal rested not on whether Judge Perry had a personal bias against me but on whether, having formed an opinion and issued a judicial finding as to my guilt to the sitting jury, he should have removed himself from hearing the second trial. The appeals court did not address this question, failing to deal with the constitutional issues. The appeals panel noted that the trial judge "clearly informed the jury that his opinion could be entirely disregarded." However, Judge Perry referred to his own opinion as a "finding," and a judge's finding is a judicial conclusion that a jury cannot disregard. Moreover, there is no way that a typed transcript could capture the cold, hostile tone of the judge's courtroom statements. No one who heard the judge that day could have doubted that Judge Perry wanted me found guilty.

I thought back to that day in front of the three judges hearing our appeal. I could see Richard Sikes nervously swallowing and stammering and weaseling out of answering any direct questions regarding his suborning perjury. I wondered how different things would have been if he had been a rising young black attorney and I had been a white government agent with a spotless record. The black attorney certainly never would practice law again, even if he was lucky enough to stay out of jail. At that point in my case, a third trial almost certainly would have ended in an acquittal. And for that to happen, the jury and the court would need to believe the government played a role in setting me up. That would have brought the Secret Service under scrutiny again, and lend credence to all the allegations I had been making for years regarding the dereliction and misconduct of the agents surrounding John Kennedy in Dallas. There was no doubt in my mind about what was at stake. My conviction had to stand undisturbed in order to silence the echo from Dealey Plaza. I knew this in my heart, but I couldn't give up the fight.

Ray Smith filed his motion for review by the full panel of appellate court judges in February 1966. Edward Hanrahan personally wrote the government's brief in opposition to our request. His argument rested, in part, on Smith's hesitancy to recommend legal action against Sikes during the oral argument.

"The government," Hanrahan wrote, "does feel that comment is imperative regarding defendant's reiterated contention that assistant United States attorney Richard T. Sikes suborned perjury in order to secure defendant's conviction. When that scurrilous accusation was suggested in oral argument before the original panel, defendant's counsel was asked no less than three times whether Mr. Sikes should be prosecuted and incarcerated as a consequence of defendant's gratuitously assumed but unsubstantiated charge. Significantly, defendant's counsel never answered those questions unequivocally. Rather, he persisted in evading the responsive answer that both respect for his duty as an officer of this court and concern for the integrity of the bar would require. Moreover, defendant's assertion is contrary to fact and completely rebutted by the credible evidence as determined by the trial court's findings of fact. Therefore, defendant's allegation is not only a factual issue improperly reargued in this petition, but also is reprehensible conduct utterly incongruous with practice before any court and merits judicial sanction."

Richard T. Sikes was, naturally, one of the signatories on the brief. It wasn't long before we received notification that the motion for a rehearing before the full court had been denied.

When Ray Smith called, angry and dejected, to tell me of the court's decision, we went over my options. I really only had two left: either I had to appeal the decision to the Supreme Court or I had to surrender to the U.S. marshals' office and begin serving the six-year sentence handed down by Judge Perry. If I chose to continue the appeal, we only had a week in which to file for a writ of certiorari from the Supreme Court. Ray explained that the next level of appeal would mean another $5,000 or so in fees, primarily for the printing of briefs, since most of the research had already been done.

By that time, I had landed a position managing the midnight shift at the Ingersoll Products factory. As it happened, the job was going well for me, and I had the impression that the company had plans for my future. Barbara, too, had improved her situation with a better-paying position at the Nabisco Company. But my beautiful and determined young wife did not need the security of some additional income to know what course of action to take. Without even blinking an eye, she insisted I go ahead and appeal to the Supreme Court.

I phoned Ray Smith and told him to go ahead and file the papers. And once again, we got on with the business of waiting.

On June 28, 1966, a bright summer day in Chicago, we learned that the U.S. Supreme Court had denied our application for a writ of certiorari and would not hear the case. Smith said that Justice William O. Douglas had written a brief statement saying the court should hear the case because there were substantial violations of my constitutional rights that needed review. Smith told me that he was preparing an emergency motion to present to Justice Douglas, asking the Court to rehear our petition in light of his statement.

At 2:30 P.M. the next afternoon, my doorbell rang. I opened the front door to find two U.S. marshals.

"Mr. Bolden," said Marshal Lowe, a man I knew a little through our law-enforcement work, "we are here to carry out the mandate of the United States Court of Appeals. Your appeal to the U.S. Supreme Court has been denied and Judge Perry has ordered your immediate incarceration."

I had no idea what was going on. "I need to call my attorney. I talked to him yesterday, and he said that we were going to ask the Supreme Court to reconsider. That's what my attorney told me yesterday."

"You can call him if you want to," Lowe said, "but that's not going to change anything. Judge Perry has ordered that you be locked up today before 4:00 P.M."

When I got Smith on the phone, he was just as shocked as I was. "Normally, they give you a few weeks before the mandate is enforced. Judges usually give defendants a few weeks to clear up their business before sending them off to prison."

"Well, they're here right now to take me to jail. What should I do?"

"You'll have to go with them, Abe, if they have a copy of the court's order. You don't have any choice other than to go. They'll probably house you in a safe place like the Wheaton County jail. You have to be brought to court before Judge Perry tomorrow before they send you to a federal penitentiary. That's usually the procedure. I'll meet you in court tomorrow," Smith added sorrowfully.

I hung up and immediately called Barbara, who raced home from work, arriving just in time to embrace me before Lowe's patience ran out.

"Okay, let's go," he said as he reached under his coat for his handcuffs.

"Where are you taking him?" Barbara asked.

"He'll be in the Cook County jail. Keep in contact with your attorney. He should know where your husband is at all times."

I turned to Marshal Lowe. "Are you going to handcuff me in front of my wife and children? I've worked with you in the past. You know I'm not going to try to run now or resist. What sense would that make now?"

"I have to follow regulations," Lowe said as he secured the cuffs around my wrists. He led me outside, down the steps of our house, and along the walkway past two rows of green hedges. As we got into the waiting car, I looked back at my home and at my wife and thought of the steel box, the woman, and the three little children of my dream.

At the county jail, Lowe led me through heavy steel doors and through rows of holding cells with prisoners behind floor-to-ceiling steel bars. I went through processing and was led into a large, filthy cell with about twenty men. The cell reeked of vomit and human waste, some of which was caked on the floor amid the scattered trash and cigarette butts, and some of which was from the single overflowing toilet. A few of the men in the cell seemed to be drunks, tossed into jail to "sleep it off."

After a few hours, a deputy called me out and escorted me upstairs to a smaller, cleaner cell with about six men. This one had metal cots lining the wall and an area where the detainees could take supervised showers. As I sat down at one of the metal tables bolted to the floor, a voice at my side startled me.

"You're Bolden, aren't you?"

I stared into the face of the young blond white man at my side and searched my memory. Had I arrested this guy? Or someone close to him? Could he have some beef with me?

"Yeah, I'm Bolden. Why?"

He must have heard the apprehension in my voice or seen it in my eyes. "It's okay, man," he said. "Nobody's going to try to hurt you in here. Everybody in here heard about you over the TV in the dayroom. Arthur Rachael is the cell block barn boss around here. You know Arthur Rachael, don't you?" The young man lit a cigarette and offered me one. Although I hadn't smoked in months, I gratefully took the smoke and lit it up.

"Yeah, I remember Art."

"He's locked up in a cell in the next unit, but by him being barn boss, he gets to do a lot of things around here. I talk to him a lot when we walk in the dayroom during the day," he explained. "Art told me something about your case when we were talking about you, and what a stupid move that guy Spagnoli made by going up against you with the feds."

"What did he say?" I asked. "I doubt Art would be trying to help me. I don't know him that well. I just saw him the day he was busted."

"Art said the judge in your case got to your jury the night they found you guilty. Spagnoli was a personal friend of one of the guys that was serving on your jury. Spagnoli and this juror on your trial pulled off a burglary together, but nobody said anything so that this guy could stay on your jury. This guy called Spagnoli the night before they started voting and asked him how Spagnoli wanted him to vote." The young man had quite a story to tell.

"What was the juror's name?"

"I don't know," the young man answered. "And that's not all that happened. Rachael told me that while your jury was in the jury room, the deputy marshal went into the room and had conversations with the jurors about the verdict in your case."

"Do you think that Rachael would talk to my lawyer?" I didn't really expect this man to be able to speak for Rachael, but wondered if he might reveal something about what Rachael was like—whether he was approachable or not.

"I doubt it, man," he answered. "Rachael's not going to do that. He's sitting on fifteen years now for passing those phony bonds, and that's a lot of time if he doesn't win his appeal. Call your lawyer—maybe he could find out who the juror was that knew this guy Spagnoli."

Sitting awake that night after lights-out, I thought about the irony of finding sympathetic ears in prison after spending so many years in law enforcement, especially now, when it seemed like people I didn't even know on the outside were out to get me. I went over what I knew. Both Rachael and Spagnoli were small-time thugs, but they were ambitious. Agent John Russell had been developing information received from the Organized Crime Division of the Chicago police that connected both men to a low-level Mafia affiliate named Vito Zaccagnini, who was caught cashing the nearly perfect $100 counterfeit bonds, and who in turn had ties to Sam DeStefano. The way we understood things, DeStefano was allegedly a territory boss for the well-known mobster Sam Giancana. After President John Kennedy was assassinated, Giancana was mentioned by several conspiracy investigators as having some part in an attempt by the U.S. government to assassinate Fidel Castro, president of Cuba. The near-perfect quality of the counterfeit bonds that had been cashed suggested to the Secret Service that organized crime had a hand in the counterfeiting operation.

In the morning, a guard came to summon me. I was due in court. Before long I was shackled and seated on a bus with other prisoners, most of whom were taken to central police headquarters in Chicago. The bus took me and one other prisoner to the Dirksen Federal Building, where the guards unshackled me and led me inside to yet another holding room. I heard a familiar voice arguing a point of law on the other side of the door, and realized I was outside Judge Perry's courtroom.

A deputy swung the door open. "Let's go, Bolden."

Inside, I saw Ray Smith standing next to the defendant's table in front of Judge Perry's bench. I looked into the spectator's gallery and quickly found Barbara's sad eyes staring at me. We nodded to each other.

Smith began an impassioned oration on my behalf, citing my outstanding record as a government agent, describing the tainted evidence and admitted perjuries in my trials, and even invoking the name of Justice Douglas and his brief in support of my appeal.

Judge Perry was only too happy to remind Smith that George

Howard's affidavit stating that Spagnoli and Jones had fixed up the case against me carried no weight at all. "I just want you to know that you can just forget what Mr. Howard said in this case. I don't give any consideration to that affidavit," Judge Perry said. "Probation? I will deny it. I have denied it, and I will," he added when Smith raised that subject.

Smith kept at it, though, insisting that my conviction was the result of perjured testimony, but Judge Perry remained adamant, insisting that I would serve the sentence he had handed down. Smith persisted, speaking about my hard work and steady performance at Ingersoll, which had sent one of its people to speak on my behalf, which Judge Perry did not allow; however, Smith was successful in receiving permission from the judge to read a letter from Dazil Lucas, executive president of Ingersoll. The letter stated that it was "our intention to appoint him as a permanent supervisor" and that "Mr. Bolden had distinguished himself in a position of union leadership and safety committeeman." The judge appeared to grow irritated as Smith pressed the argument.

"That is sufficient. No, I don't need anything more. That is the very purpose of all these trials, and I am not going to try it all over. Motion denied." Judge Perry was adamant.

Defeat showed itself on Ray Smith's face, and he changed tack, stating that the news had reported that I was being held in the Cook County jail, which housed many people whom I had arrested and who might wish to do me harm. He pleaded that I be moved to a different county jail, where my safety would not be jeopardized, until I was transported to federal prison. Again, Judge Perry refused the request, arguing that the matter was outside his jurisdiction.

Judge Perry was done, and brought the hearing to a close. I saw Barbara quietly confer with Ray Smith, who then turned to talk to one of the deputy marshals. The deputy led me down the corridor to the elevator, which we took to a small, clean holding cell, oddly situated behind a row of offices on one of the upper floors. The cell stood in a larger holding area, into which the guard brought Barbara. He left the two of us alone, separated only by the cold steel bars.

I reached through the bars to take her hand. In that instant I felt finally overwhelmed by the terrible sadness of my fate. My whole body shook with rage and tears.

Barbara looked me in the eye. "If we're going to make it through this, you're going to have to be strong. You don't have to worry about me and the children. I'm not going to let this break up our family. I saw what happened in court and how they treated you. I'll be here when you come home. You don't have to worry about that." Barbara's words were both consoling and reassuring. "You have to be strong because we are all counting on you to come back home to us. Nothing is going to happen out here, and I'm going to work and keep things together."

Barbara came close and we kissed through the bars. "No matter what happens, be strong," she said again. "I love you, and the children love you. We will be waiting for you to return home to us. Be strong."

When the guard finally led Barbara away, I washed my face and resolved to do exactly as Barbara said. From earliest childhood I had been told that grown men don't cry, and I decided then that I was finished with crying—in fact, I would be as strong as any man could be.

When they brought me back to the county jail, one of guards took me down to a basement cell block. Four cells sat separated and secluded from the rest.

"This is what they call 'Death Row,'" the guard told me. "Someone decided to keep you down here until you're shipped out to a penitentiary." He handed me over to the kindly-looking black guard who stood watch there, saying, "This is Abraham Bolden. He used to be a government FBI man."

"Yeah, I recognized him," the older guard said. The guard reminded me of my grandfather. They were about the same age, with the same small physique and medium-dark complexion, and even the same eyeglasses with clear plastic frames.

"Has anyone been threatening you upstairs?" he asked once he locked the door of my cell.

"Not really."

"Well, you watch yourself. Some of these men are real animals and will do anything to anybody." The guard asked if I had eaten dinner, and arranged to have some food sent down. He sat at his desk and swiveled his television set around so that I could see it. I watched a news report about my hearing, about Judge Perry denying probation as well as the motion to move me to a safer location. The station ran an editorial deriding the government and the Secret Service for their "harsh treatment of Agent Bolden."

Not that it could do me any good anymore. It grew late, and they dimmed the lights around me. I lay down on the small metal bunk and tried to sleep. Death Row was a very, very quiet place.

Chapter 16

Deputy Marshal Lowe and his partner arrived at my cell the next morning. The two men put me into a vehicle and we began making our way through the city.

"Where are we going?" I asked Lowe.

"We're taking you to Terre Haute prison this morning."

I turned to the other deputy. "I don't think I ever met you. I appreciate you telling my wife how to stay in touch with me when you came for me on Wednesday."

"I saw you around the building many times and heard a lot about you before I actually went to your house," the man said, not unkindly. "I'm Lowe's partner. Lowe and I work together quite a bit."

"I sure hate to meet you like this," I said, looking down at the cuffs on my writsts.

"Oh, you're going to do all right, Bolden," he answered. "Terre Haute is a good prison, and they'll probably send you to the farm camp down there. Just try to stay out of trouble while you're doing your sentence and everything will turn out all right for you."

Lowe drove past the exit ramp I always took to my house, and eventually steered us out of the city. I realized that, but for my wife and children, I felt no great sadness about leaving Chicago behind. Things hadn't worked out so well for me there, but the truth was that I'd never felt comfortable in the big city. I'd come from a small town in Illinois and gone to college in another small town in

Missouri. The gentler rhythms of those places and the brotherly warmth I'd felt among the people there were a part of me. I never got used to the daily indignities of urban life, the jostling and pushing, the loudness and the rudeness. I'd put in for transfers to other places, and even applied for managerial jobs in corporations outside the city, without any success. Part of me regretted leaving Peoria, where I'd had a good job with the state police and a nice life, but I was like a lot of other young and ambitious black men back then: when the opportunity to move up the ladder presented itself, I couldn't pass it up. I'd thought that being an agent would help me get to the top of my profession, but the steel handcuffs around my wrists told a different story.

We drove south for about an hour before Lowe pulled off the highway to stop for coffee and to use the bathroom. Lowe's partner went into the café while Lowe waited with me in the car.

"We're about halfway there now," Lowe said.

"I gotta take a leak, too," I said, "but it's hard for me to do anything with these cuffs on."

"I know how you feel, Abe, but you were a policeman for many years and you know the regulations. Whenever a prisoner is in transport, we are supposed to keep him cuffed. You know that."

"Yeah, I know the regulations. You know that I'm not going to try to escape or try to do anything stupid. The government knows everything about me. I wouldn't put your job in jeopardy by trying to run."

Lowe looked up and saw his partner coming out of the café, so he got out of the car and spoke briefly to him. When they walked back to the car, Lowe opened the door next to me.

"Hold out your hands."

As Marshal Lowe unlocked my handcuffs, he said, "Okay, we're going to trust you and take these things off you, but when we get near to Terre Haute, I'm going to have to put them back on. We're doing this as a favor to you, so don't mess up now."

I went inside and went straight toward the washroom. To my complete surprise, Marshal Lowe did not follow me, but simply sat down on a stool at the counter. The toilet stall in the washroom had a window, of course, one that opened very easily, and out of which I could see little else but rows and rows of corn. I stood on the toilet and stared out that window for one long moment, climbing down just as Lowe walked in.

"Finish up, Bolden."

Back in the car, I savored the coffee and sweet roll the two marshals had gotten for me. With the cuffs off, it seemed to me like the sun shone a little brighter and the air tasted a little fresher. I nursed this last taste of freedom as long as I could.

The first sight of the long double fence topped with glistening coils of razor wire snapped me back to cold reality. We had left the highway and driven on a series of smaller country roads before arriving at the massive complex of dark brown prison buildings. The car slowed as we approached, giving me time to take in the iron bars covering every window in sight and the forbidding watchtowers looming over the grounds.

Marshal Lowe announced himself, and we were admitted to the prison. As they helped me out of the car and walked me through those heavy doors, I could see that these were no longer the cold, businesslike officers who had knocked on the door of my house a few days earlier. There was genuine sorrow on their faces as they removed my handcuffs and prepared to turn me over to the prison guards.

"Well, this is it, Abe," said Lowe quietly. Even as he was gathering up his papers and preparing to leave, the guards began the admitting process, ordering me first to strip naked.

"I hope that you come through this all right," said Lowe, turning to leave.

"Bend over and spread your cheeks," said the intake officer.

So began prison life, with the introductory humiliation of a strip search. Next, I was fingerprinted, deloused, decontaminated, and showered before I could dress again, now in a standard-issue, one-piece white jumpsuit and cloth slippers. Finally, they hung a prisoner number, 23663, around my neck and took my photograph. I was officially a prisoner in the federal system.

I scanned the faces of the trusties and other prisoners who passed by during processing, and was surprised that I recognized a few from past investigations. I even saw the face of someone I'd seen in a mug shot and had been tracking for a long time before my arrest. Well, at least now I knew why we hadn't been able to find him in Chicago.

Guards escorted me out of intake and processing and through a maze of iron walkways and stairs to a row of cells marked "Admitting and Orientation." The lead guard signaled with his hand, and the heavy barred steel door to one of the cells rolled open. I read the number 49 in large black letters on the wall above the cell door, consciously trying to remember everything about this moment.

"Bolden, in."

I stepped into the cell: a bunk bed bolted to the wall, a small metal storage locker, a stainless steel washbasin and toilet, and a small metal desk with an attached seat that swung out from underneath. Through the bars of the door I saw a large open area with rows of moveable chairs in front of a television bolted to the wall, a Ping-Pong table, and some card tables. The ceilings were high, perhaps twenty-five feet; about five feet below the ceiling, light came in through barred windows.

You hear people talk about the walls closing in on them. Before spending just a few hours in that cell, I had thought it was just a handy expression. But that day I felt as if the size of the cell was actually decreasing. I fought back a sense of dread and claustrophobia, knowing that what I was feeling was exaggerated by exhaustion and anxiety. I lay down, listening to the sounds that in time I would even stop noticing: the muffled conversations and laughter of the guards and inmates, the harsh clanging of the metal doors, the monotonous hum of the monstrous overhead fans, and the jangling keys of the guards as they made their rounds of the cell blocks.

The impulse to scream out, to pound my fists against the steel cage, rose inside me, but eventually it passed. With my eyes tightly closed and my arms folded against my chest, I recited verse after verse of scripture, as I had learned to do as a child in East St. Louis, until finally I fell asleep.

THAT FIRST NIGHT became the first full day, and then the weekend—the Fourth of July weekend actually, and the lowest point of my life up to then. I tried to observe and learn the ways and rhythms of prison life. I marched in line with other prisoners to meals in the enormous cafeteria, where I kept my head down. I passed time in the dayroom, reading old magazines or in my cell, listening to country music on the little radio with no tuning or volume knobs that was embedded in the wall. I wrote my first letter home to Barbara and another to Judge Perry asking him to reconsider my motions for a new trial or a reduced sentence. I rolled cigarettes with the loose tobacco and papers the guard had given me, and tried to figure out how to light them, since new inmates were not allowed to have matches. I watched the guards, most of whom appeared to be Southerners of limited education, and tried to remember which ones wore the small tattoo of a flaming cross between their thumb and forefinger that signified membership in the Knights of the Ku Klux Klan.

For the most part, the new prisoners in the A&O unit hadn't been outside for days or weeks. We had no yard privileges until we appeared before the classification committee and received permanent cell and job assignments. Still, rumors spread through the cell block that because of the holiday and long weekend, the warden would allow us all some fresh air. Just after lunch on July 4, the unit guard called "Yard!" over the PA system, sending us all running to line up at the door.

The yard was slightly larger than a football field and surrounded by high fences and razor wire. Metal bleachers overlooked a softball field, a running track, and a weight-lifting and body-building area, where some men had stripped to the waist and were working out. Like me, most of the men seemed happy just to sit or stand in the warm sun and breathe the clean summer air. I had found a quiet spot off the side of the bleachers when I heard a voice calling my name.

"Hey, Abe! Hey, Abe, it's me, man. How are you doing?"

I studied the pudgy, round face of the white inmate walking toward me. I knew I had seen him before, but I couldn't match the face with a name.

"Hey, man, it's me, Lonnie. We worked together at Ingersoll. Don't you remember me?"

"Lonnie? Lonnie Bram?" I was surprised.

"Yeah, man. I heard that you were here but I didn't think that I would run into you."

Lonnie had changed a lot since I had last seen him at Ingersoll. The well-muscled and energetic young man I remembered had put on weight and gone to flab. Lonnie and I had worked closely together to unionize Ingersoll, and he had even appointed me as a member of the negotiating team when it came time to hammer out a contract. Lonnie had disappeared without warning, and rumor had him working for the union headquarters now. Now I could see that something worse may have caused his departure.

Lonnie and I talked about our time at Ingersoll. "Man, they were going to make you a big boss if you had stayed there," he said. "They really liked you, especially the vice president. He told me that he wanted to talk you into becoming a supervisor."

As I listened to Lonnie's bittersweet memories, I looked up and noticed three men walking toward us. I recognized the man in the middle: Joseph Spagnoli. One of the larger men flanking him, named

Roy, had been convicted with Spagnoli in the counterfeit bond case. They sat down on the bleachers about thirty feet from us. Spagnoli still wore the same cocky smirk on his face that I remembered from the trial.

"Do you know who that guy is sitting in the center of those two inmates?" I asked Lonnie.

"Yeah, I know him. That's Joseph Spagnoli, the guy that testified against you for the feds. Everybody here knows he's a stool pigeon, and nobody trusts him. He's on the plumbing detail."

I could feel Spagnoli's eyes on me, but whenever I turned to look at him, he dropped his gaze to the ground. I could sense that he was afraid, even as he maintained that tough-guy façade, but I resisted the urge to go over and start grilling him. Spagnoli was totally untrustworthy, and there would have been no way to believe anything he told me. Besides, he might have mistaken my intent if I approached, believing I wanted to hurt him. It was best for both of us if I just kept my distance.

Lonnie said he was going to walk around a little before we had to go back inside, and asked me to join him. "I'm not afraid to be seen walking with you," he said, making me wonder if others were afraid. I took a pass on the walk and climbed down the bleachers, walking right past Spagnoli. Not a word was exchanged between us.

Over the few days that followed, prison officials put me through a number of interviews and gave me thorough medical and dental examinations. On July 8, they transferred me to the prison camp.

TALL TREES AND a manicured lawn surrounded the brown brick dormitory of the prison camp. The windows had neither bars nor any other security restraints. From the camp, you could see the heavy smokestacks and double-row fencing of the main prison. The camp had a completely different feeling than the bleak prison. They assigned me to a large room that I shared with four other prisoners, although it could have held more. There were communal bathrooms with enclosed showers and toilet stalls. The camp had a classroom in addition to its cafeteria and other common areas. There were even private rooms for prisoners on work release or whose sentences were almost complete. Of course, this was still prison, but we did not live surrounded by bars. Most of the inmates in the camp were nonviolent offenders, many near the ends of their terms, and were allowed to move about freely and relax in the open air.

Three weeks passed before mail finally came to me in prison. Four letters, the first two of which were from Barbara, brought news of the world outside. Barbara had nothing but good news. She had told the children I was away teaching at a school. They were all doing well and missed me. The pastor at our church was writing to officials in Washington, hoping to win probation or parole for me. There was a form letter from the federal district court informing me that my letter to Judge Perry from prison asking for a reduction of sentence would be considered a motion before the court and so be docketed. Finally, a warm letter came from Ingersoll Products, affirming the company's belief in me. "We will help you in any way we can," the letter said. "After your release, we hope that you will resume your employment with our company." That gesture of support meant a great deal to me.

Barbara even managed a visit toward the end of July. She looked wonderful, and cheered me with news of the family and life in Chicago. The people at Ingersoll had stayed in touch with her and assured her that they would find work for her if ever she needed it, which eased some of our worry. Seeing her and being able to actually touch and hold her had a strange effect on me, reminding me of why I needed to stay strong and get home. But at the same time, I was reminded of how trapped I was in that miserable prison.

My first assignment was to the grounds crew at the warden's home, tending to the lawns, hedges, and flower beds. I felt energized to be working outside, but the assignment itself got under my skin. I'd stand there with a rake or clippers in my hands and silently remember the generations of ancestors forced to work as slaves in the plantation fields of the South. It didn't help that standing in the center of one of the luscious green lawns was a statue, a little black lawn jockey with big red lips, staring at me through huge round white eyes.

The work started to eat away at me. Every time I jumped up onto the moving work truck I thought about my running jumps onto the follow-up car behind the presidential limousine. I couldn't stop thinking that the hands that had once held those of President John Kennedy were now pulling weeds out of the ground at "the master's house" for fifteen bucks a month. The anger did me no good. Making trouble would just get me sent back to the main prison. I couldn't refuse the detail, but somehow I had to get a different assignment without losing my camp status.

The warden at Terre Haute was particular about the appearance of his lawn and garden. We had strict instructions about how everything should look. The swaths left by the mowers had to be uniform in width, so that the overall effect was of a nice, neat pattern, and here I saw an opportunity. One hot day in August, I started up the lawn mower and began to cut. Every time I turned to start a new row, I "accidentally" inched the mower a little bit to the side, so that none of the rows matched. When I was done, the lawn looked clean and freshly cut, but the pattern, if you cared as deeply about such things as the warden did, was random and sloppy.

I heard a lot of talk around the camp that weekend about the warden being "hopping mad" over someone screwing up his lawn. It was even rumored that someone had been sent over to recut the grass, and get it done properly. All I know for sure is that the following Monday, I was transferred from the warden's detail to the butcher shop. No one said anything to me about the lawn, but it struck me that the duty officers were keeping a very close eye on me. I'm sure that everyone considered the job on the killing floor of the butcher shop an enormous step down in status. The work was bloody, filthy, and dangerous, to be sure, but it pleased me that the work provided a service to the other prison inmates rather than our masters.

I settled into a routine, doing my assigned work and keeping my head low, working to contest my conviction, and even finding a couple of inmates with whom I formed a three-piece band. Sometimes, the duty officer let us perform during visiting hours. It was what they called "good time."

EARLY ON A November morning in 1966, I was awakened by a guard poking me with a flashlight.

"Bolden. Get your belongings together and be downstairs at the front door in fifteen minutes."

I threw on some clothes and tossed whatever I could into a pillowcase. In the office, two men in suits were waiting for me. Only a few days before, Ray Smith had let me know that Judge Perry had denied our motion to reconsider the case, so it didn't seem likely they were taking me back to court. I figured that I was being transferred, but I had no idea where or why. The two men put me into their vehicle, where a "U.S. Deputy Marshal" sign attached to the visor caught my eye.

"Where are you taking me?" I asked as we left the Terre Haute prison behind us.

"Didn't anybody tell you where you're going?" one of the deputies answered in a thick drawl.

"No, they didn't."

"Well, boy, we're taking you to a real penitentiary. You're going to Fort Leavenworth in Kansas. Since you're an ex–government man, I know that you know about Fort Leavenworth." He let that news sink in for a moment before continuing. "Won't be like that farm you just left back there. You must have torn your ass pretty good to be transferred out of a place like that into a place like Leavenworth."

I sat silent, rocked by the thought that I was going to Leavenworth, a maximum-security prison. There was a prison camp there, but as far as I knew, it was only for military personnel.

The drive to Leavenworth took us within sight of the great arch on the riverfront in St. Louis, and past East St. Louis, where I had spent my childhood. Each exit along the highway brought to mind familiar names and memories of streets, houses, and sandlot ball games. Farther down the highway, we passed Jefferson City, where I had gone to college, and many of the smaller towns in which our little college dance band had played. It was, literally, as if my life was passing before my eyes. I was dead to the free world. My dream was becoming reality.

At first sight, the penitentiary at Leavenworth did not seem so different from Terre Haute, but as we drew nearer, it seemed to grow more immense, more forbidding, and more terrible. This was the Leavenworth I had heard so much about. Like everyone said, it was everything that a good policeman would hope for and the dread of those who had run afoul of the law.

The intake officers ran me through the now-familiar procedures and led me, as they had in Terre Haute, along cold corridors and steel walkways, and up steel stairs. Leavenworth was built like a wheel, with each cell block representing a spoke, all of them meeting at a large central rotunda, like the great rotunda in the old federal building in Chicago. Eventually, we came to cell 208, and as the barred door rolled shut behind me, I knew I had come to the end of this particular journey.

Of the five bunks in the cell, the only one that didn't appear to be occupied was just a few feet from the toilet. Nobody answered when I asked if it was taken, so I cleared off the piles of old magazines and newspapers and got myself settled. I didn't need anyone to explain the general routine, and when chow time came, I fell in line like everyone else and marched into the cafeteria. My first meal in Leavenworth had an eerie similarity to the first one at Terre Haute. As I walked through the room with my food, looking for a seat, the murmur that had filled the room suddenly quieted. I looked around to make sure it wasn't my imagination, and saw many of the inmates staring at me. I didn't know if they treated every new prisoner this way or if they recognized me from the news reports, but I had no doubt that I was the main attraction that night. I felt very uneasy and was greatly relieved when the meal ended and I could return to my cell. But as we marched back, I heard a voice call out from one of the upper tiers of cells.

"Abraham! We know you're down there, and we're going to get you. This is Crazy Joe out of New York. You put me in here, and now I'm going to get you."

I couldn't see anything, or even tell exactly where the voice came from, but the threat unnerved me. I knew that I had been responsible for sending men to the penitentiary and that just being there was dangerous, but I didn't know anything about any Crazy Joe from New York. I ran through the possible cases or investigations that could have indirectly caused trouble for someone in New York. I had worked an undercover case in Buffalo, but nothing tied to that case came to mind.

Exhausted from the trip and apprehensive about unseen dangers in Leavenworth, I kept to the cell when the guard allowed us to visit the dayroom later. I was sitting quietly at the table when one of my cellmates returned. As we were alone in the cell, I kept a cautious eye on the well-built black man.

"You don't remember me, do you?" he asked.

"No, I don't."

"I talked with you back in '61, in Chicago," he said. "You were with Mitch in the Robert Taylor Homes on Forty-third and State. I talked to Mitch in his car, and you were sitting in the front seat next to him."

"I don't remember anything about it, and I don't remember seeing you before," I insisted.

"My name is Jimmy," he continued. "I'm out of Chicago, and I know a lot about you. I'm sure that it was you who was in the car when I talked to Mitch back in '61."

"Mitch" would have been Illinois state narcotics agent Mitchell, and while there was no way I would have recognized Jimmy from a brief meeting five years in the past, he had his facts right about my being with Mitchell that night. We talked after that. Jimmy told me he was doing ten years on a drug charge, and I surmised from what he told me about his relationship with Agent Mitchell that Jimmy had probably turned state's evidence at some point against some of his partners. *Once a stoolie, always a stoolie,* I thought.

Jimmy had some useful things to say. "We heard a few weeks ago that the agent that was involved in the Kennedy murder was coming here. The rumor was circulating all over the yard. This is a dangerous place for you, and nobody that I talked to could understand why they would send you to a hellhole like this."

"I guess they want to teach me a lesson."

"I doubt it. You'll be out of here in a little while. They won't keep you around for long. It's too dangerous for you in this place. These guys kill each other over a pack of cigarettes. You'll never know when you're going to run into someone who knows you, just like you ran into me. I recognized you, but you didn't remember me. If I had wanted to do something to you, it would have been easy." I could tell Jimmy's warning was sincere. "You should call your lawyer or your relatives or whoever you know that can help get you out of here." Jimmy clammed up when the rest of the men returned to the cell.

Sure enough, I got my first hint of trouble the next day in the yard, where I found myself being approached by a group of three men. All three men wore prison blues, and one was noticeably smaller than the others, with streaks of gray in his hair and long side-burns. He took a few steps in front of me as if to block my path.

"Hey, Abraham, remember me? I'm Crazy Joe, out of Buffalo, New York."

My eyes went down to the three men's hands, to see if any of them carried a weapon.

"Now we're on even terms," Joe said.

We eyeballed each other for a long moment, and I felt the rage boiling up inside me. I realized right there that I didn't care if I lived or died, but I wasn't about to be bullied by this weasel, or any other convict.

"Look, man," I shouted, getting right in his face, "I've never seen you and I don't know you from Adam! Even if I did know you from somewhere, man, I was an agent doing my job. Like you said, we're in here together now. I'm a convict in this hellhole just like you. Both of us are trying to do this time. Now if you have some grudge to set-tle, let's settle it right here, right now, because I'm not going around ducking you or anybody else while I'm locked up in here."

Just then, one of the guards shouted over at us. "Hey! You men move it along there, now!" Crazy Joe and his buddies moved off in a hurry, leaving me standing there shaking with tension. I tried to calm myself and sort out whether blowing my top in that situation had been a good thing or a bad thing. Was I truly ready to kill or to be killed?

The next thing I knew, there was a man at my side, a small black man with a little black tam on his head. He looked to be in his for-

ties, with smooth skin and clear eyes, and seemed to have material-
ized out of nowhere.

"Come on," he said. "Let's take a walk."

There was something gentle and kindly about this man, and I
went along with him.

"You handled that just right. I was watching the whole thing.
Now, you watch yourself, because there are a lot of fools in here just
like Joe."

"Oh, you know Joe?" I asked, thinking I'd get some information.

"I know almost everybody in here," he answered. "I've been
locked up here for over thirty years and probably will be here another thirty years more. I'm doing three hundred sixty-five years."
He offered the last part almost casually.

This guy didn't look old enough to have been locked up that
long. I looked again at the tam, and it occurred to me that nobody I
knew wore hats like that anymore.

"You must have been a teenager when you came here," I said,
trying to get his story out of him.

"I was forty years old when I came here. I'll be seventy years old
my next birthday."

"Seventy!" I blurted out. "You must have really been taking care
of yourself."

He wasn't interested in that subject. "I heard that you are going
to another place from here," he went on. "You got that one guy off
your back, but there will be others who are going to hurt you because you were a cop outside. There are guys in here that just want
to kill a cop . . . any cop. Everyone in here was sent here by a cop.
Take my advice: don't come back out into this yard again. If they decide to keep you here, ask them to put you in the camp outside of the
walls. There are too many men out here that would think nothing of
doing you in. It's too dangerous for you to be walking around out
here. Stay around your cell inside until they move you out of here."

I thanked this stranger profusely, and as he walked away, I asked, "What's your name?"

"It doesn't matter," he said with a slight smile. "It doesn't matter." I watched him as he disappeared back into the prison.

I took his advice to heart, and from that moment on stayed out of the yard and, except for meals, remained close to my cell.

Chapter 17

THE KINDLY LIFER at Leavenworth had been right. On a gray and rainy November day less than a week after I arrived, I found my-self sitting in handcuffs and leg irons on a bus with barred windows, pulling away from that infamous prison. Again, nobody ever told me where I was going, but from the routes we were taking and the chatter of the other prisoners on the bus, I guessed our destination: Springfield Medical Center for Federal Prisoners.

The move didn't surprise me in the least. I knew well what the government had in store for me. I'd seen how they dealt with other personnel who dared to speak out on sensitive subjects. As I understood it, the government could declare that I was mentally imbalanced or unstable or insane or whatever term they chose to use, at which point the actual length of my sentence no longer mattered. They could keep me in "treatment" until such time as their doctors decided I was "cured." Then, I would be ready to continue serving the sentence of the court. None of the time spent in psychiatric care would count toward the completion of my sentence. I understood that I was facing a whole new kind of peril, and more than ever, I needed to keep my wits about me.

Intake and processing were by now routine, and I went through it all passively. It wasn't until I got to my cell that I realized how different things had become. I was to be alone, in a tiny, windowless cell, about seven by eight feet, with nothing but a bench, a washbowl, and a toilet. The door was solid steel, with a tiny viewing window at eye level and a long, narrow slot through which they could pass a tray of food. The door clanged shut for the first time, and I peered through the window but could see nothing but another cell door and some blank wall. I could see no other human being.

Suddenly, I felt myself beginning to sweat and I felt weak. I lay down on the bunk and rested my head on the thin pillow as a wave of nausea swept over me. This was it: the realization of the dream I had when I was thirteen. A rectangular steel vault with a tiny glass window. Me on the inside, and a woman standing with three children on the outside. No escape. I felt as if I were standing face-to-face with living death. Holding my body rigid, with my arms folded across my chest, I closed my eyes and started to pray, hoping to drive away the terrible vision and fight back the tears I felt gathering inside me.

The crisis passed after a while, but I knew there would be more to come. A guard brought me a meal, which I welcomed, and gave me paper and pencil and envelopes when I asked. I spent my first night writing letters to the outside world. I spent several days in that cell, in virtual isolation except for an hour of walking every day, a few trips to the guard station to fill out paperwork, and a shower. My restlessness was growing into desperation until one day when I was escorted into a room where three middle-aged white men in suits sat at a long mahogany table. This was a hearing to classify me and determine my permanent status.

"Mr. Bolden," one of the men began, introducing himself as my caseworker, "I see that following a plea of not guilty, you were tried and found guilty of crimes that you are alleged to have committed during your duties as an agent of the federal government. You have been sentenced to serve a term of six years in the custody of the U.S. attorney general. Is that correct?"

"Yes, sir."

"I also see from the summary that you appealed your case through the courts in Chicago and all the way to the Supreme Court of the United States. Is that correct?"

"That is correct, sir."

"Your case was recently heard before the sentencing judge in Chicago in, let's see . . . October, I believe it says here. Your motion for a reduction of your sentence or retrial of the case was denied. Is that correct?"

I affirmed that all the contents of the file were correct, and he asked if I had concluded all the court action in my case.

"No," I answered.

A prisoner at Springfield could be classified in four different ways. He might be there for medical reasons, or for psychiatric problems, or because he was too difficult to handle at other federal prisons and needed to be held under maximum security conditions. The last classification was prison camp status. No reason was given in my case. I was simply sent there. I was allowed to gather up my few things from that claustrophobic little holding cell, and was escorted through a maze of corridors and passageways to a large central room surrounded by smaller dormitory rooms. At the center stood a guard station, an enclosure made of heavy steel with wire-reinforced glass windows. It was mid-November, and although I was relieved to be there and not in that terrifying isolation cell, I was taken aback by the stark contrast with the airy camp at Terre Haute in midsummer. The camp here was darker and bleaker, with grates over the windows to remind us where we were. Still, I breathed easier, and was cheered by the sight of the Holy Bible on my bunk, apparently left by the previous occupant.

I had been at the camp for less than a month, working an easy job at the officers' mess, when Barbara came to visit for the first time. She had finished her shift at Nabisco, and then ridden all night on a bus in order to be in Springfield by eight-thirty in the morning. It pained me terribly for her to see me in this prison so far from home, reminding me that I had not measured up, not become the husband she deserved

"Don't believe anything they tell you about me from here," I began. I needed Barbara to understand Springfield represented a life-and-death situation for me. "If they say something has happened to me, contact Attorney John Hosmer and come here as soon as you can." I had been unable to reach John Hosmer, whom I had asked to represent me if I was ever sent to Springfield, so Ray Smith was still listed in the prison files as my lawyer. As emotionally draining as it was for me to see my wife, I spent a lot of our visit telling her about the dangers there and the different ways I thought the government would try to break me. And then she was gone.

I settled fairly quickly into a routine at Springfield. I had learned a thing or two about how to do time. I got involved in drafting and public-speaking classes available there, and spent time in the library doing legal research in preparation for filing a petition for a writ of habeas corpus. More important, I made some real friends. Every day, I walked in the yard with Elijah, with whom I would discuss spirituality and religion. As a member of the Israelites, African Americans who claimed a historical Jewish heritage, Elijah had a perspective on the world that was new to me.

A few bunks down from me in the dormitory, I found Exindine, a Native American from Oklahoma, sitting cross-legged on his bunk, reading the Holy Bible. We struck up a conversation and became fast friends. Exindine would tell me how much his people loved John Kennedy. As an Indian, he could empathize completely with the civil rights movement and the struggle of black Americans, but he never fully accepted the idea of nonviolent protest. After all, the "blue-eyed devil," as he referred to all European inhabitants in America, had taken away the lands of his people through years of bloodshed.

And finally, there was Gus, whose bunk was next to mine. A former boxing promoter who admittedly had been mixed up with underworld characters, Gus had plenty of his own troubles with the government, but it turned out that he had followed my case so closely that he had a scrapbook of clippings about me from the papers in Cincinnati, his hometown. He never imagined that he'd actually meet me. Gus warned me about life at Springfield. "This is a bad place to be in," he would say. "This is hell." He told me about an inmate who simply disappeared from the camp domitory one night. "The next time I saw him in the hallway," Gus told me, "the guy was so doped up that he didn't know me. Watch out for these people. They don't care about anybody around here."

Barbara brought the children to visit me around the New Year's holiday, and a week or two later, my mother came, along with my younger sister. The moment Mom saw me when I walked into the visitors' room, she burst into tears. My innocence or guilt didn't matter to her. I had brought shame to us all, and my confinement was taking a toll on her. Seeing her devastation, I grew even more determined to get back into court and challenge my conviction. I had to protect myself from any sudden "disappearances" while at Springfield, and I had to get Hosmer up to speed.

IN THE YEARS just after that terrible day in Dallas, the American public became increasingly obsessed with the circumstances of Kennedy's assassination. For many people, the release of the Warren Commission report in 1964 failed to settle any questions, and even raised some new ones. Conspiracy theorists published countless books and articles speculating on the unseen forces behind the crime. Three of those books mentioned my treatment at the hands of the government when I became a potential witness. One of these was Mark Lane's *Rush to Judgment,* which challenged the commission's finding that Oswald had acted alone, and went on to become a best-seller. Lane detailed how the Secret Service had tricked me into returning to Chicago from Washington and what had followed, based

on interviews he had conducted with me secretly while I was appeal-
ing my case to the U.S. Supreme Court. At the time, I had shared
with him my fears of how the government might try to deal with me
once I was incarcerated.

In early 1967, Mark Lane happened to call my home while visiting Chicago, and learned that I was being held in Springfield. Lane
was no novice, and knowing what Springfield might mean for me, he
called a news conference in which he announced where I was being
held, and described his fear that the government might try to silence
me further by declaring me insane. Mark Lane's statements were
broadcast widely.

About a week later, John Hosmer showed up at Springfield Medical Center with a man he introduced as Mr. Burt. Hosmer looked
nothing like what I had imagined. He was an older man and very
tall, with unkempt gray hair, and he wore a black patch over one eye.
Mark Lane's appearances on television had reminded Hosmer that
he was to act as my attorney if the government sent me to the Springfield Medical Center.

The other man, Burt, turned out to be a young lawyer from Jim
Garrison's office in New Orleans. Garrison, the district attorney
there, fervently believed that the Warren Commission had been methodically deceived by a malicious conspiracy hatched by agents and
officers operating within and on behalf of the government. Convinced that Oswald had not acted alone and that the government
was conspiring to cover up evidence of a plot to assassinate the president of the United States, Garrison had launched his own investigation. Hosmer had contacted Garrison about my case, and this young
lawyer seemed to be well acquainted with my predicament.

I gave the two men a detailed account of everything that had
happened to me up to that point, and then expressed my main fear:
that the prison officials would try to classify me as a psychiatric patient in order to discredit me. This would undermine any future tes-

timony I might give about the Secret Service's failure to protect the president. I needed people on the outside to be aware of my physical and mental status at all times and to be prepared to mount an immediate legal challenge if the government attempted to reclassify me as an inmate undergoing psychiatric treatment for any reason.

Hosmer and Burt held a news conference of their own after our visit. Burt mentioned me by name and stated boldly that "Bolden's imprisonment inside the medical center is very suspicious in light of Bolden's charges against the Secret Service." At Springfield, we were able to see the reports of the conference on the dayroom television, and I became something of a celebrity within the prison. Rather than shunning me as an ex-agent of the government, inmates sought me out to hear about my experience in the White House and ask what it was like to work next President Kennedy. A few realized that I had some knowledge of the law and enlisted my help with paperwork and letter writing in their court cases. In three cases, I actually helped a few inmates get their sentences reduced to time served.

Around that time, in 1967, William Manchester's book *The Death of a President* joined the growing body of literature that challenged the findings of the Warren Commission. Manchester made much more than some previous authors about the Secret Service's inadequate protection of Kennedy. When James Rowley, the chief of the Secret Service, testified before Congress and refused to answer any questions about the reportedly outlandish conduct of the agents in Dallas, one congressman angrily upbraided him, saying that his attitude "was strange in light of statements in William Manchester's book" about the drinking and late-night partying on the night before the assassination. Rowley deflected the questions by saying that the agent who had made those accusations "was in prison for other crimes," but the congressman wasn't buying it, and forced Rowley to promise that the "Secret Service would issue a white paper explaining their side of the issue."

All of this received plenty of attention from the news media, and so prison officials clamped down on me right away at Springfield. My caseworker accused me of misusing my visiting privileges by contacting authors and lawyers who were writing articles and books that put the government in a bad light. I hadn't written or contacted anyone in Jim Garrison's office or anyone else who was trying to embarrass the government, and I told them so. Nonetheless, they limited my visitors from then on to family members and John Hosmer, now my attorney of record.

Indeed, my family did come and visit in April 1967. It had been nearly a year since my children and I had seen one another. They were growing so fast, both physically and mentally, and I felt sure that my ten-year-old daughter and my eight-year-old son had figured out that the bars on the windows and the uniformed guards meant something, and that maybe I wasn't away "teaching," as they had been led to believe. I can't describe how much I wanted to get up and walk out of the prison with their little hands in mine, but that was not to be.

It wasn't long after the family's visit that I saw a story on the evening news about my case. "Former Secret Service agent Abraham Bolden has filed a writ in court charging the government with soliciting perjured testimony and other illegal activity used to convict Bolden and sentence him to prison," said the correspondent. John Hosmer appeared in the story, reiterating that my conviction and confinement at Springfield had been engineered to silence my criticism of the Secret Service.

My friend Elijah found me in the yard later and spoke sternly to me. "That guy is just using you to fill his pockets," he said, referring to Hosmer. "He wants you to think that he cares about you, but when push comes to shove, he wouldn't do one day of your time for you. You have to reach into yourself and find that power that God gave us. It's inside of you." Elijah's voice rose, either in anger or in inspiration. "It is you who are standing in the way of your own destiny. You have the inner power, and that's what they are afraid of."

That same night, a guard came and found me at my bunk.

"Come with me, Bolden."

I reached toward my cabinet, but he quickly stopped me. "Don't worry about bringing anything. We can take care of that later. We will bring you anything that you need from here."

I followed the guard through the prison until we arrived at what was obviously a hospital floor, with male and female nurses and attendants hustling about the spotless corridor. I was placed in a small hospital room, bare except for a bed and some medical equipment attached to the wall.

"Where are we?"

"You are in section 1-2A," one of the guards explained. "You were sent here by order of the associate warden." The guard informed me that the warden had ordered me confined there for my own safety until further notice. I wasn't fooled in the least by the hospital surroundings. I was in "the hole," receiving punishment as if I had violated prison rules. There was no evidence anywhere of any threat to my safety within the prison. I could not leave the room except to use the bathroom, and even then I needed a guard to escort me. Walking the hallways was forbidden, as was going out into the yard. The door of my room remain locked at all times. Even my meals were brought to me there.

On the second day of this confinement, I asked to see the warden but was told I had to start at the bottom of the chain of command, which meant speaking to Sergeant Ennis. I complained to Ennis that I was being held in virtual isolation and wanted to be returned to the camp dormitory. Sergeant Ennis didn't try to cover up the truth, and told me straight out that the order to segregate me resulted from all the "publicity about your connection to the Kennedy thing." He added that nothing could be done about the isolation until some decision was made by the administration regarding my status at the medical center.

The conversation with Sergeant Ennis motivated me to write to Judge William Collinson, who was handling my petition for a writ of habeas corpus in the Springfield district court. In my letter, I provided the judge with a detailed account of how I had been sent into isolation after the publicity about my filing the petition, and how prison personnel had acknowledged to me that my involvement in "the Kennedy thing" was to blame.

In June, Judge Collinson took under consideration the motion for a writ. In his decision December 18, 1967, he noted that he was unable to "overturn a conviction that has been upheld by the other Courts that the plaintiff has petitioned. Although the case is out of the ordinary, the petition must raise substantial constitutional issues that have not been litigated elsewhere in order to overturn your conviction. Plaintiff has presented enough evidence for this court to question whether or not you should have been convicted by a jury, but plaintiff has failed to present the kind of new evidence that would be necessary for this court to rule against the government's motion for a summary judgment. Said petition should be filed in the U.S. District Court in Chicago and that the U.S. District Court in Springfield, Missouri, could take no action on his complaint," the judge concluded.

I don't know why I thought anything different might happen, but I had let myself get my hopes up. The judge's decision devastated me. When I got back to prison, I found out that for some reason they had decided to send me back to the camp. After a week spent in almost total isolation and the crushing disappointment of the judge's denial of my petition, going back to the camp felt wonderful, as if I had been let out on parole. Funny how the mind works.

LIFE BACK AT the camp didn't remain peaceful for very long. A few weeks after I had returned, I witnessed the murder of one inmate at the hands of another. I had gone from the officers' mess in the basement to the main cafeteria to deliver some food. An inmate I had never seen before was standing at the back of the elevator when I got on to return downstairs. When the doors opened again at the basement, another inmate rushed past me in a blur. He threw himself on the young man standing in the elevator, stabbing him repeatedly in the belly. The screams, the blood, the terror in both men's eyes— these were horrible things to see, and the images will never leave me. I walked away as the doors of the elevator closed with the two men inside. I was trembling at the thought that I could have been killed as well. Word got around about what had happened, but I never said a word to anyone about what I'd seen.

The next confrontation involved me directly, and had serious ramifications. One day, a burly young inmate with sandy hair named Kenny came to work in the kitchen. The rumor around the prison was that Kenny had beaten another inmate with a bat during a prison baseball game and had been sent to the psychiatric wing of the prison. Indeed, he had a P number, identifying him as a psychiatric patient, but his behavior wasn't too different from that of a lot of regular inmates. It was common to hear men muttering to themselves from time to time. Keeping your distance from other inmates could be as much a necessity of survival as a sign of antisocial behavior. Kenny did his job well, mopping the floors of the kitchen and officers' mess. Most of us gave psychiatric inmates a wide berth, and the guards tended to cut them more slack than the regular prisoners.

One day I had just finished washing dishes and pots and was preparing to clean up the floor in my area, by filling a mop bucket with hot water, when I heard a voice behind me.

"What the fuck are you doing with my bucket?"

I turned around to see Kenny glaring at me. There were two mop buckets in our area of the prison that were plainly different from each other, and I was not using Kenny's bucket.

"Oh, is this the bucket you use?" I asked, knowing it wasn't but trying to placate him.

"You know that that's my goddamned bucket!" Kenny shouted. "Why you keep fucking with me?"

I could see that Kenny was either delusional or trying to start a fight with me, so I continued to try to make peace.

"I'm not fucking with you," I said. "This is the bucket I've been using, but if you want it, I'll go get the other one."

"Why you keep fucking with me?"

Kenny stood blocking the door. As he took a step toward me, I saw that he was holding a long knife against his leg. Instantly, I lifted the bucket of hot water and drew it back, as if to throw it.

"What the hell is the matter with you, man?" I shouted back at him. "If you take another step toward me, I'm going to throw this fucking hot water in your face and burn all the skin off your body." He stopped, but the commotion had attracted several other inmates, and Mr. Angland, who ran the kitchen.

"What the hell is going on here?" Angland demanded. He looked first at me, saying, "Put that bucket down!"

"Kenny's got a knife," I protested. "He came at me with a knife. I'm not going to put this bucket down until you take that knife from Kenny."

Mr. Angland reached his hand out and said, "Kenny, give me that knife." Kenny did as he was told. He also obeyed Angland's order to return to his ward, but not without first shooting me a menacing look.

Angland turned back to me. "I want to see you in my office, Bolden."

When we sat down in his office, Angland started in on me. "Bolden, you know that you can't threaten the patients around here. You know better."

"He came at me with a knife. What am I supposed to do? Just stand there and not defend myself because he's a patient?"

"The way I saw it, the two of you were threatening each other," Angland said. "You had the bucket of water and he had the knife. The two of you threatened each other, and that's what I saw."

"But you didn't see the whole thing," I insisted. "I was in the back room doing my work, and suddenly this guy is standing in the doorway talking about a mop bucket. I know that he's a patient, but I'm going to protect myself. He came at me with the knife, and that's when I picked up the bucket of hot water to throw on him."

"Well, you can't discipline these patients. You should have come to me. You can't threaten these patients. I'm going to have to write you up for it," he stated angrily.

"You can write me up all you want to, but I'm not going to stand there and let any of these patients stab or butcher me with a knife. If I could have gotten out of the room, I would have come to you, but Kenny had the door blocked, and he was talking out of his mind about a mop bucket."

"You go back to the dormitory now. You'll be off tomorrow. When you come in Wednesday, you, me, and Kenny will get together and straighten out this problem," Angland concluded.

In the yard later that day, I told Elijah what had happened with Kenny. Elijah didn't say much, but he had an odd half-smile on his round, pockmarked face.

"You might as well get ready," he finally said.

"Ready for what?"

Elijah swept his hand around at the surrounding enclosures. "You see all of these fences and wire? You are in the devil's pit. This is the blazing furnace of the holy scriptures. Anything that the government wants to happen in here, it can make happen, unless you have the power of God on your side." Elijah's voice rose with emotion. "You don't think that Kenny came at you because he's crazy, do you?"

"Well, he is a mental patient, and—"

"No, he's not the mental patient you think he is. You're the mental patient. He is doing what he was sent here to do, but you refuse to do what God created you to do. That's why you're in this trouble. You're going to stay in trouble until God breaks you down and you submit." Elijah had been speaking with great passion, but now he grew quiet again. "We are God's children," he said. "The power of the living God is within you."

On Wednesday morning, Angland sent me to see Julius Nicholas, the chief of classification and parole. Nicholas turned out to be a black man, but one of those who acted and looked so much like a white man that corporations and government offices loved using them to fulfill their new minority hiring requirements.

"I understand that you had a misunderstanding with one of the patients Sunday morning," he began.

"Yes, sir," I answered, as politely as I could. "One of the patients, Kenny, drew a knife on me while I was at work in the dish-washing room."

Nicholas leaned back in his chair. "What did you do to trigger off that kind of reaction from him?"

"Nothing," I said emphatically. "I was working in the back room when Kenny walked in and shouted something about a mop bucket. I looked around and saw him standing behind me near the doorway claiming that I had his mop bucket. I wasn't about to argue with him about a mop bucket, so I told him he could have it. The next thing I know, the guy has a knife in his hand. So I grabbed the mop bucket full of hot water and told him that if he came any closer to me, I would throw the hot water in his face."

"So, you threatened him with the bucket of hot water?" Nicholas asked.

"Yeah, I threatened him after he pulled the knife on me. I was going to protect myself the best way that I knew how and—"

"Weren't you a state policeman and an FBI agent? Didn't they teach you how to disarm a person who was threatening you with a knife?"

"What's my past employment got to do with what happened in the kitchen?" I blurted out, frustrated by Nicholas' accusatory tone. "It's your job to govern these inmates, not mine. Kenny came at me, and I have every right to defend myself."

"That's not the story that Kenny told. Kenny said that you took the bucket that he was using to mop the floor. He went looking for his bucket and when he saw you had it, he asked you for it, and you exploded, calling him all kinds of filthy names. Kenny told us that he saw a knife lying on top of a silverware tray that you had just taken out of the washer. He said he picked up the knife because you threatened him with the water."

"That's ridiculous," I argued. "There was no silverware tray in the room. Kenny brought the knife into the room with him. I'm not the patient here. Kenny is the one who was hallucinating or something. He just went crazy, like he did in Arizona or wherever he beat that other inmate with the baseball bat."

"Look, Bolden, don't raise your voice at me. I'm not Kenny. I know that you've been under a lot of pressure. I read the papers. Sometimes when an inmate is under pressure about things on the outside, he does a lot of things that he wouldn't normally do." Nicholas' tone became sympathetic. "I'm just trying to help you adjust to these conditions."

"Help me adjust? Help me adjust to what?" I demanded angrily. "I don't need any adjustment. I have not had one argument with any other inmate since I've been incarcerated. I haven't had one write-up about my conduct or anything, and I've been locked up over a year now."

"Well, what do you think we should do with you?" Nicholas asked.

"Just give me another job assignment. I don't want to work in the officers' kitchen if Kenny is going to be there. I think that will be the best solution."

"Okay, Bolden. You can go back to work now. I'll tell you what we decide."

I hadn't even made it back to my bunk when I heard my name called over the PA system. I had been summoned by Dr. Kinsel, one of Springfield's staff psychiatrists. Kinsel, a young, light-skinned black man with soft hands, introduced himself and began his questioning.

"Mr. Nicholas asked me to talk to you about what happened Sunday. He seems to think that you have a feeling that you are being persecuted. Do you feel that someone is out to get you or that you are being watched?"

"Of course I feel like I'm being watched. I'm in the penitentiary. Everywhere I go, everything I do is being watched," I snapped. "As far as me being persecuted, the incident Sunday has nothing to do with persecution. Kenny cannot persecute me because he does not have any authority over me. Persecution is an act of abuse of authority."

"You know that there has been a lot of talk about how the government framed you and how the witnesses lied in your trial," Kinsel said. "In your letters to your wife, you constantly give the impression that you are being persecuted. That's what I read into them."

I was sensing something was wrong, and started to get defensive. "I thought that you sent for me to talk about what happened in the cafeteria. What I have been complaining about in my letters to my wife are matters verified by court records. These are documented charges that have been all the way to the Supreme Court, and the government has yet to deny any of them. It's not unusual for black people to be persecuted, if you want to call it that."

"Bolden," Kinsel shot back, "your problem is that you have a big mouth. You may be right in what you are saying, but you need to learn to keep your mouth shut. You had a good job and messed it up because you talk too much for your own good."

"If we're going to talk about my case or what was said in court," I told him, "then I think you should allow me to call Attorney Hosmer into this conference. You call me in here and say we are going to talk about what happened Sunday and Kenny's threats against me, but you're asking me about what I said in court. I need to be represented by an attorney if you are going to keep talking about something that has nothing to do with Kenny," I said, struggling to keep my anger in check.

"I think you are being used by people who don't mean you any good, Bolden," Dr. Kinsel said.

"Well, for my part, I think that you and Mr. Nicholas are being used by people who don't mean me any good, too."

"Are you claiming that I'm part of some kind of conspiracy? Is that what you're saying?" Kinsel rose from his seat.

"I didn't say any such thing and you know it. I'm reciting the facts, and the facts are that I was approached by a man who threatened me with a knife for no reason whatsoever. I get called into Mr. Nicholas' office and the whole incident gets turned around to make it seem that I was responsible for Kenny's conduct. Then you send for me and I sit here listening to you insinuate that I have some kind of persecution complex and a big mouth. We could settle this whole thing by removing me or Kenny from the kitchen. I don't think that I can feel safe working with him anymore."

Kinsel didn't respond directly. "You're very emotional, aren't you, Bolden?"

"Who wouldn't be emotional under these circumstances?"

The room got quiet for a moment as I watched Kinsel leaf through my file.

"I see where you had a problem with the athletic department at the university you attended. Is that right?"

"I didn't have any problem with the athletic department. My problem was with the unfair way that scholarships were given at

Lincoln University. That's the only problem I had," I explained. "The university didn't like the fact that I wrote a letter to the school newspaper and helped put pressure on the university to change its scholarship policy. The dean threatened to kick me out of Lincoln University for writing that letter, but I ended up graduating cum laude and third in a class of ninety-seven."

"Bolden, here again, I am concerned about your compulsion to delve into things that are not your business. These types of comp—"

"Excuse me, sir," I interrupted. "I didn't have a compulsion to do anything. I saw a wrong and tried to do something about it. I wouldn't call that a compulsion. I'd—"

"And you're very defensive," Kinsel continued. "You are going to have to learn to control your compulsions. They are the cause of what I see as antigovernment and sociopathic behavior."

I realized then that I had to keep quiet. Even if this doctor couldn't get me to lose my temper, any response I made would be twisted into another reason why I should be given some kind of abnormal psychological classification. I sat there stonily until Kinsel looked up from his file and dismissed me. Back in the dormitory, I gathered my friends Elijah, Gus, and Exindine and told them, in as much detail as I could remember, about my meetings with Nicholas and Kinsel. I needed people to have that information in case something should happen to me.

The next day, a guard told me I didn't have to report to the officers' kitchen. I assumed I was getting a day off in preparation for reassignment to a new job. Elijah was happy; he didn't believe that Kenny had a mental problem, which as far as Elijah was concerned made Kenny more dangerous than I had imagined.

Chapter 18

THEY HAD PLANS to reassign me, as I found out the next day, but not to a new work detail. A guard poked me awake with his flashlight in the early morning, told me to get dressed, and marched me deep into what seemed like the bowels of the prison. We ended up in a corridor lined on both sides with heavy steel doors. The only windows visible were the tiny viewing windows above the tray slots in each of the doors. There was an awful stench, and the sounds of muffled screams and sobbing filled the corridor. I knew where I was without anyone ever telling me: the dreaded 2-1 East, the psychiatric ward.

I shot questions at the guards. Why was I there? Had I been reclassified? Did anybody seriously think there was something wrong with me? But nobody would answer my questions, telling me to talk to the doctor when he came by. The guards took my belt and shoelaces and put me in a small, dark cell. Amazingly, this cell was actually a physical improvement over the isolation cell; it had a window that I could open to let in fresh air, and its own washroom facilities.

The door to my cell slammed shut, leaving me alone with my thoughts. The only thing I knew for certain was that I had to let Barbara and my attorney, John Hosmer, know what had happened to me. There was no way I could sit quietly while the government locked me away interminably in some kind of asylum. The situation seemed ominous.

Before long, the prison added something new to my routine. Four uniformed officers entered my cell. One of them, a particularly burly guard, carried a tray filled with tiny white paper cups.

"Medication time," he said, holding out a little cup in his big, meaty hand.

I felt suddenly weak and dizzy, as if I were caught in some terrible dream. I couldn't move or speak.

"Come on, boy. We ain't got all day," he drawled.

"There's got to be some mistake," I said. "I'm not a patient. There's got to be a mistake."

"We ain't makin' no mistake, boy. The doctor ordered this to calm you down, I guess."

"What is in that cup?" I asked.

"It's something that the doctor ordered. It's Elavil, to calm you down."

"I'm not taking any medication until I talk to my lawyer," I said defiantly. "I'm not a patient and I don't need any medication. I'm a camp—"

"Oh, you gonna take it, all right. You can either take it the easy way, out of this cup, or we can give it to you in your ass. Either way, you gonna take it. I didn't say you gonna like it, but you damn sure gonna take it, one way or the other."

I looked at the four guards and understood that I wouldn't be able to resist. That would probably make things even worse for me, anyway. I took the cup and put the pill in my mouth. Taking the little cup of juice he offered to wash it down, I slid the pill under my tongue to hide it. Apparently, I wasn't the first one to think of that.

"Open your mouth and raise your tongue," he ordered.

Having no choice, I swallowed the pill, and they left.

Dr. Kinsel showed up later in the day. "How are you feeling today?" he asked.

"I think that I'm doing all right." Trying to sound calm, I added,

"I was wondering why I've been sent over here. I'm not suffering from any mental illness, and I don't know why I'm over here."

"Oh, we just felt you needed a rest, and we wanted to make you as secure as possible. We wanted to give you a chance to pull yourself together," he answered in a dismissive tone.

"I don't need any rest. All I need is to go back to the camp and be assigned to another job. That's all I need. I was doing fine until I had the run-in with Kenny, and now I wind up over here because he threatened me."

Kinsel wasn't going to give me any straight answers. "It's not all about Kenny. You seem to be under a lot of pressure, and we need to get to the bottom of your compulsions and paranoid behavior."

"I haven't been classified as being paranoid. Nobody has ever told me that I am paranoid. I'm paranoid about what?"

"We won't go into that now," Kinsel said testily. "You'll be here for a while, and I have prescribed medication for you to take. It should help you sleep."

"I don't need any medication or drugs. There's nothing wrong with me, and you know it. Who ordered me to be sent to this place? I need to contact my attorney and let him know that I've been moved out of the camp."

Kinsel stopped me. "Just relax, Abraham. You'll be here for a while, and we will decide where you go from here. Just settle down and relax and take the medication that I ordered for you." With that, he turned and with his soft, delicate steps left my cell.

From the window of my cell, I could see the patients from the pysch ward wandering about the yard under the watchful eyes of a number of guards. So many of them seemed dazed and off-balance, shuffling and stumbling about in the evening sunlight. Others sat motionless, some in wheelchairs, staring blankly into the distance. As precarious as my situation had been, something new was troubling me. Both Nicholas and Kinsel were black men. My mother used to have a saying about feeding Uncle Toms with a long-handled spoon, because they couldn't be trusted. These two men were "house Negroes," only too happy to do their master's bidding. There was a time when I would have thought that having two black men as authorities above me in the prison would work to my advantage, but clearly that wasn't the case now. I suppose I had been a "house Negro" for a long time myself. Now I knew something that Nicholas and Kinsel hadn't figured out yet: you can put in a day's work for your master and never complain and never give him any trouble, but at the end of the day he's still your master, and he can do with you any damn thing he pleases.

After a few days, I could feel the effects of the Elavil. I hated the way it made me feel, like I was a little high and a little parched. One day, the pill made me feel so dizzy and nauseous that I passed out. I realized then that I needed to keep those pills out of my system, or else I'd become one of those walking zombies in the yard. The sick feeling in my gut sparked an idea. The guards had stopped waiting in my cell for me to take the medication, although I knew they could watch me through the little viewing window. But I figured out that there was a blind spot, a corner of my cell that could not be seen through the window. I came up with a plan: I would eat only a little of the breakfast they brought me, and hide the rest in the blind spot. When they gave me the medication, I would swallow it, but force myself to vomit it up as soon as the guards had moved on to the other cells. Then I would quickly eat the hidden portion of the breakfast, both to keep up my strength and to keep the guards from getting suspicious. I knew they would punish me if they caught me, but I had to take the risk. I felt like my life depended on it. I put my plan into operation the next day, and found very quickly that it worked.

IT'S DIFFICULT TO describe the cruelty of isolation. It attacks you on every level: physically, emotionally, even spiritually. I was unshaven and unclean and my body ached. I felt bereft, not merely lonely—that was a given—but ignored, almost forgotten. Whenever I would see Dr. Kinsel in the corridor outside my cell and rap on the window to get his attention, he would refuse to respond or acknowledge me, as if trying to make the point that I didn't really exist.

Strange things started to happen in my head. One night, after a week or two on the psych ward, I was awakened in the middle of the night by a sound, a quiet but crisp snap. I looked around the room and saw nothing. When I heard another snap, I followed the sound and saw a tiny spark of light, as if from a cigarette lighter. As the spark grew brighter and brighter, I felt my limbs become numb, frozen. I couldn't move. The light became so intense that I couldn't bear to look into it. I thought for sure that I was losing my mind.

Suddenly, the outline of a human face formed in the center of the light. It began as a small black dot and then grew, taking form as a shadowy outline. It had long hair, but I couldn't make the features out clearly enough to know if it was a man or woman.

"What is your name?" the figure asked in an otherworldly voice more clear and full than any human voice I had ever heard.

"Abraham," I answered.

"How many children do you have?"

"Three."

"Fear not," the beautiful voice said. "God be with you."

The face shrank back into the light, which dimmed until both were gone, leaving only darkness in that corner of my cell.

I felt sensation returning to my limbs and was about to get up and go to the bathroom when I heard the jangling keys and heavy footfalls that always announced the arrival of guards. They stopped outside my room and shone a flashlight through the viewing window, raking the beam over every corner of the room. I had believed that the face was a vision or a hallucination, but clearly the guards must have heard something or seen something. They left quickly, and I lay awake most of the rest of the night, trying to make sense of the vision.

In the morning, as I was washing up, I smelled a faint odor of smoke. I could see no sign of fire outside my window, but through the small viewing window in the door I thought I detected a slight haze in the air of the corridor. Suddenly, a guard rushed down the corridor, shouting, "Fire! Fire in the cell block!" I heard another officer shout that one of the rooms at the end of the block was on fire, and then heard another answer that those rooms were unoccupied. Another odd and inexplicable circumstance.

The guards opened our cell doors and evacuated all of us to the dayroom. I felt so happy to be out of my little room—free, if you want to call it that, for the first time in over a week—that I didn't react to the grotesque sight of so many drugged and possibly deranged men, dragged from their beds in various states of undress, draped over the tables and chairs. The fire was extinguished quickly, but I was allowed to linger in the dayroom for a while. As I looked around the room, I suddenly found myself staring into a familiar face. A man was gazing back at me intently and purposefully. He didn't seem to be overmedicated or crazy; he seemed to recognize me. It was the man who had stabbed the other inmate to death in the elevator in the basement by the officers' kitchen.

He rose and walked to my table. I could see that he had gained some weight and wore his hair cut much closer to his head, but it was definitely the same man.

"Haven't I seen you somewhere before?" he asked as he sat down across from me.

"I don't think so."

"My name is James. What's yours?"

"I'm Abraham."

James let out a soft laugh and began to eat. I could see bits of food tumble out of his mouth as he chewed, which I knew to be a sign that he was heavily medicated.

"I've been over here since that day," he said.

"What day?"

"You know," James said. "The day that little punk motherfucker tried to kill me on the elevator. I had to protect myself."

"Oh, yeah," I said. "I remember you getting on the elevator, but I didn't see what happened. I heard that something happened, about some young guy getting into a fight on the elevator. Was that you?"

"Yeah, the motherfucker pulled a knife on me, and I took it from him and used it on him. That's what I did."

"Well, I didn't see what happened," I repeated, "and nobody asked me about any fight. If they did, I would just tell them the truth. I didn't see anything."

Just then, a guard's voice rang out above the din. "Dayroom is over. Dayroom is over."

The very next day, it seemed like everything had changed. The guards who gave me my medication didn't stay around to watch me take it, and I was able to simply flush it down the toilet. One guard left the door to my room unlocked for half an hour, just to let me have some air. And surprisingly, they let me have lunch in the dayroom with the others. I had no idea if all this newfound freedom was connected to my vision of the night before or perhaps somehow to the fire, but I was so glad for it. After lunch in the dayroom, I even persuaded the other inmates, as drugged and sluggish as many of them were, to join me in a sing-along. Over the next few days, I was allowed out in the yard, and to take all my meals in the dayroom. Even though it made me happy to be released from my room, being able to see the other patients on a regular basis reminded me of what could happen to me if I ever let down my guard.

I wrote letters to both Barbara and Hosmer, in each of them using the secret code we had devised before I went to prison. I had told them that if they ever saw the letter *i* dotted with a five-pointed star in any written communication from me, it would mean that I thought I was in grave danger, regardless of what the letter actually said. I had no way of knowing whether my letters ever made it out of the prison, but on my tenth full day of confinement in the psychiatric ward, a guard roused me from my cell. A visitor had come to see me. It was my lawyer, John Hosmer. They told me to wash up, and let me shave for the first time since I'd been on 2-1 East, then brought me to meet him.

"I got your letter, Abe," Hosmer said as he shook my hand. He introduced me to another man who had come with him, William Blanc, another investigating attorney working with Jim Garrison in New Orleans. Hosmer told the guards to leave us alone so we could confer in private, and as soon as they had left, he asked, "What the hell is going on?"

I explained everything that had happened—the incident with Kenny, the meeting with Nicholas, and then the interview with Kinsel. I described how Kinsel had told me I was paranoid and that I had a big mouth, talking too much about things that didn't concern me.

"Do you think that he was talking about the Kennedy assassination?" William Blanc asked.

I answered that I believed that what was going on was somehow connected to my involvement with the Kennedy assassination. "They've been giving me a hundred and fifty milligrams of Elavil every day since they put me in here."

"You sure don't look drugged to me," Hosmer said, with Blanc nodding in agreement.

"That's because I didn't take all of that garbage," I said. "Once they get that stuff into my system, it's all over for me."

"Did anyone tell you why you are being medicated?" Hosmer asked.

"The only thing Kinsel told me was that it's to calm me down and help me rest."

"Have you been before the classification committee, or have they changed your status here?"

"No. As far as I know, I'm still assigned to the camp."

We talked awhile longer about my life in 2-1 East. Blanc was particularly interested in whether or not any of the administrators had tried to discuss the Kennedy assassination with me or had told me to keep quiet about my criticism of the Secret Service.

I hadn't really had any specific conversations, and told him so, but I explained that I felt fairly certain that Kinsel had been referring to the Kennedy case when he told me I had a big mouth. In addition, my caseworker, Mr. Tindall, had given me a hard time about my contact with authors and researchers on that subject, which led me to think that my comments about the Secret Service were largely to blame for my predicament.

The guard cut our conversation short, informing us that our meeting had ended. The very same night, a guard unlocked the door to my room and spoke the words that had now become too familiar to me.

"Bolden, get your things together and come with me."

I HAD LEARNED that in the prison system, you never knew where you were going until you got there, and that even after you got there, you still might not know where you were. On this particular occasion, my new home turned out to be C Unit. At least that's what the sign above the two heavy steel doors said. I thought they were perhaps finally taking me to the "hole," but when I asked, a guard told me, "This isn't the hole, but it is one of our segregation units." I would soon find out that C Unit was a transitional cell block, like the one they had put me in on my first night in Springfield. Prisoners on their way out to another institution, or recently arrived prisoners, bided their time in C Unit until they were classified or assigned more permanent status. Some inmates were there awaiting medical or psychological evaluations, or to recuperate after release from the hospital ward.

I learned the routine quickly on C Unit, where I had considerably more freedom than I'd had in the psych ward. We ate our meals in the dayroom and had privileges to use a small exercise yard. The guards were not as watchful as in 2-1 East, which made it easy for me to fake swallowing the Elavil. I even made the acquaintance of a kindly officer, named Sweet, who brought me a few of my things from the camp, including my copy of the Bible.

I escaped into that Bible, spending hours reading and rereading it. With the slide rule that Sweet had also brought me, I explored some of the mathematical relationships within the Bible that I had learned about years ago when I joined the Masonic Temple. These exercises and studies kept my mind sharp and provided a kind of sanctuary for me when things got ugly, as happened when a young inmate a few doors down drowned himself in his own toilet.

"What a hell of a way to die," one of the guards had said. Those words stuck with me. A hell of a way to die, and a hell of a place to be in.

Time ground on at C Unit. The endless days were broken up once by a visit from Barbara, but by that time, the utter mortification I felt when she saw me in that terrible cell block, smelling funky and unshaven like some B-movie madman, made her visits almost more painful than comforting. I retreated more and more into my Bible, choosing to remain in my room or in the dayroom when the others were exercising in the yard. This is the kind of behavior, of course, that makes prison officials nervous. I imagine that anyone observing me from a distance would have wondered about my sanity at that point. Looking back at myself now, I have to wonder, too. I know that some part of me believed that my immersion in the Bible had the power to establish a connection with the angels and spirits who dwelt in its stories.

On a stifling hot night in early August, something woke me out of deep sleep. I immediately recognized the same snapping sound that I had heard one night in 2-1 East. I looked around and saw nothing, but when I tried to move my arms and legs, I found that I could not. I couldn't even turn my head from side to side. I felt myself on the verge of some extraordinary experience, and felt both awe and terror. Suddenly, I thought I perceived a slight movement in the darkness, and in the next moment, a tiny speck of light began to grow in one of the dark corners of the ceiling. The light grew brighter, and within it, some kind of mass began to take shape. I understood that I was having another vision, like the one in the psychiatric ward. I was so afraid that I was on the verge of insanity.

The mass arranged itself into identifiable shapes. The upper portion appeared to take the form of a swinging rope. Toward the center of the brilliant light, the rope thickened into a knot, and beneath that knot at the end of that swinging rope, there appeared the shadowy image of a man's head. The head swung back and forth across the width of the ball of light. Then, as mysteriously as it had all appeared, the shapes began to dissolve and the light to fade. As it vanished, I broke free from the paralysis in my body and was able to sit up. My entire body was soaked with sweat.

As before, the vision must have triggered something to alert the guards. I heard the sound of their footsteps rushing toward my room before I had even collected my thoughts. Again, a guard shone a flashlight through the viewing window, peering into my face and around the room. I kept still, and soon enough the guards were gone.

In the morning, I went to breakfast, but stayed in when the other inmates went out to the yard to escape the heat inside. I knew they'd all take this as a sure sign that I had lost my grip, but I no longer cared. I felt like I was fighting for my life. The figure in my first vision had said, "God be with you." Perhaps that was a signal that I was under God's protection, but perhaps it was an omen that I would soon be with my maker. The prison staff must have thought so; the fact that a guard was checking on me now through the viewing window at least every fifteen minutes meant that they had put me on a suicide watch. Even Dr. Kinsel, who had barely acknowledged me in recent weeks, visited me in my cell and let me know he was concerned about my "lack of interaction." Strangely, their fear that I might hurt myself could have become a self-fulfilling prophecy. I hadn't thought a great deal about it before, but now that it was in my head, the idea of suicide seemed like a viable alternative to life in that hell.

Obviously, I did not take that road. Life in prison, random and unpredictable until then, took another odd turn. On Friday of that week, two days after the nighttime apparition, I was brought up before the prison classification committee. Kinsel, Tindall, and all the other officials I'd been dealing with, including Associate Warden Grunska, were there except Nicholas, the chief of classification, even though he had called the meeting. I had steeled myself for a fight, believing that I would have to argue hard to keep myself out of isolation or psychiatric care, but amazingly, I never got the chance to make my case. Grunska needed no convincing and was prepared to send me back to the camp immediately. By that afternoon, I was back with my friends.

It may be difficult to understand what joy I felt to be back at the prison camp. I knew I was still in the penitentiary, but the specter of endless confinement in a mental ward, forgotten by the world, had at last disappeared. I felt in my heart that the worst was behind me now and that I would be safe.

The gang in the camp greeted me with some bizarre news. Julius Nicholas, the chief of classification, had died the night before, an apparent suicide. Gus ran to get me the papers, all of which carried the story on the front page. Nicholas had become enraged during an argument with his wife. He had threatened to kill her, and even shot at her, wounding her in the leg, and then secluded himself in their home. When the police broke into the house, they found Nicholas dead—hanging from the ceiling.

The news left me numb. The vision on Wednesday night was of a hanging. On Thursday, Nicholas hanged himself. On Friday, his absence from the committee meeting derailed the process of getting me committed to psychiatric care, and thus saved my life.

I REMAINED ANOTHER year at Springfield Medical Center, after which the Bureau of Prisons transferred me to the prison camp at Maxwell Air Force Base in Montgomery, Alabama.

There were minimum-security prisons much closer to Chicago, but I understood they wanted to make things difficult for me. The tide of suspicion regarding the Warren Commission and the speculations about conspiracies in the Kennedy assassination were gathering force around the country. The Secret Service still had their jobs to protect, and nobody wanted people like me adding to the public outcry.

On September 25, 1969, with just four months to go before I would have completed my entire sentence and been freed from any further obligation to the government, I was granted parole. Of course, by paroling me, the government could keep me under their jurisdiction for another two years.

It was three-thirty in the morning when my Greyhound bus pulled into the station near Clark and Randolph Streets in Chicago. I could see the figure of a beautiful young woman, her form illuminated by the headlights of the bus, almost glowing in the fresh night air. I climbed down the steps of the bus and fell into Barbara's arms. That embrace told me, finally, that my ordeal had come to an end.

My wife drove us south on Clark Street, crossing over to Michigan, steering us home. I remember opening the back door of my house, my own house, and being met by the happy squeals of my children, already awake and expecting me, bouncing all over the house, giggling with joy and shouting, "Daddy's home! Daddy's home!"

Daddy was home.

Epilogue

My reentry into the life of an ordinary citizen went relatively smoothly. I fell into the rhythms of my family and became reacquainted with my children. At the same time, I saw to it that religion played a more central role in all of our lives. I returned to Ingersoll briefly, but left when I heard rumors that the company was relocating out of Chicago. I remained in the machining industry, holding management positions in the quality control departments of two different companies, both of which I helped turn around into very successful ventures.

Twice, in 1974 and 1976, I petitioned for a pardon to the United States attorney general. Both requests were denied well before they would have been submitted to the president for his signature. Of the key players in my drama, Agent Cross left the Secret Service shortly after I went to prison. I don't think he ever opened that saloon, but went instead into financial management or real estate. Joseph Spagnoli served about five years of his fifteen-year sentence. The government never brought any charges against him despite his admission of perjury in a federal trial.

Thinking that I would pursue further legal action, I tried to purchase transcripts of all my trials, hearings, and appeals. I went downtown to the Dirksen Federal Building and filled out all the necessary paperwork. In August 1973, the clerk of the federal district court called me on the phone and told me that none of those transcripts could be located. They had been ordered through the

court of Judge J. Sam Perry, but the clerk never received them
for copying. They would not be able to fulfill my request for certified
copies. It had been less than ten years since my conviction, and all the
relevant transcripts were missing.

By that time, a decade had passed since the murder of John
Kennedy in Dealey Plaza. They were dramatic and turbulent years,
marked by race riots, war protests, an exploding youth countercul-
ture, and palpable shifts in power and influence. Men had walked on
the moon. America in 1973 looked very different than it had on that
bright November day in Dallas. In just another year a president
would resign in disgrace, and a year after that, we would make our
ignoble exit from Vietnam. For a public openly distrustful of government and authority to an unprecedented degree, the suspicions and
insinuations swirling around Kennedy's assassination were like raw
meat to hungry lions. Americans couldn't get enough, and the mur-
ders of Martin Luther King Jr. and Bobby Kennedy in 1968 only
sharpened the national obsession. In 1976, Congress established the
House Select Committee on Assassinations for the purpose of investigating these crimes in greater depth.

In January 1978, two investigators from that committee asked to
meet with me, to hear my statement of my recollections and concerns
about the protection that John Kennedy had received. I met them at
a motel in Chicago, where they questioned me extensively about the
conduct of the agents of the Secret Service White House detail during
my temporary assignment there in 1961. The investigators also
wanted details about the threats against Kennedy that had been investigated in Chicago shortly before the assassination. I'd endured so
many years of abuse and degradation for having spoken out on these
questions, but the United States government finally had come to seek
me out, and to listen with respect. It felt like victory.

In its final report, released in March 1979, the House Select
Committee concluded:

On the basis of the evidence available to it ...
President John F. Kennedy was probably assassinated as a result of a conspiracy. The committee is
unable to identify the gunman or the extent of the
conspiracy.

The Secret Service was deficient in the performance of its duties.

The Secret Service possessed information that
was not properly analyzed, investigated or used by
the Secret Service in connection with the President's trip to Dallas; in addition, Secret Service
agents in the motorcade were inadequately prepared
to protect the President from a sniper.

No actions were taken by the agent in the right
front seat of the Presidential limousine to cover
the President with his body, although it would have
been consistent with Secret Service procedure for
him to do so.

Everything that I had said more than ten years before was finally
confirmed in an official government report. I know I should have felt
vindicated, but I found that I still could not let the matter rest. The
committee's findings did not erase the injustice committed against me,
and with the transcripts nowhere to be found, I had no documenta-
tion, no record of the travesty that my journey through the legal and
penal system represented. I needed that record to show my children
and my children's children, so they could know what their mother
and I had endured. So that they would always know the truth.

In the years since, not a day has passed that I haven't relived some piece of my arrest and unlawful conviction. The frustration built up inside me until I knew that I had to take some action, one last effort to have my conviction overturned, rather than let it eat away at me.

In July 1994, I contacted Ray Smith, my attorney for part of the time I spent in prison, and asked him to help me track down the missing transcripts. Most significantly, I needed to know if there was any certified record of what Judge Perry had said to the jury on the night George Howard and I were locked out of the court building during the second trial, while the jury remained inside, deliberating. Smith did what he could, making a formal request to the National Archives in Washington. The National Archives responded as follows:

> To: Ray Smith
> From: Christine Ross
> Date: August 15, 1994
> Re; Status of Abraham Bolden citation requests 64
> CR 324; No. 14907
>
> In searching for the information requested by
> Abraham Bolden, I have run into many obstacles.
> The District Court Records Center did a search for
> the file and could not find it. I then checked the
> National Archives Center, which found that the file
> was checked out on August 21, 1973, and has never
> been returned. Scott Forseyth assisted me in the
> search at the Archives, and he believes the file
> was presumably checked out by the court. There is
> no indication as to who exactly checked the file
> out, Scott informed me that files rarely
> "disappear," but it does sometimes happen,
> especially with older cases.
>
> The District Court Records Center is currently

looking through old paperwork to see if the file was possibly sent back to Archives under a different accession number. The search is extremely time-consuming and tedious. A gentleman named Wally is currently searching through the old paperwork, and he will let me know if he finds anything.

The National Archives Center does have the Court of Appeals record. I went to search through the file, and it did not contain any transcripts. The District Court informed me that transcripts will normally be in the appellate record if they were in the original record. But with older cases, such as this one, sometimes a file would be shipped out to Archives without the transcripts. In such a case, the transcripts would normally be in the District Court's Exhibit Area. Unfortunately, there were no transcripts from this case in the Exhibit Area.

In order to see if the transcripts were part of the original record, I have made an appointment to go back to the Archives Center to look at the district court's docket this Wednesday, August 17.

When I searched the appellate record at the Archives Center, I did find information in the government's appendix and the appellant's appendix. I had the information copied. It includes: 1) the judge's opinion of guilt, 2) the trial judge's jury instructions in the first trial, and 3) Maurice G. [Martinez'] testimony. The case was orally argued before the Court of Appeals on October 11, 1965.

I did not find any reference to the trial judge's
exclusion of evidence because a "representative of
government was not present," nor did I find any
reference to Sikes taking the 5th amendment before
the Court of Appeals.

From the evidence at hand, I had to conclude that the transcripts
had been checked out of the archives by the district court one month
after I requested certified copies of them in July 1973. Only the district court in which I was convicted had the authority to order the
transcripts removed from the archives and brought before the court.
The transcripts would have to have been delivered to the court of the
Honorable J. Sam Perry or to some district court acting on his behalf. Once they were checked out by the court, the transcripts, exhibits, and other important records of the two trials and oral
arguments before the Court of Appeals could no longer be found.

Acting as my own attorney, I filed a motion to expunge my conviction in federal court in August 1994. Without the actual transcripts to cite in the motion, I did my best with the documents
available to me: written court briefs, records and appendices filed by
my attorneys or the government. Naturally, these papers carry less
weight than the trial and hearing transcripts, and they did not contain everything I needed to make my case. I knew I had little chance
of success in those circumstances, but I had to keep trying.

To my surprise, the government responded to my motion in January 1995 by asking for a continuance. It seemed that the transcripts
had turned up after all, in a midwestern branch of the federal
archives. I wasted no time renewing my request for a certified copy of
those transcripts, for use in my legal efforts, but my request was denied. In fact, Judge William T. Hart, who was to consider my motion
to expunge, formally censured me when I wrote him a letter asking
for a conference to discuss the transcripts and the government's

stalling actions in the case. He admonished me for not using proper legal procedure and not filing the correct paperwork. I have no doubt that he was right according to the letter of the law. My problem was that I had neither the training nor experience to work the system according to the rules and regulations, and I could no longer afford to pay a lawyer to do it for me.

Judge Hart denied the motion in October 1995. A year later, his decision was upheld in the Seventh Circuit Court of Appeals. I made one last attempt to clear the record, petitioning for a writ of certiorari before the United States Supreme Court. In February 1997, the highest legal authority in America denied my petition, bringing my long journey to an end.

I HAVE SACRIFICED too many years of my life to this quest for justice. I would give anything to have those years back to spend with my young children or simply to live peacefully, without the cloud of bitterness and indignation that followed me for so long. Still, I could not have done anything differently. I never could have rolled over and accepted my fate. I could not have accepted punishment gracefully, knowing that my only crime had been to hold my fellow agents to the same standards I set for myself, and which our government and our president expected of us.

I have told the story with the same accuracy and attention that I brought to my work for the government and elsewhere, and with the same honesty I owe my loved ones. I have shared what I believe to be the truth of my life, and also the truth about a small but significant chapter in our nation's history. I can move beyond it now and enjoy the peace of my retirement, but without my heroic wife, Barbara, who passed away suddenly on December 27, 2005. For my children and my grandchildren, the haunting echo from Dealey Plaza has been quieted.

Notes

Chapter 3

18 **Executive Order Number 10925 . . .:** http://www.jfklink.com/speeches/jfk/
publicpapers/1961/jfk137_61.html.

24 **"I hand-copied the text of the memorandum . . .":** United States Government
Office Memorandum, reproduced from my original hand-copied copy, visit of
the President to Palm Beach, Florida, File No 3-11-602.111, dated June 6,
1961.

Chapter 6

47 **"I flew to Washington at the request of the . . .":** Secret Service attachment,
Bolden expense voucher, Freedom of Information Act File dated June 26, 1979,
page 2, November 17, 1963.

59 **I radioed the office from the car . . .:** *Chicago Tribune,* "Counterfeiters Use
Church," Section 1, page 7, February 14, 1964.

Chapter 9

108 **The government had simply gone ahead and indicted me . . .:** *United States of
America v. Abraham W. Bolden,* Docket No. 64 CR 324, United States District
Court, Northern District of Illinois, indictment returned May 21st, 1964 violation of Sections 201, 371, 1505, United States Code, pages 1–5. For brevity, citations to the transcripts hereinafter will consist of a shortened notation: *U.S. v.
Bolden.* Quotations occurring in the set of transcripts from the 1st trial (July 6
through July 12th, 1964, will be so noted. All transcript citations not designated
as 1st trial occurred in the 2nd trial (August 3 through August 12, 1964).

Chapter 10

111 "The defendant enters a plea of not guilty, Your Honor . . .": *United States of America v. Abraham W. Bolden,* Case No. 64 CR 324, Federal District Court for the Northern District of Illinois, 1964.

113 The overt acts alleged were that . . . : *United States of America v. Abraham W. Bolden,* Case No. 64 CR 324, United States District Court for the Northern District of Illinois, copy of indictment filed May 21, 1964, pages 1–5.

113 "defendant Abraham Bolden is not guilty of . . .": *United States of America v. Abraham W. Bolden,* 1st trial, pages 102–06.

113 "We intend to show by evidence . . .": *U.S. v. Bolden,* 1st trial, pages 102–6.

114 "Spagnoli told me . . .": *U.S. v. Bolden,* pages 688, 689.

116 "I hadn't mentioned that . . .": Ibid., pages 695, 696.

116 "Bolden told me that . . .": Ibid., page 697.

116 Sikes had no more questions.: Ibid., pages 703–7.

116 Martineau insisted that he had no knowledge of . . . : Ibid., page 725.

117 Under direct examination, Jones . . . : Ibid., pages 246–52.

117 "Those cases are still pending . . .": Ibid., page 249.

117 "Bolden said that this prisoner . . .": Ibid., page 252–56.

117 "Bolden said that the file would be valuable . . .": Ibid., page 257.

118 "He took this typewritten piece of paper out of his briefcase . . .": Ibid., page 257.

118–19 "Is this the paper . . .": *U.S. v. Bolden,* page 259.

119 "Yes, it is . . .": Ibid., page 259.

119 "The address was 5301 Quincy, in Chicago.": *U.S. v. Bolden,* page 260.

119 "I told him that the man wanted fifty thousand dollars.": Ibid., pages 262–66.

120 "I gave Spagnoli my home telephone number . . .": Ibid., pages 269–71.

120 Jones added that he had called . . . : Ibid., pages 273–78.

120 " 'You don't know nothing' . . .": Ibid., pages 278, 279.

120 "When I was arrested . . .": Ibid., page 280.

121 "He wrote the address of Joseph Spagnoli . . .": Ibid., page 281.

121 "I want to finish with this witness . . .": Ibid., page 282.

122 "I discussed it with Agent Bolden . . .": Ibid., page 334.

123 "When you gave the statement to the Secret Service . . .": Ibid., page 349.

123 "Objection sustained . . .": Ibid., page 349.

123 "What has this got to do with the cross-examination?": Ibid., page 322.

123 "Mr. Jones testified that it was . . .": Ibid., page 329.

124 As the trial continued, the government . . . : Ibid., page 522.

124 . . . however, when questioned . . . : Ibid., page 540.

124 "No, sir, I did not": Ibid., page 540.

125 "These objections are made for the reason that . . .": *U.S. v. Bolden*, 1st trial, page 659.

125 "We take the position it is . . .": *U.S. v. Bolden*, 1st trial, page 659.

125 "If the jury finds that Bolden was in no way associated . . .": *U.S. v. Bolden*, page 710.

125–26 She went on to testify that . . . : Ibid., page 428.

126 She said that on May 12 . . . : Ibid., page 427.

126 She told the jury . . . : Ibid., page 428.

126 Her attempt to conceal evidence . . . : Ibid., page 441.

126 He said that when he'd asked me if agents took money . . . : Ibid., page 461.

127 "He told me that he wanted fifty thousand for the whole file.": Ibid., page 468.

127 "Mr. Q gave me his telephone number and told me . . .": Ibid., pages 470–72.

128 "I told her that if she saw him . . .": Ibid., pages 472–75.

128 ". . . you say that you are indicted under case docketed as 64 CR 300 . . .": Ibid., page 495.

128 "Let his answer stand . . .": Ibid., pages 495–96.

128 "No . . .": *U.S. v. Bolden*, 1st trial, pages 435–37.

129 "Did this man, Mr. Q . . .": *U.S. v. Bolden*, 1st trial, page 445.

129 " 'I don't want her. I'm not interested.' ": *U.S. v. Bolden*, pages 498–99.

129 "May it please the Court . . .": *U.S. v. Bolden*, page 502.

130 "Regardless, morning or afternoon, I talked to a woman over there.": *U.S. v. Bolden*, 1st trial, pages 439–41.

131 Russell said that on April 28, 1964 . . . : *United States v. D'Antonio et al.*, 64 CR 300, United States District Court for the Northern District of Illinois, 1964.

For brevity, this case will be shortened to *U.S. v. D'Antonio* followed by the transcript page number.

131 He said that prior to Spagnoli's arrest: *U.S. v. Bolden*, page 151.

131 "Spagnoli is a defendant in that case.": Ibid., pages 123–25.

131 "The arrests of Joseph Spagnoli and Arthur Rachael actually took place . . .": Ibid., page 126.

131 "Agent Noonan was to make the arrangements . . .": Ibid., pages 128–30.

131 "Abraham Bolden spoke up in agreement . . .": Ibid., pages 130–32.

131 "On May 13, Special Agent in Charge Mr. Martineau . . .": Ibid., pages 134–35.

132 "A copy which I identified for Agents Bolden and Cross . . .": Ibid., page 151.

132 "With the exception of the introductory words . . .": Ibid., pages 122–23.

132 Later during Russell's testimony, Howard and I examined the two exhibits together . . . : U.S. Secret Service, Freedom of Information Act File dated June 26, 1979, Secret Service report, "Abraham W. Bolden," dated May 25, 1964, page 4.

133 "No, at that time . . .": *U.S. v. Bolden*, pages 164–65.

133 "The dyeing of Sandra's hair and the fact that she . . .": Ibid., page 182.

Chapter 11

136 Sikes asked Cross if he had "received . . .": Ibid., page 195.

136 "On May 8, Bolden came into my office . . .": Ibid., page 196.

136 "We were conducting investigations on the South Side of Chicago . . .": Ibid., page 202.

137 "Around May 15, Michael Torina came to my office . . .": Ibid., page 214.

137 "No, I didn't . . .": Ibid., pages 209–14.

138 "Because I knew I didn't have it . . .": Ibid., page 214.

138 "The objection will be sustained and the questions and answers will be stricken . . .": *U.S. v. Bolden*, 1st trial, pages 618–21.

138 "When I sustain an objection, Mr. Witness . . .": *U.S. v. Bolden*, pages 222–23.

139 "Bolden told me that Agent Russell would not tell him . . .": Ibid., page 660.

139 "When Bolden hung up the telephone . . .": Ibid., pages 661–64.

140 "He said Agent—no, he didn't tell me that.": Ibid., pages 665–66.

140 "Well, it was common knowledge that she was an informant . . .": Ibid., page 667.

140 Dunne objected once again . . . : *U.S. v. Bolden*, pages 671–73.

140 After a brief discussion . . . : Ibid., pages 674–76.

142 "Yes," Walters answered. "I said that.": Ibid., page 564.

142 "I don't know. All I know is this . . .": Ibid., pages 573–76.

143 "I was alone with Bolden in the United States attorney's office.": Ibid., page 738.

143 "When I asked Bolden who had said anything about red hair . . .": Ibid., page 740.

145 "The motion is denied and the defendant directed to proceed . . .": Ibid., page 759.

147 I described my meeting with Kennedy at McCormick Place . . . : *U.S. v. Bolden*, 1st trial, page 733.

147 "Between 1962 and 1963, I had many conversations with Jones.": *U.S. v. Bolden*, page 774.

148 "Monday morning, the 11th of May . . .": Ibid., page 774.

150 "I never told Walters that I had five hundred dollars for anyone who killed Jones . . .": Ibid., pages 761–830.

152 In an attempt to discredit my contention . . . : Ibid., pages 843–44.

152 He positioned himself in front of the jury box . . . : Ibid., pages 831–65.

153 And yet by getting me to repeat . . . : Ibid., pages 852–65.

153 When he finished, I managed to say . . . : *U.S. v. Bolden*, 1st trial, page 909.

154 Everyone in the room watched her . . . : *U.S. v. Bolden*, pages 971–73.

Chapter 12

156 "The government has met its burden . . .": *U.S. v. Bolden*, closing argument, Richard Sikes, pages 986–1011, August 11, 1964.

157 "When Jones tells you that this agent . . .": There are no transcriptions of the closing arguments made by Howard for either of the two trials. The text of

Howard's closing argument is as recalled by Bolden at the time that the argument was made in the first trial, July 11, 1964. Transcripts of the second trial in August contain the complete closing arguments by government prosecutors Richard Sikes and Arthur Dunne but as to closing arguments by Howard merely states that at the request of the judge, "whereupon Mr. Howard argued on behalf of the defendant after which the following proceedings were had; to wit." See *U.S. v. Bolden*, page 1011, August 11, 1964.

158 **"Did Bolden prove that any of the witnesses were liars?":** *U.S. v. Bolden*, closing argument, Arthur Dunne, pages 1012–27.

160 **"This might, in my opinion, give the jurors the impression . . .":** *U.S. v. Bolden*, 1st trial, jury deliberation, page 4, July 11, 1964.

160 **"If you should fail to agree on a verdict . . .":** *U.S. v. Bolden*, 1st trial, jury deliberation, pages 5–6, July 11, 1964.

161 **"Ladies and gentlemen of the jury . . .":** *U.S. v. Bolden*, 1st trial, jury deliberation, page 6, July 11, 1964.

161 **"Now, with that in mind . . .":** *U.S. v. Bolden*, 1st trial, jury deliberation, page 6, July 11, 1964.

161 **"I now discharge the jury . . .":** *U.S. v. Bolden*, 1st trial, jury deliberation, pages 7–8, July 11, 1964.

162 **"Judge Perry brought the jury out . . .":** *Chicago Sun Times*, "Predicts Bolden Acquittal," July 13, 1964, reproduced in Appellant's Appendix, Case No. 14907, United States Court of Appeals for the 7th Circuit, page 14.

162 **"I'm not going to take the word of two confessed criminals over the word of that agent.":** ABC network television, Channel 7 evening news interview, July 11, 1964. Transcripts of Anna B. Hightower's July 11, 1964, interview are unavailable.

162 **"She has a son who is an agent . . .":** *Chicago Sun Times*, "Predicts Bolden Acquittal," July 13, 1968, reproduced in Appellant's Appendix, Case No. 14907, United States Court of Appeals for the 7th Circuit, page 14.

163 **"No, it is not, but we do have that prerogative . . .":** ABC network television, Channel 7 evening news interview, July 11, 1964. Transcripts of Judge Perry's July 11, 1964, interview are unavailable.

Chapter 13

168 **I understood, in that moment, that the Secret Service . . . :** U.S. Secret Service Memorandum dated July 23, 1964, "Abraham Bolden, et al," received on June 26, 1979, under the Freedom of Information Act, confirms that on July 21, 1964, agents from the Secret Service visited the Dwyer Real Estate office. Other contact with Dwyer and Richard Sikes' recommendations to obstruct Dwyer's potential appearance as a witness for the defense are included in the three-page report.

169 **Sikes did not have an argument to make . . . :** Motion for continuance (transcript of proceedings), pages 1–3, July 27, 1964.

172 **"Your Honor, this petition . . .":** Motion for continuance (transcript of proceedings), pages 1–3, July 27, 1964.

172 **"Yes, sir . . . I think that the court was completely . . .":** *U.S. v. Bolden*, motion for substitute judge, page 3, July 31, 1964.

173 **Richard Sikes argued that . . . :** *U.S. v. Bolden*, motion for substitute judge, pages 5–6, July 31, 1964.

173 **The judge agreed . . . :** *U.S. v. Bolden*, motion for substitute judge, page 11, July 31, 1964.

176 **I had testified in the first trial that . . . :** *U.S. v. Bolden*, page 137.

177 **"Bolden testified in July 1964, at his . . ."** Ibid., page 400.

178 **"On July 6, 1964, I tried to show you . . ."** Ibid., page 368.

179 **"You owe it to your client not to . . .":** Ibid., page 371.

179 **"All right . . . Let us remember . . .":** Ibid., page 372.

179 **"If you gentlemen wish to take action . . .":** Ibid., page 372.

182 **"That's what he is objecting to . . .":** Ibid., page 894.

182 **"If we put that evidence as a defense . . .":** Ibid., page 895.

182 **"Now just a second . . . We are not going into a . . .":** Ibid., page 895.

182 **"Mr. Howard, will you reserve your arguments . . .":** Ibid., page 896.

183 **"Ladies and gentlemen . . . you believe that testimony under oath . . .":** Ibid., page 1024.

185 **"It's been a long day . . .":** No transcript of the judge's remarks can be found; however, a copy of the judge's notes prepared for the clerk of the court are in

the judge's handwriting and confirms that on August 11, 1964, "jury in-structed, alternate juror discharged & Marshals sworn. Jury to consider of its verdict. By agreement jury to sign, seal, & separate & polling of jury waived." No transcript of any of the judge's instructions or conversations with the delib-erating jury can be found in the official records and transcripts of the August trial. Mysteriously, there are no transcripts of any communications between the judge and the jury between the closing-argument phase of the trial on Au-gust 11 and the opening of the sealed verdict on August 12, 1964.

187 **"We, the jury, find Abraham Bolden guilty . . .":** *U.S. v. Bolden*, jury verdict, pages 2–3, August 12, 1964.

188 **"Have mercy . . . In the name of God, have mercy.":** *U.S. v. Bolden*, jury ver-dict, page 6, August 12, 1964.

Chapter 14

196 **"I can make no comment . . . 'No comment whatsoever' . . .":** *Chicago Ameri-can*, "U.S. to Probe Perjury in Bolden Conviction," January 21, 1965.

196 **"Bolden's attorney, Raymond J. Smith . . .":** Ibid.

198 **"That's Sikes' handwriting . . .":** Exhibit 36 was reproduced from *U.S. v. Bolden*, Case 14907, appellant's additional appendix, U.S. Court of Appeals, 7th Circuit, 1965, page 18.

198 **The transcripts told a remarkable story.:** All transcriptions pertaining to *U.S v. D'Antonio et al.*, 64 CR 300, are referenced from *United States v. Bolden*, appellant's additional appendix, by Raymond J. Smith and James F. Ward, Case 14907, U.S. Court of Appeals, 7th Circuit, 1965.

199 **"So I would remember what to say in the Bolden trial . . .":** *U.S. v. D'Anto-nio*, 64 CR 300, page 6269, January 20, 1965.

199 **"After he wrote it up, did he give it . . .":** Ibid., page 6272.

199 **"I took it.":** Ibid., page 6272.

199 **"To remember the lies . . .":** Ibid., page 6272.

199 **"No.":** Ibid., page 6274.

200 **"That was false . . .":** Ibid., page 6282.

200 "Attorney Sikes.": Ibid., page 6284.

200 "That's all I can remember right now.": Ibid., pages 6285–6.

201 "stated that the testimony given by him . . .": United States Secret Service, Freedom of Information Act Memorandum, "Abraham W. Bolden," January 21, 1965.

202 "Yeah, and that's not all . . . He said that he would name names.": *U.S. v. Bolden*, Case No. 14906, appellant's supplemental appendix, affidavit of George Howard, page 19.

205 "Your Honor, if there is a hearing to be held . . .": *U.S. v. Bolden*, motion for new trial, Federal District Court for the Northern District of Illinois, page 5, March 2, 1965.

205 "I'm going to docket this case for March 22 . . .": *U.S. v. Bolden*, motion for new trial, Federal District Court for the Northern District of Illinois, page 6, March 2, 1965.

205 "Your Honor . . . Attorney Sikes has filed an affidavit . . .": *U.S. v. Bolden*, motion for new trial, Federal District Court for the Northern District of Illinois, page 3, March 2, 1965.

206 "refresh his memory . . .": *U.S. v. Bolden*, motion for new trial, March 22, 1965, affidavit of Richard T. Sikes, page 2.

206 . . . they had recovered his previous testimony . . . : *U.S. v. Bolden*, motion for new trial, March 22, 1965, affidavit of Richard T. Sikes, page 1.

207 "would be brought to the attention . . .": *U.S. v. Bolden*, motion for new trial, March 22, 1965, page 48.

207 "Your Honor . . . Attorney Sikes has not denied . . .": *U.S. v. Bolden*, motion for new trial, March 25, 1965, page 2.

207 "This case is continued . . .": *U.S. v. Bolden*, motion for new trial, March 2, 1965, page 5.

208 "Your Honor, prior to making a decision . . .": *U.S. v. Bolden*, 64 CR 324, motion for entry of findings, March 25, 1965, page 2.

209 "I am going to enter them . . .": *U.S. v. Bolden*, 64 CR 324, motion for entry of findings, March 25, 1965, page 6.

209 "Your Honor . . . so that we may be clear on this . . .": *U.S. v. Bolden*, 64 CR 324, motion for entry of findings, March 25, 1965, page 7.

209 "a plot by the witness . . .": *U.S. v. Bolden*, Judge's Finding of Fact, dated March 25, 1965, referenced from *United States v. Bolden*, appellant's additional appendix by Attorneys Raymond J. Smith and James F. Ward, Case 14907, U.S. Court of Appeals, 7th Circuit, 1965, page 29, paragraph 13.

210 That this court expressly finds . . . : Ibid., paragraph 13.

210 "the witness Joseph Spagnoli did not recant . . .": Ibid., paragraph 12.

211 "purge himself of any impropriety . . .": *U.S. v. D' Antonio et al.*, 64 CR 300 Federal District Court for the Northern District, Illinois, January 20, 1965, page 6282.

211 "We are not going into what it was.": Ibid.

211 "I told Mr. Oliver not to go into that subject . . .": *U.S. v. Bolden*, hearing on motion for new trial, March 22, 1965, page 18.

Chapter 15

215 "I ask the question again: did you solicit perjured testimony . . .": No transcript of the proceedings before the U.S. Court of Appeals (14907) could be located. However, on June 29, 1966, *U. S. v. Bolden*, 64 CR 324, motion to reconsider the sentence under Rule 35, page 8, Smith told the court, "We also have in this case, Your Honor, the fact. And I point out once again that it is Spagnoli that made this statement that he accused the Government of subornation in this case, and the fact remains that to this day, two appeals to the Supreme Court, there is a question by the Chief Judge of the United States Court of Appeals that charge by Spagnoli has never been denied, and we have this as another cloud over the case."

215 "Your Honor . . . I refuse to answer . . .": Ibid., USCA, October, 1965, 7th circuit.

219 "Spagnoli's livelihood was clearly . . .": *United States of America v. Abraham W. Bolden*, case 14907, 355 F. 2d 453 (7th Cir. 1965), opinion and finding, page 11, paragraph 1. Note: Hereinafter, citations to the opinion and findings

of the Court of Appeals will be notated as *U.S. v. Bolden*, USCA, opinion, page number, and paragraph location.

219 **"the record amply supports the district judge's . . .":** *U.S. v. Bolden*, USCA, opinion, page 11, paragraph 2.

219 **"Trial Judges are invariably called upon . . .":** *U.S. v. Bolden*, USCA, opinion, page 5, paragraph 4.

220 **"The defendant says that the motion should have been granted . . .":** *U.S. v. Bolden*, USCA, opinion, page 5, paragraph 3.

220 **"Nor do we find any merit in it.":** *U.S. v. Bolden*, USCA, opinion, page 5, paragraph 3.

220 **"clearly informed the jury that . . .":** *U.S. v. Bolden*, USCA, opinion, page 5, paragraph 2.

221 **"The government . . . does feel that comment is imperative . . .":** *U.S. v. Bolden*, USCA, Government Motion to Deny Hearing en Banc, page 2, 1966.

221 **"defendant's allegation . . . merits judicial sanctions.":** *U.S. v. Bolden*, USCA, government motion to deny hearing en banc, page 2, 1966.

227 **"Probation? I have denied it . . .":** *U.S. v. Bolden*, 64 CR 324, motion to reconsider sentence, page 19, July 29, 1964.

227 **"our intention to appoint him . . .":** *U.S. v. Bolden*, 64 CR 324, motion to reconsider sentence, page 11, July 29, 1964.

227 **"Mr. Bolden has distinguished himself . . .":** *U.S. v. Bolden,* 64 CR 324, motion to reconsider sentence, page 11, July 29, 1964.

227 **"That is sufficient. No, I don't need anything more.":** *U.S. v. Bolden,* 64 CR 324, motion to reconsider sentence, page 15, July 29, 1964.

227 **"That is the very purpose of all these trials . . . Motion denied.":** *U.S. v. Bolden,* 64 CR 324, motion to reconsider sentence, page 15, July 29, 1964.

227 **Again, Judge Perry refused the request . . .:** *U.S. v. Bolden*, 64 CR 324, motion to reconsider sentence, pages 19–22, July 29, 1964.

Chapter 17

253 "Secret Service would issue a white paper . . .": http://www.aarclibrary.org/publib/jfk/wc/wcvols/wh5/pdf/WH5_Rowley.pdf, pages 453, 454, 455.

256 "Said Petition should be filed . . .": U.S. Secret Service, FOIA Memorandum, Abraham Bolden petition before Judge Collinson, dated December 28, 1967.

Epilogue

281 "The Secret Service was deficient in the performance of its duties . . .": http://www.history-matters.com/archive/jfk/hsca/report/contents.htm.

Index